COMPOSING(MEDIA) =
COMPOSING(EMBODIMENT)

COMPOSING(MEDIA) = COMPOSING(EMBODIMENT)

bodies, technologies, writing, the teaching of writing

Edited by

KRISTIN L. AROLA
ANNE FRANCES WYSOCKI

UTAH STATE UNIVERSITY PRESS
Logan, Utah
2012

© 2012 by the University Press of Colorado

Published by Utah State University Press
An imprint of University Press of Colorado
5589 Arapahoe Avenue, Suite 206C
Boulder, Colorado 80303

The University Press of Colorado is a proud member of

 The Association of American University Presses.

AAUP 1937 / 2012

The University Press of Colorado is a cooperative publishing enterprise supported, in part, by Adams State College, Colorado State University, Fort Lewis College, Metropolitan State College of Denver, Regis University, University of Colorado, University of Northern Colorado, Utah State University, and Western State College of Colorado.

Cover design: Anne Wysocki
Cover photo: "Fertile Graffiti, Montmartie" by Zander Wextendarp. Used by permission

ISBN: 978-0-87421-880-0 (paper)
ISBN: 978-0-87421-881-7 (e-book)

Library of Congress Cataloging-in-Publication Data

Composing(media) = composing(embodiment) : bodies, technologies, writing, the teaching of writing / edited by Kristin L. Arola and Anne Frances Wysocki.
    p. cm.
  Includes index.
  ISBN 978-0-87421-880-0 (pbk.) — ISBN 978-0-87421-881-7 (e-book)
1. English language—Rhetoric—Computer-assisted instruction. 2. Online data processing—Authorship—Study and teaching. 3. English language—Rhetoric—Computer network resources. 4. Report writing—Study and teaching—Data processing. 5. English language—Rhetoric—Study and teaching. 6. Report writing—Computer-assisted instruction. 7. Mass media—Authorship—Study and teaching. 8. Report writing—Computer network resources. I. Arola, Kristin L. II. Wysocki, Anne Frances, 1956-
  PE1404.C617574 2012
  808'.0420285—dc23
                    2012014285

CONTENTS

ACKNOWLEDGMENTS

This book has its roots in early dissertation coffee shop conversations with my then chair, and now colleague and coeditor, Anne Frances Wysocki. Without those conversations, which continue today, this book would not be possible. And here's to mindful conversations, to our generous and patient authors, to our encouraging editor Michael Spooner, and to Jeff for keeping me nourished and filled with wonder.

Kristin

Calling to bodies, yes, this book held on through a long move and a slow death, and so for their patience I thank Kristin and all this book's writers, whose generosity and gifts of time helped me through boxes, tape, and hospital rooms. And here's to you, readers, thanks for your hands, eyes, and curiosity: here's to what you make and give.

Anne

COMPOSING(MEDIA) =
COMPOSING(EMBODIMENT)

INTRODUCTION
Into Between—On Composition in Mediation

Anne Frances Wysocki

These are physical things, he had come to understand, memories. All that we feel, pain and hatred and love and happiness, they aren't some existential experiment of the mind, but they played themselves out in the body mainly, and the thoughts came after, a justification of what the body already knew.
—Patrick Thomas Casey, *Our Burden's Light*

. . . There can be no history of the body that is not at the same time a study of the various media that constitute embodiment as such.
—Bernadette Wegenstein, *Getting Under the Skin*

The following writing, put down a few days after my father died, reminds me of hearing his last breath. He was in the family room, where we'd put his hospital bed; from his bed he could see out into the green and azalea backyard where, in earlier years, he'd moved and worked so often. This writing also tells me about ways I have learned to feel:

> Life leaving a body still looks like a leaving, like breath or movement or ani-mation removing itself. The body does seem discarded, an emptied out shell or container or glove. No wonder we once said, "I have a body" instead of "I am a body."
>
> Seeing a body go from alive to not, how can we then believe that bodies are other than things that hold us—some real us? How can we not believe that bod-ies are what keep us from being what we are meant to be?
>
> Seeing a quiet death of another goes a long way toward explaining Plato's belief that our life's task is to master the body so that we can attend to the inter-nal. We are to make our bodies tractable rather than demanding; we are to focus on what within that body but separable from it seems most truly human.

In the days following my father's death, I would write at the dining room table, surrounded by varying numbers of family. I was trying to keep up with an online class and other work, and I was also writing to reflect and to plan, given my new familial responsibilities. In memory those evenings are silent and still, at least from my perspective, focused as I was on my writing while some jumble of my mother, my siblings, and my nieces and nephews chatted or made dinner.

In the days following my father's death, I also made many phone calls. Months later, I can recite from memory the list of questions that the United States Social Security Administration asks, questions that can require almost twenty minutes of phone keypad letter typing and that can still end in frustration when the machine at the other end cannot translate 7-2-4-9-3-3-2 into my father's mother's maiden name. I can also still feel—my body remembers—my back slump when I had to redial and go through the process again. I still feel the delight of getting things set up right, finally, for my mother.

■

The protests in Madison, Wisconsin during February and March 2011 were primarily intended to insert views like those below into current political discussions. People were there to be to be seen together—and by being so unitedly visible, they were there to have effects on a legislature that otherwise seemed to feel no need to pay attention because (evidence suggested) those with much more money and so access were shaping the law.

■ ■ ■

Two related sets of assumptions about bodies and media ground this collection's essays. The first has to do with the first paragraphs above, about the feelings of embodiment; the second explores tensions between those feelings and the knowledge that we are also experienced from outside, observed and shaped as part of a culture and its institutions.

I develop these two sets of assumptions in this introduction to explain how this collection came together and the ordering of chapters in its two parts and also to explain why we think considering composition through media and embodiment matters now in writing classes.

ASSUMPTION SET 1: MEDIA = EMBODIMENT

As philosopher Merleau-Ponty argued, your body is your primary medium—taking *medium* here in its grounding sense of that which is between, in the middle. Without our bodies—our sensing abilities—we do not have a world; we have the world we do because we have our particular senses and experiences. But this is not to say that we come to be with finished bodies and then start sensing, or that some unmediated way of being exists prior to or grounding our sensuous experiences; N. Katherine Hayles, for example, is careful to distinguish between such a static notion of a body and the processes of embodiment: "In contrast to the body," she writes, "embodiment is contextual, enmeshed within the specifics of place, time, physiology, and culture, which together compose enactment" (*How We Became Posthuman* 196). For example, the doctors described in a recent *New York Times* article, "As Physicians' Jobs Change, So Do Their Politics," do not seem to have changed their politics only or primarily because of rational deliberation with others; instead, it is the felt, often nondiscursive particularities of their embodied experiences of mothering or shift work that affect the doctors' temporalized opinions and actions: "Because so many doctors are no longer in business for themselves," the article argues, "many of the issues that were once priorities for doctors' groups, like insurance reimbursement, have been displaced by public health and safety concerns, including mandatory seat belt use and chemicals in baby products" (Harris).

"Embodiment," in this understanding, calls us to attend to what we just simply do, day to day, moving about, communicating with others, using objects that we simply use in order to make things happen . . . until those objects break or don't do what we want and so tease us into a different attitude: we try to take the objects apart—to analyze—their parts and processes so that we might fix them. Heidegger's distinction between the "ready-to-hand" and the "present-at-hand" not only names the difference in attitude we have about a hammer that works and one whose head has separated from its handle; Heidegger's distinction urges us toward acknowledging this difference and understanding that our ways of being are most often simply engaged with getting things done: we act through the various understandings we acquire through moving and interacting and engaging, using—being—the bodies we are.

Heidegger did not name technologies and media (now to use the more general sense of *media* as books, magazines, films, television shows, radio programs, web pages) as extensions of our bodies— that was McLuhan. For McLuhan, technologies and media enable us to extend what we can do with our given sensory apparatus. Our relations with our technologies and media are not one way, however. Not only does a hammer or a piece of writing, for example, enable us to extend our reach but it also modifies our sense of engagement: it shifts how we feel what is around us or how we sense those with whom we communicate; our senses reflex and shift in response to these mediated engagements, and in further response we then modify our media toward our shifting ends. Given the contemporary range of media objects with which we engage, W.J.T. Mitchell and Mark Hansen argue, in their introduction to their collection of *Critical Terms for Media Studies,* that—when we speak now of media— "what is at stake is more than the form of a specific content," more than any medium serving simply as a carrier for content; instead, we are discussing "something that opens onto the notion of a form of life, of a general environment for living": "Media Studies can and should designate the study of our fundamental relationality, of the irreducible role of mediation in the history of human being"(xii).

> The media revolution so transformed the notion of medium and reality that our body—formerly declassed as merely a medium of, or means to, the real (hence subordinate, reflective, distortive)—now gets elevated, as our central medium, to the status of constructor and locus of the real . . . . Once reality is seen as a construction, the media that construct it can no longer be disdained. (Shusterman 144)

And so, again, our bodies—our primary media, to draw on the first sentence and observation of this section—are not fixed; they are mutable. We come to be always already embedded—embodied—in mediation. Our relations with our media matter, in other words, and (this is one lesson we take from the philosophers and thinkers just mentioned) we therefore need to consider our engagements with our media if we and the people in our classes are to learn about our embodiment and so what we consider ourselves to be and to be able to do in our worlds.

Those of us who teach writing need, then, to consider media that use the alphabet and to ask how such media engage with our senses and contribute to our embodiment. We need to do this both theoretically and in praxis. This introduction climbs into the theory as a way toward praxis; the other chapters often mix both, while the pedagogical activities we offer in this book provide students openings for exploring how the media with which they work encourage certain embodiments.

To take on the media with which we writing teachers seem most clearly related, we can start with Ong's arguments from *Orality and Literacy* about books, and with the simple descriptive recipe he gave: a book is made of

> lines perfectly regular, . . . all justified,
> everything coming out even visually. (121)

The repetitiveness of the visual patterning of books, made possible by printing technologies, led Ong to argue that books give us a "hypervisual-ized noetic world" (127). Like McLuhan, Ong attributed much to the spatial relations that printed pages convey to our eyes and so to our behaviors: for example, the intense regularity and evenness of a page of print shows us and so creates for us "an insistent world of cold, non-human facts" (122). Ong argued that another "consequence of the [book's] exactly repeatable visual statement was modern science" (127), that print "fostered the desire to legislate for 'correctness' in language" (130), and that print "was also a major factor in the development of the sense of personal privacy that marks modern society" (130). You are probably familiar with such claims about how books, as they extend us toward each other but then work back on us, can be understood to shape how we are embodied in our worlds.

But a limitation colors these particular forays that consider how print media work on us, for with them it is as though bookish effects are limit-ed to the attitudinal and not the sensuous. Under the descriptions of both McLuhan and Ong, sight is a passive sense: it is as though, for them, we open our eyes and stuff just pours in; it pours in and works on us directly, causing all that other stuff. Under this telling, sight itself is unchanging and unaffected by mediation, and so there is only one way for it to function; it is assumed here that everyone sees in the same ways and so will be affected in the same ways by what they see, everywhere and at all times, ahistorical-ly, aculturally, apolitically.

In response, here (for example) is the political philosopher Iris Marion Young, characterizing and calling into question a certain "logic . . . in Western philosophical and theoretical discourse" (98), in which

> rational thought is defined as infallible vision; only what is seen clearly is real, and to see it clearly makes it real. One sees not with the fallible senses, but with the mind's eye, a vision standing outside all, surveying like a proud and watchful lord. This subject seeks to know a Truth as pure signifier that completely and accurately mirrors reality. The knowing subject is a gazer, an observer who stands alone, outside of the object of knowledge. (125)

And—discussing the development of modern science—here is Donna Haraway, similarly questioning that notion of seeing that allows us to think we can be (if we are male) "modest witnesses":

> Enhancing their agency through their masculine virtue exercised in carefully regulated "public spaces," modest men were to be self-invisible, transparent, so that their reports would not be polluted by the body. Only in that way could they give credibility to their descriptions of other bodies and minimize critical attention to their own. This is a crucial epistemological move in the grounding of several centuries of race, sex, and class discourses as objective scientific reports. (*Modest Witness* 32)

What both feminist philosophers point to (as many other theorists have, feminist and otherwise) is how vision—as it is conceived by McLuhan and Ong, as it has tended to be conceived in the West—is more complex and changeable than conceived and, as conceived and applied, has consequences we should not wish blindly to accept.

In place of the singular vision presumed by McLuhan and Ong, Haraway writes that she "would like to insist on the embodied nature of all vision, and so reclaim the sensory system that has been used to signify a leap out of the marked body and into a conquering gaze from nowhere" (188). In somewhat parallel fashion, Martin Jay has argued that "the privileging of any one visual order or scopic regime" ought to be replaced by "ocular eccentricity": Jay encourages "the multiplication of a thousand eyes, which, like Nietzsche's thousand suns, suggests the openness of human possibilities" (591). Jay has argued, for example, that people living in the Baroque period had different ways of seeing from people living during the Italian Renaissance, who saw differently from those who lived at the same time in northern Europe; each of these ways of seeing articulated, Jay argues, to epistemological and so ontological habits of the time.

Others extend these arguments still further, to try to get us not only to the possible multiplicities of sight but also to the multiplicities of our other senses. Anthropologists Constance Classen and David Howes, for example, have individually and in edited collections described the sensuous hierarchies of other cultures in other times and other places—with, instead of sight, some cultures privileging hearing, smell, or a sense of heat as the primary epistemological sense—and they have told of the mortal consequences that can result when cultures with different sensuous epistemologies and cosmologies come up against each other. (Think here of theories of the Great Divide played out not only attitudinally but with guns.) Other writings about the sensuous also show how the work of McLuhan and Ong has, over time and (importantly) woven together with the calls that arose with identity politics in the 1960s to attend to differences in bodies, opened our eyes not only to a needed critique of sight but also has turned our attentions to other senses, their actions, and their locations: look, for example, at the long bibliography on these matters at the end of Howes's edited collection *Empire of the Senses* or at Madnar and Vodvarka's book *Sensory Design*, Marks's book *Touch: Sensuous Theory and Multisensory Media*, or Caroline Jones's edited collection (with pieces by Latour, Haraway, Turkle, Stafford, and Classen, among others) *Sensorium: Embodied Experience, Technology, and Contemporary Art*.

In *Bodies in Code*, Mark Hansen argues that to "expand the scope of [our] bodily agency . . . transforms the agency of collective existence" (20). Hansen argues that—when we use digital technologies *not* for their "representational or simulational capacities" (25)—digital technologies can shift our sense of bodies-as-primarily-eyes to sensing how embodiment is also through skin and other senses; such expansion can happen, that is, when we use digital technologies not for their visual capacities but for their "enactive potentialities" (25). When we shift, he argues, from observational to operational engagement within our worlds, digital technologies can "facilitate new kinds of world-construction and intersubjective communication" (31). Hansen's examples of digital works that do this sensory expansion are primarily installations; the other books listed above similarly point to artworks and to science-art collaborations as the places where we can re-engage and experiment with sensory connections other than the relentlessly visually reductive.

Compositions that move us out of printed books as the primary means of communicating with each other, that is, are the compositions that these various scholars argue we need if we are to move away from a way of being in the world that focuses (literally) our attentions in limited, reductive, dangerous-to-Others ways. These scholars are not arguing for us to do away with books, of course, for they make their arguments in books—but they do ask what other sorts of arguments are possible when we broaden our senses of the texts we can make for each other through the possibilities of the digital. What might be possible if we encouraged a democracy of the senses in our teaching instead of a hegemony of sight?

> Written literature has, historically speaking, played a dominant role for only a few centuries. Even today, the predominance of the book has an episodic air. An incomparably longer time preceded it in which literature was oral. Now it is being succeeded by the age of the electronic media, which tend once more to make people speak. At its period of fullest development, the book to some extent usurped the place of the more primitive but generally more accessible methods of production of the past; on the other hand, it was a stand-in for future methods which make it possible for everyone to become a producer. (Enzensberger 272)

But that is getting somewhat ahead of the work of this edited collection you hold in your hands. What you hold in your hands, still and after
all, is a book and so participates in and is limited to certain mediations—
as our first chapter, "Drawn Together: Possibilities for Bodies in Words and
Pictures," explores explicitly in its considerations of the embodying differences between words and pictures on book pages and how only a mix of
words and pictures enables, now, a particular sexual orientation.

◆ In this book,
    our work (to summarize the assumptions I have laid out
        in the previous pages) is
    to offer further arguments, tied to analyses of differing
        kinds of media,
    that what any body is and is able to do
    —and how any one body differs from other bodies in its
        affective and physiological capabilities—
    cannot be disentangled from the media we use
    or from the times and cultures in and technologies with
        which we consume and produce texts,
    especially texts (given that we are mostly writing teachers)
    composed with some ratio of words.

This collection can thus be considered groundwork toward wider sensuous engagements in writing classrooms. For that reason, we take seriously
a need to engage with a wide range of media that use alphabetic text (with
their entangled technologies and their histories) in order to explore how
they participate in mediating our embodiments. In addition to the comics
explored in "Looking like a Body of Words," then, the chapters of this book
discuss *Wikipedia*, maps, computer interfaces, powwow
regalia, queerness and multimodality, research methodologies, transgendered bodies and writing, blogging,
art posters, "normal" writing, videogames, and videos.

And how can the
domination of both old
(television) and new
(computer interface) media
by old white pricks be
resisted? (Nakamura 103)

In addressing such a range of media, we do not in
this book argue that digital technologies profoundly change our possible embodiments; we leave those
arguments to others (such as has been implied by my
quotation from Hansen or upcoming references to Stiegler or Wegenstein)
precisely because we do work with writing, that old medium: we wish to
understand writing's particular and varying embodying possibilities, as
in the chapter on comics or in the chapter that follows it, Paul Walker's
"Pausing to Reflect: Mass Observation, Blogs, and Composing Everyday
Life." "Pausing to Reflect" compares the mass observation movement of

the 1930s with current blogging practices, advocating for us to reflect on "how any technology may have the capability to increase everyday life's influence on collective knowledge" (44) and so on the mediating possibilities of attending to embodiment as we live it. The anthropologists who organized the mass observation movement asked "ordinary, hardworking folk" (46) to write on specific days over a number of years; Walker argues that these writers, "by their reflection and our knowledge of their words, achieved a degree of authorship and validity by consciously, even enthusiastically, projecting their everyday life—and its infrastructure—during their 'ordinary' lifetimes." Their writing offers insight into why bloggers write now and challenges us, in our uses of digital media, "to compose ourselves meaningfully, balancing how we embody everyday practices, power, literacy, want of attention, culture, and identity" (59) through understanding how we have and can use written words in shaping our lives with other individuals.

As Walker's chapter compares diaries to blogs, Matthew S. S. Johnson's chapter compares the processes of embodiment assumed in composition textbooks to those assumed in computer game manuals and games. As players choose the qualities through which they will understand themselves while playing, they come to understand the possibilities of experiencing complex, ready-made worlds from different perspectives. Johnson argues that

> perhaps recognizing where playing a game and practicing academic discourse (a binary in many of our students' minds if there ever was one) intersect—in consciously formulating and exploring identities and/or various manifestations of the "self"—we can re-evaluate a stagnant set of ideals for which both audiences (teachers and students) have traditionally privileged the one over the other. (70)

Johnson thus suggests strategies we might use to help students consider differing embodiments across differing media, with the hope that this will encourage more exploration in writing activities.

As Walker's and Johnson's chapters show, writing opens possibilities into understanding relations between writing and newer-media technologies—but it also potentially shuts down potentials of new media. David Parry, in his chapter on *Wikipedia*—"How Billie Jean King Became the Center of the Universe"—argues that, for now, "*Wikipedia* is valued precisely because it fulfills librocentric criteria" (76): it addresses older concerns—and in so doing forecloses the new. Similarly, Jason Farman's chapter—"Information Cartography: Visualizations of internet Spatiality and Information Flows"—demonstrates how current mappings of the internet can offer "no entry point for embodied interaction that resembles the user's process of navigation"(85) because such mappings do not attend to the embodied understandings viewers bring from their experiences with earlier media. Both of these chapters challenge us to consider our attitudes toward mediation as we work with new (and old) media in our teaching and research.

In "Multimodal Methods for Multimodal Literacies: Establishing A Technofeminist Research Identity," Jen Almjeld and Kristine Blair describe what happens when—in the processes of Almjeld's dissertation's being written—feminist theories, very much concerned with embodiment, overlap with a committee's disembodying approaches to new media and theorizing. In its reports on the potentials for mediation within the dissertation process, the chapter raises questions about the limits of control over mediation not only for feminist scholars and for scholars researching online technologies but also for those of us who direct dissertations.

Finally, for fleshing out and pursuing our first set of assumptions about embodiment that shape our book, there is Jay Dolmage's chapter "Writing against Normal." Dolmage asks, reflectively and through examples from students who used a wiki for revision, whether "a composition pedagogy that ignores the body might actually limit our ability to make meaning" (125). The class activities Dolmage describes have students up and moving in space but also engage them in much messy and emotional response and thought, leading Dolmage to argue that

> to "compose" the body is to examine the shadows and scissions that differentially constitute embodiment. Likewise, if we want to truly understand embodied writing, perhaps what we need to most closely study are not ideal, complete texts, but the messy and recursive process of composing, as we break our ideas apart through language. (125)

Dolmage writes his chapter "not to proscribe a process, but to find ways to emphasize the situatedness and partiality of communication, to draw attention to relationships and choices and the feeling for moving across ideas, genres, and mediums" (124); he writes therefore to emphasize the necessary embodiedness of teaching if it is to encourage students toward curiosity about their own embodiments through the mediations of learning and writing.

Through describing such teaching, Dolmage's chapter turns our attentions to the next set of assumptions that shape the second part of this collection. This next set of assumptions pushes us to ask not only how media and mediation embody us but also how—and why—we ourselves should mediate bodies, including and especially our own.

ASSUMPTION SET 2: MEDIATING BODIES ∧ MEDIATED BODIES

The second set of assumptions that underlie the work of this book's chapters is characterized by the differences between the two stories with which

I opened this chapter. This set of assumptions engages with a tension between the two stories, a tension between the felt experiences of an interior—being a body that composes, writes, and communicates—and a bodily exterior, of being one person among many, subject to study and impress from above or outside, mattering only because of one's part in composing the many. This tension plays itself out in our composition classes as we decide whether to teach

ONE: that writing is about expressing one's particular experiences.
or
TWO: that writing is always and inescapably part of larger social, cultural, and political structures, institutions, and systems and that individuals and (perceptions of) agency are always and only effects of those structures, institutions, and systems.

You are probably stuttering at me now over the broadness of those two perspectives. I imagine that you are articulating, in response, your teaching position that fine-tunes and particularizes across what I have just offered. But I doubt that your position disengages from the tension between *the felt experience of being an individual body that can act* and *the achieved-through-research-and-observation-and-experience outlook that we operate (and are operated) only within larger systems that determine what we can be and what we can do.* And we cannot deny that this tension has structured and continues to structure the field of rhetoric and composition.

In 1994, this tension was the subject of John Trimbur's review essay, "Taking the Social Turn: Teaching Writing Post-Process." Discussing books by Bizzell, Knoblauch and Brannon, and Spellmayer, Trimbur writes that

> one might say that these books result from a crisis within the process paradigm and a growing disillusion with its limits and pressures. When process pedagogy emerged on the scene in the late 1960s and early 1970s, process teachers and theorists sought to free themselves from the formalism of current-traditional rhetoric and return the text to the student composer. But the distinction between product and process, which initially seemed so clarifying, not only proved conceptually inadequate to what writers do when they are writing, it also made writing instruction appear to be easier than it is. As Bizzell notes, by polarizing "individual creative talents" and "the oppressive institution" of schooling (182), the process movement led teachers to believe that they could simply step outside the institutions and discourses of schooling in order to release an authentic language from their students. (109–110)

There is, of course, also the debate between Bartholomae and Elbow on precisely these matters, published in 1995; there is also—ten years later in 2005—Richard Fulkerson's essay "Composition at the Turn of the

Twenty-First Century," which argues that two "theories of value" shape pedagogy in Rhetoric and Composition: "an expressive one" and "the newest one, 'the social' or 'social-construction' view, which values critical cultural analysis" (655). In classes shaped by the first set of values, writing "is a means of fostering personal development, in the great Socratean tradition of 'knowing thyself'" (667); in classes shaped by the second set of values, "students read about systemic cultural injustices inflicted by dominant societal groups and dominant discourses on those with less power" (659).

This tension, structuring our field between expressivist and social-constructionist/cultural studies approaches, is equivalent to a tension that has structured philosophy and psychoanalytic theory in the last century. Let me explain this other tension, and then explore it through a historical tracing of media studies, to suggest what might as a result be useful for rhetoric and composition.

His body throws two shadows:
One onto the table
and the piece of paper before him,
and one onto his mind.

(from "In His Own Shadow,"
Li-Young Lee)

To describe this other, equivalent tension, I can turn to philosopher Richard Shusterman, for example, who argues that the wide range of approaches to our bodies that he studies can be classified as *experiential* or *representational*: the first focuses "not on how the body looks from the outside but on the aesthetic quality of its experience" while the second "emphasizes the body's external appearance"(142). Or I can turn to media and film theorist and documentary filmmaker Bernadette Wegenstein, who in her book-length study of our contemporary understanding of bodies writes that both psychoanalysis and phenomenological approaches have worked with an understanding that there is a separation of

> the subject of the body (the body as it is perceived through one's own body) from the objectified body (the body as it is perceived by the world)—a distinction between the subject of perception and the socially constructed body, between the psychoanalytic *I* and the *Me*. (29)

Wegenstein shows how Lacan, for example, argued that we come to "perceive our bodily selves . . . through a deceptive image that is framed by somebody else's gaze (in the beginning, the mother's or her substitutes), or by the frame of a screen or interface of some kind (mirror, computer interface, television screen, etc.)," and that through this externalized recognition we come to a sense of "corporeal unity" and so self (26); for Bergson, a "body is at the same time mirror or screen for the images [attached to it as identities] from the outside and the perceptive center"(29). Both Lacan and Bergson, then, like Merleau-Ponty, understood our embodiment to happen through culturally developed identities being placed on us by

others while at the same time we come to experience ourselves as sensing interiors. Rhetoric and
Composition is not alone, then, in trying to work
with what Wegenstein argues is a historically situated—mediated—sense that we are fragmented between a perceiving and a perceived body,
between a potentially expressive mediating body
and a body that exists only in mediation by others.

*To note, then: we understand
"identity" as externally available
categories for social belonging; one
can take up identities and perform
them, and they become part of one's
embodiment, shaping one's sense of
body and its relations to others—
but they are not comprehensive of
embodiment.*

Let me then examine one strand of considerations from Media Studies of this tension
between mediating and mediated bodies, to
help me situate the chapters of this book's second part and to suggest
productive approaches for working with this tension in Rhetoric and
Composition. Note that I use "productive" carefully in the preceding sentence for it is a concept that repeats itself in the several pages that follow
and that shapes the arguments I will make; in what follows, please watch
for movements from productive to passive and back to productive in analyses of bodies mediated by the new communication technologies of the
early twentieth century.

Formative twentieth-century European studies of media asked us to
attend to how the then new media of photography and film were not simply
a superstructural aftereffect of economic change; instead, such media were
capable of changing our sensibilities. Theorists like Benjamin, Adorno and
Horkheimer, Debord, Enzensberger, and Baudrillard (all of whose writing will soon be discussed) understood not only that the new mass media,
because of their scales of production and distribution, required mass audiences and large amounts of capital, but also that the structures of these
media—their particular compositions and modes of production as well as
their industrial articulations—enabled new relations between audiences
and texts and hence new sensory registers, new embodiments. Please bear
with me in these few pages as I summarize and present their observations.

Benjamin, in "The Work of Art in the Age of Mechanical Reproduction,"
for example, argues that, because they are no longer tied to tradition and
the singularity of paintings—to the "aura" of paintings—photography and
film (to quote from a commentary on Benjamin)

> have the ability to brush aside the precarious legacy of bourgeois art and
> nineteenth-century culture, namely the stratifying rhetoric of genius, unique-
> ness and awe, which in Benjamin's eyes had become conceptually untenable
> and politically dangerous in a time of totalitarian rule. And because the struc-
> tural logic of film, because of its constitutive technique of cutting and editing,
> privileges discontinuity over durational extension, rapid interruption over

contemplative stillness, shock over awe, it produces viewers and consumers who do not submit to the authority of artistic work but instead seek to assimilate it into the itineraries of their social and political life outside the theatre. The media of industrial culture convert the meditative and absorbed viewer of the nineteenth century into deliberate and active users of cultural materials. (Koepnick and McGlothlin 9)

Distracted by rapid discontinuity, that is, those audiences were thus potentially deliberate and active users of culture, given Benjamin's understanding of film logics. He noted, however, that (and now I use Benjamin's words), society "has not been mature enough" to make good use of those deliberate and active users:

> If the natural utilization of productive forces is impeded by the property system, the increase in technical devices, in speed, and in the sources of energy will press for an unnatural utilization, and this is found in war.

Benjamin's prescience of war strengthens his arguments at the same time it saddens.

Following World War II, in "The Culture Industry: Enlightenment as Mass Deception," Adorno and Horkheimer similarly found that film's structures rendered audiences distracted, but rather than audiences then becoming actively engaged with culture they become passive receptors: for Adorno and Horkheimer, culture and entertainment *are* industries, seeking "standardization and mass production" like any other industry and supported by the capital of "the most powerful sectors of industry—steel, petroleum, electricity, and chemicals." Media audiences are therefore treated as consumers, reduced by what they watch:

> The stunting of the mass-media consumer's powers of imagination and spontaneity does not have to be traced back to any psychological mechanisms; he must ascribe the loss of those attributes to the objective nature of the products themselves, especially to the most characteristic of them, the sound film. They are so designed that quickness, powers of observation, and experience are undeniably needed to apprehend them at all; yet sustained thought is out of the question if the spectator is not to miss the relentless rush of facts.

Consumers, as products of this industry, are themselves subject to mass production and standardization; the industries of media production, for Adorno and Horkheimer, are so large that any possible idiosyncrasy or individual creative productivity, before it can start,

> has already been suppressed by the control of the individual consciousness. The step from the telephone to the radio has clearly distinguished the roles. The

former still allowed the subscriber to play the role of subject, and was liberal. The latter is democratic: it turns all participants into listeners and authoritatively subjects them to broadcast programs which are all exactly the same. No machinery of rejoinder has been devised, and private broadcasters are denied any freedom.

Audiences—consumers—under this telling are kept from activities that are productive on their own behalf.

From 1967, Debord's "Society of the Spectacle" analyzes the media situation when passive, placid consumerism is all there is. See, for example, his thesis 160—"The spectator's consciousness, immobilized in the falsified center of the movement of its world, no longer experiences its life as a passage toward self-realization"—or thesis 43:

> At this point the humanism of the commodity takes charge of the worker's "leisure and humanity," simply because now political economy can and must dominate these spheres as political economy. Thus the "perfected denial of man" has taken charge of the totality of human existence.

But there are implications here of what should be the case instead of passivity: consider thesis 203—"To effectively destroy the society of the spectacle, what is needed is men putting a practical force into action." Action and production are what then enable individuals to stand up to the pacifying structures of the mass media.

Enzensberger, in a piece published in 1970 and analyzing "the industry that shapes consciousness" (261), is overt in his calls for certain kinds of action, as when he writes that

> every use of the media presupposes manipulation. The most elementary processes in media production, from the choice of the medium itself to shooting, cutting, synchronization, dubbing, right up to distribution, are all operations carried out on the raw material. There is no such thing as unmanipulated writing, filming, or broadcasting. The question is therefore not whether the media are manipulated but who manipulates them. A revolutionary plan should not require the manipulators to disappear; on the contrary, it must make everyone a manipulator. (265)

Observing that the then new "electronic techniques recognize no contradiction in principle between transmitter and receiver" (262), Enzensberger urges "a collective, organized effort" (267) for taking advantage of these "subversive potentialities of the electronic media" (269): audiences will become transmitters of their perspectives rather than passive receptors of the mass media. Before I say more about this turn toward production, let me bring in Baudrillard's response to Enzensberger. Baudrillard, in a piece published in 1972, criticizes Enzensberger for taking up the transmitter-message-receiver coded model of communication and for then simply calling for that model to be reversible, as though receivers should become transmitters and transmitters should become receivers. For Baudrillard, this "fails to place the mass media system in check" (286) for it does not allow response. Instead, Baudrillard offers graffiti as it was used in the 1968 demonstrations:

> Graffiti is transgressive, not because it substitutes another content, another discourse, but simply because it responds, there, on the spot, and breaches the fundamental role of nonresponse enunciated by all the media. (287)

Baudrillard is not denying the need for audiences to be producing texts; he is arguing over how that production should function.

I have, of course, shortchanged each of the essays I have so quickly summarized in the last few pages and I have shortchanged their differences, but not to the extent, I believe, that the point I want to take from them is incorrect: through the response of these essays to each other and to the mass media, we see acknowledgment of the tension with which I started this section and arguments about how that tension needs to be sustained. That is, in understanding that we are (to use Wegenstein's formulations) each a subject—a body perceived through itself, through its own mediations—at the same time we are each also objectified through others' mediations of us, the essays I have just reviewed argue against any tip in the balance between those two positions. In reading from Benjamin through to Baudrillard, we see burgeoning awareness that the mass media, while potentially setting up structures that could change our relations with a stultifying past, instead have been set up to deny subjects their own perceptions and any abilities to produce their own media and mediations based on those perceptions. In other words, under some conditions (which should be changed), mediation happens in only one direction, from structures and institutions onto individuals.

Why should production matter so much in the thread I just traced through the media theorists I summarized? For one possible answer, we need to turn back to a specific nineteenth-century philosophic concern; then we can once again pick up this book's response.

Each media theorist I summarized was educated in the European philosophic tradition that grew out of Marx, who was in turn grounded in Kant and Hegel. Part of that intellectual tradition is a notion that ideas develop historically and systematically, such that those ideas—reason, for example—can be traced in a logical development that manifests itself in human institutions and beliefs. For example, Hegel presented all of human history as a process of Reason coming to know itself in the world: he understood the development of democracies out of monarchies, for instance, as a spreading of Reason from one person (the monarch) into individuals who therefore come to know themselves as reasonable and so know themselves as active individuals free to make decisions in the world and so free to develop as moral agents. Marx, alert to the stunted and exploited lives of working people in the nineteenth century, shifted the ground of historical change away from reason: he came to understand, instead, that economic processes provide the base for how all other institutions and processes intersect and act—including relations among humans and including human sense of self and possibility. Like Kant and Hegel before him, he believed that the end (in the sense of pu rpose) of human existence is freedom; Marx defined freedom as the ability to be productive in the world, to choose and shape what one does as work—and to shape how one's work moves through the world in its uses by others. Josef Chytry (quoting Marx from the *Economic and Philosophical Manuscripts of 1844*) describes Marx's understanding of how being an individual is inseparable from being a producer: "Marx's concept of the object . . . culminates in a focus on the objectifying, creating activity of human being as individuality" (242). And (again from Chytry, now quoting what Marx wrote in response to James Mill's *Elements of Political Economy*):

> labor creates a product which brings enjoyment to its recipient while the laborer takes pleasure in fulfilling another's needs. This act of exchange thus makes the laborer aware of the mediation between the other and the human species as a whole; and to the extent that the other person senses his own essence as a member of the species, he confirms the laborer's being in his "thought and love." Finally, the laborer realizes the value of his individual activity by recognizing it as the actualization of his own communal nature. (244)

And, finally, words directly from Marx and Engels, from *The German Ideology*: "Only within the community has each individual the means of cultivating his gifts in all directions; hence personal freedom becomes possible only within the community." For Marx, roughly, the production of objects out of the stuff of nature gives us an understanding of ourselves within nature and within human community: human freedom is the freedom to do productive work in one's community. We cannot be fully human if we cannot work and see how the results of our work connect us with others.

At the time he was writing, however, Marx saw that historical developments had separated—alienated—laborers from their work: the bourgeoisie (factory owners, managers) took over from laborers all decisions about who would make what objects and how those objects would be circulated; the objects made by productive humans were turned into commodities—objects not with the value of use but with the value of exchange—and so the real work of humans was made less real by being set free to circulate outside their control. This is what results (for Marx) when the bourgeoisie take over all the structures—the modes—of production.

What underlies the productive concerns of the media theorists I summarized, then, is some echo or memory of this understanding of what it is to be a free human: it is to be a being who can mediate from its particular embodied position within its community.

And this is not a perspective that has disappeared. In his chapter in the Mitchell and Hansen collection I cited earlier, for example, Bernard Stiegler describes two kinds of memory that function now, one embodied and individual, the other embedded in external media. Note not only that these two forms of memory align with the division between the mediat*ing* subject and the mediat*ed* objectified subject that has motivated this section of our introduction, but that Stiegler argues that this division is political, playing out in what we now (thanks to Deleuze) understand to be control societies in which what is at stake is, in no small part, the determination of what is remembered. Stiegler's writing thus echoes that of the earlier media theorists in, first, its concern that earlier mass-media structures put the control of memory construction-and-keeping in the hands of industry and, second, in its arguments that we need each and all to be producers and consumers of media at the same time, engaged in "interlocution," which Stiegler argues is possible with digital media.

Or consider Rita Raley's writing on tactical media, digital network-enabled "interventions and disruptions" of dominant regimes (6) that are meant to "provoke and reveal, to defamiliarize and to critique" postindustrial society and neoliberal globalization, with "uncertain and unpredictable" outcomes (7). Citing Hardt and Negri, and Virno, among others, to acknowledge that only resistance and dissent and not revolution seem possible, Raley describes tactical media as needing "a multitude of different creative agents, a multitude that fuses or is situated between the individual and the collective" (10); tactical media's epistemology is that "we are meant to interact and engage while simultaneously becoming aware of our own limitations and our own inability to make an immediately perceptible impact on the project as it stands in for the socioeconomic and political system" (18). What Raley describes is the mediating subject whose actions both acknowledge and resist the objectifying mediations of institutions.

What we end up with, finally, from all these writings that consider a mediating subject in tension with structures and institutions that (also through mediation) objectify that subject, is no dissolution of the tension that shapes this section as it has shaped Rhetoric and Composition. In the pages above in which I have tracked media theorists' descriptions of an audience pacified by media alongside hopes for productive, mediating audiences, the subjectifying and the objectifying processes of media stay active—but some sort of balance of mediations is sought.

◆ In this book, then,
> *we assume*
>> *—alongside our first set of assumptions about what constitutes*
>> *embodiment and about a corresponding need for engagement*
>> *with a range of media—*
>>> *that embodiment has to be acknowledged*
>>> *as both active and passive,*
>>>> *felt by us as well as produced by us.*

Mediation is not to be performed only *on* one; one is to be actively engaged with mediation, with attending productively to one's own felt experiences and with learning how to compose media out of those experiences, media for circulating and eliciting engagements with others. This book is not about subtle analyses of the differences between (for example) Baudrillard's notions of response and Stiegler's notions of interlocution; we are, instead, collectively concerned with how, as writing teachers, we help both students and ourselves experience mediation both productively and reflectively. Because the ability to produce media objects and so to shape mediations has culturally been with corporations, industries, and institutions (an observation that grounds every media theorist I quoted),

> *our collection emphasizes*
>> *what it is that enables subjects*
>> *—those on the "inside" of felt embodiment—*
>>> *to take on productive, mediating actions*
>>> *through written, textual possibilities.*

For those reasons, this collection includes "Activities" sections. These sections offer classroom activities (primarily designed for undergraduate audiences but extendable to graduate classes) in which analysis and production are mixed: with these activities we hope to engage students with differing media in order that they might alertly mediate their own experiences and so feel—and not only see (to return now to a concern of our first set of assumptions)—the potentials of their particular embodiment. How is it to construct and disseminate their own embodied memories?

Individual chapters of this collection also take up the particular assumptions of the past few pages, as when, in her chapter "Crafting New Approaches to Composition," Kristin Prins considers writing through the tradition of craft, which interweaves with this introduction's tilt to a Marxian tradition of production. In her chapter, Prins asks us to think of writing not as the often abstract process of designing but as *making*, and, in so doing, directs our attention to our mediating capabilities when we produce media that differ from what corporations offer and when we engage in crafting, which

> implies a maker, tools used to shape materials into a made object, a user or users for that object, the time it took for the maker to learn how to use the tools and work with the materials, the time it took to make the object, relationships between the maker and thing made, as well as between maker and users. (152)

Following Prins's chapter, Aaron Raz Link—in "Bodies of Texts"—crafts an essay that demonstrates writing strategies for how to mediate against objective and limiting identities. At the same time, the writing calls its own assumptions about embodiment, theorizing, and writing into question as it discusses embodiments that look one way but have been arrived at through very different means. As a meditation on and mediation of a transgendered and ambiguously ethnic body, Raz Link's chapter wonders what is truly possible with written (especially written academic) mediation when none of its available means come close to satisfying the embodied being doing the writing.

In "Whose Body? Looking Critically at New Interface Designs," Ben McCorkle, working under the assumptions that we do want the thick sorts of situations for mediating bodies that Prins and Raz both describe, questions how writing teachers can then approach digital interfaces. After describing how some interfaces "assume unquestioned subject positions for the user" (174), McCorkle questions what embodied interfaces might be; he makes recommendations for how teachers of writing might actively engage in the processes of producing such interfaces so that the interfaces do not, finally, only "facilitate real-world practices of silencing and marginalization, in effect essentializing difference"(186).

Jonathan Alexander and Jacqueline Rhodes's chapter returns our attentions specifically to the acts and potentials of productive mediating bodies: in arranging their chapter so that it visually holds two narratives at once, narratives that curl around each other and sometimes foil our learned reading habits, Alexander and Rhodes demonstrate possibilities for "figuring the queer" (188). They also analyze two of Cocteau's films as another vector for questioning what it is to figure the queer, specifically through multimodality, and they present us with other mediations of their particular embodiments, showing us and discussing websites and photographs they have produced. They write that

> we make use of our converging alienations, our mesh of desire and want, in order to position ourselves to be—if only for a particular, rhetorical moment—and,

more to the point of this particular work, to be sexual. Through the constant exchange/deferral of need, this self-positioning increases and sustains itself through its desire, serving as the engine of its own perpetual visibility. It is thus a generative, multimodal techne of self, with both somatic and representational consequence. (211)

Their chapter, then, both analyzes and demonstrates mediation that pushes against an external, objectifying mediation that would normalize and so limit embodiment—as does the chapter that follows it, Kristin Arola's "It's My Revolution: Learning to See the Mixedblood."

Arola considers the difficult external positionality experienced by mixedblood people in the United States, caught between Indian and white identities. Against that background, Arola also considers powwow regalia, which "function as an expression of dancers' lives and represents a range of the dancer's experiences: families, hobbies, dreams, and religious beliefs" (218): "It as an embodied visible act that evolves and changes, and that represents one's history, one's community, and one's self within that particular moment" (218). Regalia thus "firmly positions one within a shifting continuum of embodied identities" (219) and Arola argues—as Alexander and Rhodes do with their multimodal explorations—that regalia thus enables its wearers, especially mixedbloods, to mediate their embodiment outside traditional, usually restrictive, possibilities. Given that, she asks and analyzes how we might think of online social networking sites as regalia rather than as templates that encourage only those restricted possibilities for embodiment.

"Visible Guerrillas," Karen Springsteen's contribution to this book, shows us what mediations were needed for women to make a place for themselves in the art world of New York City from the late twentieth into the early twentieth centuries. Springsteen describes how the feminist activist group the Guerrilla Girls used media strategies of what Springsteen calls "appropriative reproach": it is a taking "possession of a commonly accepted or normalized form and altering it such that it is implicated in a design that disgraces, discredits, shames, or blames an offender"(234), a kind of culture jamming—and a kind of "powerful writing" that is "quite literally an effort to change how we see" (235). Springsteen's chapter, like the others I have discussed in line with the second set of assumptions that shape our book, offers examples of mediating bodies refusing to be seen only through the object positions held by others.

The final chapter of our collection is Kristie Fleckenstein's "Affording New Media: Individuation, Imagination, and the Hope of Change." Fleckenstein uses Coco Fusco's multimodal one-act drama *The Incredible Disappearing Woman* both as an example of how new media can be used toward social ends and to initiate strategies for nondisembodied teaching and learning of new media. To ground her understanding of Fusco's drama and so her teaching, Fleckenstein turns to "what legal ethicist Drucilla Cornell calls the minimum qualifications of individuation: bodily integrity, access to symbol systems, and protection of the imaginary domain" (239). Fleckenstein's chapter ends with examples of two blogs produced by students, each of which demonstrates those qualifications and shows how the students have learned—through the qualifications—to mediate their experiences and engage with others.

As it emphasizes that embodiment is both active and passive, felt by us as well as produced by us through our own mediating practices, Fleckenstein's work thus also circles us back to our initial assumptions for this collection, that embodiment is an ongoing process to which we need attend and for which we need engagement with a range of media. Our writing classrooms similarly need to work across all these assumptions if we and the people we teach are to have thoughtful participation in our own mediating and mediated embodiments.

In this book—as we ask you to attend to writing as a technology that enables us to experience our bodies as *our* bodies while at the same time writing mediates those bodies in line with existing institutions—we hope we have offered both theoretic and practical support for helping us and students enact and reflect upon our embodied and embodying writing.

PART 1

MEDIA = EMBODIMENT

How do differing media encourage—
or discourage—particular senses of
bodies in the world and bodies in
relation to others?

How have changes in media, over
time, entwined with differing
possibilities for bodies and relations
with others?

How can we work with available media
and media technologies to open new
possibilities for embodiment?

1 DRAWN TOGETHER
Possibilities for Bodies in Words and Pictures

Anne Frances Wysocki

A few years back, in an interview published in *JAC*, Stuart Hall suggested one reason production has always mattered to writing studies: Hall ties production to identity. He says that "there is no final, finished identity position or self" to be reflected in one's writing; instead, as he describes the process of producing a written text, he says that

> while it's true that you may have a very clear notion of what the argument is and that you may be constructing that argument very carefully, very deliberately, your identity is also in part becoming through the writing. (qtd. in Drew 173)

For Hall, that is, "We therefore occupy our identities very retrospectively: having produced them, we then know who we are" (qtd. in Drew 173). It is not that we find our selves in our work because there was a unified self that preceded the work and that only needed being made present somehow in the work; it is rather that what the work is—its status as a shaped object in front of us—makes visible to us "what we are." "I think only then," continues Hall, "do we make an investment [in the produced position], saying, 'Yes, I like that position, I am that sort of person, I'm willing to occupy that position" (qtd. in Drew 173). One could also just as easily say, "No, I do not like that position . . . how can I rework it?"—but in either case the position has had to be constructed—produced—before it can be so judged.

That is, we see ourselves in what we produce. We can look at what we produce to ask, "Is that who I (at least in part) am? Is that who I want to be? Is that a position through which I want to be seen?"

■

In this chapter, I want to consider (altogether too quickly to be anything more than suggestive, given the space here) what kinds of identities and bodies can be constructed when one can use not only words but also pictures—as in comic books and graphic novels—in composing.

In composing the selves-to-be-considered that Hall describes, we can only work with available cultural categories for shaping texts if we wish to be understood by others, as the New London Group describes when they argue that any composition must begin in "available designs" (the existing social systems of conventions, grammars, and genres upon which all text composers rely) or as Kaja Silverman describes when she writes, drawing on Lacanian psychoanalytic structures, that "all subjects, male or female, rely for their identity upon the repertoire of culturally available images" surrounding them at any time (295). The argument I build here about words and pictures as available designs or culturally available images depends on understanding words and pictures not as having essential, formal functions but as having histories. And because of the particular histories words and pictures have had relative to each other, and because of how then comics and graphic novels have come to have a particular cultural place at this moment, certain kinds of visible identities—and questionings of identities, and understandings of bodies—are possible, for now.

The available designs of words and pictures, that is, come with attached discourses. How one articulates words and pictures, then, can play with—or against—those discourses.

■

In *The Gutenberg Galaxy*, published in 1962, Marshall McLuhan argues that the serious and repeated look of printed book pages homogenize (some) people. In the book there are men who build nations together because they see similarities in themselves as they learned to see book pages; in the book there is abstraction, but nothing of bodies; there is science and philosophy, but nothing of the quotidian; there are men and words, and men and words only. It is in McLuhan's earlier *The Mechanical Bride*, first published in 1951, that there appear women, children, class distinctions, cars, nylons, Mennen Skin Bracer, pictures, advertising, and "sex, gunplay, fast action" (14); in this second book, McLuhan claims that

> A huge passivity has settled on industrial society. For people carried about in
> mechanical vehicles, earning their living by waiting on machines, listening much
> of the day to canned music, watching packaged movie entertainment and cap-
> sulated news, for such people it would require an exceptional degree of aware-
> ness and an especial heroism of effort to be anything but supine consumers of

processed goods. Society begins to take on the character of the kept woman whose role is expected to be submission and luxurious passivity. (21)

Whether or not one agrees with McLuhan's claims (which align with the media theorists discussed in the introduction) that mass media encourage passive receptivity, McLuhan articulates words, when they are alone, to thought and men; pictures align with no thought and women.

These particular dichotomous articulations were not new with McLuhan, of course. The dichotomies were presaged even by the Pythagoreans and their list, quoted by Aristotle, of the ten pairs of opposites the Pythagoreans believed shaped all existence—

limit and the absence of limit

odd and even

one and many

right and left

male and female

rest and motion

straight and curved

light and dark

good and bad

square and oblong

(John Robinson 119)

In *Iconology: Image, Text, Ideology*, W.J.T. Mitchell discusses the shifting tensions among conceptions of word and image in the writings of G.E. Lessing, Edmund Burke, Karl Marx, Nelson Goodman, and Rudolf Arnheim. For one example, Mitchell offers a table that shows the "oppositions that regulate Lessing's discourse" (110):

Poetry	Painting
Time	Space
Arbitrary (man-made) signs	Natural Signs
Infinite range	Narrow Sphere
Expression	Imitation
Mind	Body
Internal	External
Eloquent	Silent
Sublimity	Beauty

Ear   Eye

Masculine   Feminine

And Mitchell characterizes Lessing's position toward these oppositions:

> Paintings, like women, are ideally silent, beautiful creatures designed for the gratification of the eye, in contrast to the sublime eloquence proper to the manly art of poetry. Paintings are confined to the narrow sphere of external display of their bodies and of the space which they ornament, while poems are free to range over an infinite realm of potential action and expression, the domain of time, discourse, and history. (110)

Or, as Mitchell writes in a later work, under such tradition the "image is the medium of the subhuman, the savage, the 'dumb' animal, the child, the woman, the masses" (*Picture Theory* 24).

And here, finally for now, is not another list but a description of a solitary reader set off against a group of television watchers, as Robert Romanyshyn turns a psychologist's perspective to how the word and picture opposition shows itself in our actions and attentions (while adding new terms to either side of the above dichotomizing lists). Romanyshyn's work, from 1992, echoes McLuhan:

> Distraction, triviality, and passivity are the judgments . . . of a book consciousness watching television. They are the diagnosed symptoms of the serious reader who has distanced herself or himself from the vulgar. The headless nuclear family watching television is the nightmare of the bodyless reader, the terrible image of what we become when we lose the book. We need to remember, however, the kinship between the two, the connection between that kind of thinking which, in splitting off the serious from the vulgar, the mind from flesh, reason from emotion, first creates a mindless body and its needs for distraction, and then produced the means to do it. (348)

My quick travel through Western takes on word and picture, male and female, mind and body, reason and emotion, is quick, but establishes, I hope, that conceptually, these terms have been treated as connected essentials with ethical weight: word and picture are not simply conceived as neutrally different available choices for communication; they are conceived as discrete and unitary kinds of objects that articulate to highly valued categories that have been and are used to define what and who we might be and do in our lives with others. The reach of the articulations encourage us to judge others in relation to how well those others fit to one side or the other of these lists. If one chooses only words for composing a self, then and for example, it is not that there is something inherent in words that makes one look smart or male; it is that a cultural history supports one in so believing, seeing, and making sense of one's body.

Comic strip panel from the chapter 'Lost and Found' in *One! Hundred! Demons!* by Lynda Barry, © 2002 Lynda Barry, published by Sasquatch Books and used courtesy of Darhansoff & Verrill Literary Agents.

In response to his considerations of how others have conceived word and image, Mitchell argues that any tension or difference we see between words and images is a "struggle that carries the fundamental contradictions of our culture into the heart of theoretical discourse itself. The point, then, is not to heal the split between words and images, but to see what interests and powers it serves" (*Iconology* 44). Precisely because one of their defining characteristics is that they hold words and pictures together on a page (on this defining characteristic, see, for example, McCloud; Hatfield; Varnum and Gibbons), comics offer a site for exploring how the historical and particularly valued articulations of word and picture move beyond the conceptual and into questions of interests and powers. Several snapshots from the history of comics can show, then, how these media are not inherently less serious than print-only texts but how their mediating potentials can be shaped by political and social decisions.

"The marijuana of the nursery, the bane of the bassinet, the horror of the house, the curse of the kids, and a threat to the future" is how John Mason Brown, a drama critic for *The Saturday Review of Literature*, described comics in a 1948 radio debate called "What's Wrong with Comics?" The name of the debate (which was sponsored by the ABC radio show *America's Town Meetings of the Air*) suggests that the direction of the debate was shaped beforehand: those speaking against comics could be on the attack from the start but those speaking in favor had to be on the defensive, needing to prove nothing was wrong with comics. In addition to calling them the "marijuana of the nursery," Brown also called comics "the lowest, most despicable, and harmful form of trash," because they made reading "too easy" (Nyberg 44).

This debate was not an isolated event, but rather part of an on-going concern in the 1940s and 1950s in the US—and around the world—over the effects comics were having on youth and, implicitly, on adult readers. (See both Lent's "Comic Debates," and the edited collection for which that article served as an introduction, for a sense of just how international the debate over comics was in the 1940s and 1950s.) I want to consider such criticisms of comics against the backdrop of the word-picture articulations I outlined previously, to argue that when comics are criticized for not being serious enough, for not teaching serious reading and writing abilities, or for not teaching serious thinking, it is not because the pictures have somehow won out over the words; it is instead because their critics fear comics are too serious. Comics have come under attack, I argue, not because they necessarily cause people to think poorly or live as though they are bodies only but because their appeal to large audiences can potentially make them a threat to the existing social order if their content is not controlled. Because arguments to decide means of social control rarely claim social control as their explicit end, however, the arguments about comics instead get focused on their formal aspects, on their uses of words and pictures together: comics are argued to be demeaning and infantilizing and then are made to be so, their words and pictures simplified and reduced from what they could otherwise be.

A dip into the history of comics will thus help make clear how the potential mediations of comics—of words and pictures—are not fixed.

Although some writers find the origins of comics in cave paintings, Egyptian hieroglyphics, Mayan illustrated books, or old European tapestries that show sequences of illustrations with words explaining what is in the illustrations (McCloud; Nielsen and Wichmann; Jerry Robinson), some pages that look like what we now call comics appeared in illustrated educational magazines of the first half of the nineteenth century. These magazines, such as *Penny Magazine* and *Penny Cyclopedia* produced by the Society for the Diffusion of Really Useful Knowledge, were published for the working classes. As Adrian Johns, a researcher into book history, argues, the society was founded out of a long-standing fear that even books innocuous enough in restricted settings could take on dangerous, even seditious, meanings in the hands of a mass proletarian audience. So [the Society] resolved to swamp the country with cheap periodicals containing "nothing to excite the passions." (630)

Worried, that is, that working-class people who read the same books as the upper classes would get ideas about what their lives should be, the society provided to the lower classes magazines with simplified information (which relied more heavily on illustrations than on words) about (for example) natural history and mathematics; by 1832, the magazines had one million readers. As for the story magazines—called "penny dreadfuls" because of, as Roger Sabin describes, "their lurid subject matter" about wild boys, criminals, and murderers—these too were "designed for a working class audience" and "were read primarily by young men" (*Comics* 14). Sabin writes that they were at one time in the nineteenth century

> feared to be so politically subversive that a censorship campaign was initiated to ban them. Officially, the reason for the clampdown was given to be their violent nature: in fact, anti-establishment story lines were considered much more of a threat. (*Comics* 14)

Similarly, Kress and van Leeuwen understand processes of cultural— class—differentiation in the nineteenth century to have included differentiation between the value of word and picture; they connect this differentiation to the entrenchment of capital at a particular time and to the development of more visual texts explicitly for mass consumption:

> This development beyond the densely printed page began in the late nineteenth century mass press, in a context in which the ruling class, itself strongly committed to the densely printed page, attempted to maintain its hegemony by taking control of the popular culture, commercializing it, and so turning the media *of* the people into the media *for* the people. Their own comparable media—"high" literature and the humanities generally—became even more firmly grounded on the single semiotic of writing. Layout was not encouraged here, because it undermined the power of the densely printed page as, literally, the realization of the most literary and literate semiotic. The genres of the densely printed page, then, manifest the cultural capital ("high" cultural forms) controlled by the intellectual and artistic wing of the middle class, to use Bourdieu's terms. (185; emphases in original)

Kress and van Leeuwen thus argue that pages attentive to layout and variety are aimed at "'the masses,' or children" (186), so that pages of words only can be used by others—the "ruling class," "the middle class" that is aspiring "upwards"—to show their particular and happy social positions and their maturity. From the first mass reproduction of printed texts, then, the formal content of pages—their proportion and arrangements of words and pictures—became visual markers of class differentiation and, as Johns and Sabin argue, their formal content was shaped to be less stimulating or complex than it could have been; so shaped, their purpose became educating particular bodies toward passivity.

In Britain the first mass-market comic to use a recurring character, *Ally Sloper's Half Holiday*, told of a man who liked to drink, who avoided both work and the rent collector, and who therefore, according to Roger Sabin in his history of comics in Britain and the US, "articulated a side of working-class life rarely touched upon in other publications" (*Adult Comics* 17–18). This comics magazine was inexpensive, and became "the largest-selling penny-paper in the world"—in part because, Sabin argues,

> as an expression of the new working-class culture, it was ultimately quite conservative. There was no suggestion of class struggle, and the depiction of the rich was comic rather than hostile, with no reference to the source of their income. (18)

Ally Sloper, Sabin writes, was the "'little man' who 'knows his place'" (19). Because it allowed working-class people to see hard aspects of their lives but in a way that didn't threaten the social order, Sabin argues that this comic was allowed to continue from 1884 until 1923—and its popularity gave rise to many competitors and to the printing of comics in newspapers as well as to comics for children.

Comics developed similarly in the United States. There were, first, comic magazines; newspaper publishers then starting putting comics into their papers. In the United States, the comic strip that started the boom is considered to be the Yellow Kid, which appeared in 1895 in the *New York World* newspaper: the Yellow Kid was "big-eared, bald, and beady-eyed" (Daniels 2) and the "setting was the city slums, squalid tenements and backyards filled with dogs and cats, tough characters and various ragamuffins" (Jerry Robinson 12); according to Daniels, the Yellow Kid

> existed in a world that was crude, noisy, sordid, and eccentric, and he commented disdainfully on it, first with wry expressions on his idiot's face, later with phonetically rendered slang inscribed on his expansive nightshirt. (2)

That the Yellow Kid was no threat to any person or social order is clear in how his creator, Richard Outcault, described him:

> The Yellow Kid was not an individual but a type. When I used to go about the slums on newspaper assignments I would encounter him often, wandering out

of doorways or sitting down on dirty doorsteps. I always loved the Kid. He had a sweet character and a sunny disposition, and was generous to a fault. Malice, envy, or selfishness were not traits of his, and he never lost his temper. (Wood)

The Yellow Kid was such a success that his picture was "soon on buttons, cracker tins, cigarette packs, and ladies' fans; eventually he was a character in a Broadway play" (Becker, qtd. in A. Berger 24). The success of the strip led to other newspapers developing similar strips, to the Sunday comics sections, and—eventually—to bound editions of these comics. This led to comic books, standing on their own as continuing stories about children, animals, families, spies, detectives and crooks, ghosts, and superheroes.

In the 1940s, various surveys reported that anywhere from 83% to 100% of children between seven and seventeen years of age in the United States read comic books, some reading two comics "regularly," some twenty-three (Lent, "Comic Debates" 14–16). In the mid-1950s, sales of comics approached 60 million per month—with some fair amount of those sales going to adults, many of whom, according to a 1954 government-sponsored survey in one Ohio town, averaged eleven comics a month; in 1949 there were 120 different romance comics one could buy; in 1953, 130 horror comics (Sabin, *Adult Comics* 144, 147, 152, 154).

In the early days of comic strips in US newspapers, there were, as Sabin reports, complaints about the comics similar to those in Britain: comics

> were accused of being crass, ephemeral, and detrimental to reading: that they were often more popular than the actual news-pages in the papers was considered by some a national outrage. . . . Because Hearst, Pulitzer, and other tycoons were using the strips to reach an ever-wider audience (often an immigrant audience), they were branded as "low-class" and accused of "dragging the press down." (*Adult Comics* 137)

Just as earlier, comics were designed with simplified words and pictures in accord with how some perceived the immigrant and other feared or denigrated audiences; for neither comics nor audience did the words or pictures reflect any essential qualities—but they instead were worked to create a sense of the essential.

The years between World War I and World War II are often considered the "golden years" of comics in the US. In those years, as conditions lead up to World War II, the actors in comic books shifted:

> Superman and Batman were born . . . . They mirrored the spirit of the era and America's attitude towards political problems; they expressed the idea that America was the savior and preserver of all true social values, guardian of democracy, deliverer of the oppressed from the bondage of Fascism and National Socialism. (Reitberger and Fuchs 117)

During World War II, comics about military life and the war proliferated. One survey estimated that 44% of men in military training camps regularly read comic books; comic books outsold other magazines ten to one at military stores. The army approved 180 periodicals—of which almost 50 were comic books—that could be distributed without having to be checked for political content (Zorbaugh 198–199). After the war, however, comic books again came under attack, as the radio debate that opens this section shows.

In 1954 psychiatrist Frederic Wertham published *Seduction of the Innocent*, in which he argued that there existed a direct connection between reading comics—and being exposed to the violence in them—and juvenile delinquency. To support his claims, Wertham used examples:

> A fifteen-year-old boy was accused of having shot and killed a boy of fourteen (the authorities chose to consider this accidental), of having thrown a cat from a roof, of having thrown a knife through a boy's foot, of sadistic acts with younger children, of having shot at a younger girl with a BB gun. After a full study of the psychological and social background, we came to the conclusion that the fact he was an inveterate reader of comic books was an important contributing factor. (qtd. in Nyberg 51)

Wertham's criticisms helped galvanize concerns over the effects of comics to the extent that congressional hearings were held. Some who have written about this situation argue, however, that it was more than fears about the effects of comics on children that underlay the criticisms. Les Daniels, for example, describes what brought disfavor on crime comics:

> The documentary-style crime comic books depicted without restraint the gang-life of the Depression and the psychopathic aberrations of the postwar liberation. In a medium where fantasy was the standard fare, the crime comics exposed some unpleasant truths about our society. Their honesty, we may assume, made them unpleasant. In any case, they came under attack for what they were only reporting, even as bearers of bad tidings might be executed by resentful rulers. (86)

In response to the attacks and hoping to avoid external censorship, the comics industry developed its own self-regulatory Code of the Comics Association of America, Inc. to govern what could and could not be shown in comics and how what could be shown would be shown. The code stated, for example, that "in every instance good shall triumph over evil and the criminal shall be punished for his misdeeds," and "although slang and colloquialisms are acceptable, excessive use should be discouraged and wherever possible good grammar shall be employed." (The full original 1954 code is easily found online; see Lavin, "Comics Code," for example.) As a result, comics were sanitized to pose no threat to the proper ethical or educational upbringing of the young. Many comics publishing companies went out of business, the industry consolidated into the hands of a few companies, and—some argue (see Daniels or either Sabin book, for example)—the subject matter of comics became more juvenile than before.

The historical sketch above focuses on class: comics have been shaped to meet producers' notions of what was appropriate for readers perceived not to need intellectual stimulation or challenge. In matters of gender, perceptions of audience desire are suggested by lines in the Comics Code—"Females shall be drawn realistically without exaggeration of any physical qualities" or "the treatment of love-romance stories shall emphasize the value of the home and the sanctity of marriage"—or by this summary about the appearance of women in Golden Age Comics:

> Powerful super-heroines like DC's Wonder Woman or Marvel's She-Hulk may easily overcome the most overwhelming threats and obstacles, but they are invariably depicted as alluring objects of desire, wearing the scantiest of costumes. These twin themes of dependence and sexual desirability have permeated the comic book medium from its earliest days. . . . (Lavin, "Women")

How audience desire was perceived in matters of ethnicity is suggested by these lines from Leonard Rifas's article "Racial Imagery, Racism, Individualism, and Underground Comix," in which Rifas describes how *Seduction of the Innocent*, mentioned above, contained

> an extensive section condemning American comic books for indelibly impressing on their young readers that there exist "natives, primitives, savages, 'ape men,' Negroes, Jews, Indians, Italians, Slavs, Chinese and Japanese, immigrants of every description, people with irregular features, swarthy skins, physical deformities, [or] Oriental features" who are inferior to tall, blond, regular-featured men, and are "suitable victims for slaughter."

I wish to repeat that it is not because words and pictures have some essential form or mediating function that the portrayals above appear.

The alternative comics movement that started in the 1960s—giving rise to what many label "comix"—is "defined by its insistent, even strident, opposition to the normative practices and clichés of 'mainstream' comic books" (Hatfield 18) that resulted from the Comics Code. These alternatives to

the mainstream—epitomized first by the work of R. Crumb and then by
Art Spiegelman's *Maus*—oppose themselves to publishing practices of
the large commercial comics presses: published by independent presses,
they are most often both drawn and written by one person instead of a
company-built team of writer, artist, and inker, and they emphasize "cor-
rosive reexamination of familiar tropes" (18). These books and the production practices behind them are originary for "graphic novels," first so
called by Will Eisner in his 1985 book *Comics and Sequential Art.* In spite of
the opposition of both comix and graphic novels to the more traditional comics publishers, however, they are still most often analyzed in the
United States in terms of their formal linkings of word and picture: consider the title of Robin Varnum and Christina T. Gibbons's edited collection *The Language of Comics: Word and Image,* for example, or look through
Scott McCloud's highly influential *Understanding Comics* or *Making Comics*
to see the emphasis placed on the possible formal patterns of word and
picture interaction.

■

from Moore and Gibbons's
Watchmen. © DC Comics

The passages I quoted from Hall at this paper's beginning encourage us
to imagine a writer mediating him- or herself in the content of the words
on a page—but what I have written following that beginning suggests, I
hope, that such content cannot be separated from the physical material
without which we cannot communicate. To compose a words-only page

here and now is to take up, along with a keyboard and a white surface, the whole set of articulations and attitudes outlined above for words. Through the look of our pages and our splittings between words and pictures, we make visible cultural beliefs about the places and representations of class, gender, ethnicity, and other identities and embodiments. But what if one fits into none of the received possibilities of words or pictures?

The dichotomies of mind and body, male and female, reason and emotion, and light and dark to which words and pictures have been articulated *have* been questioned for how they limit and constrain those identified with one side or the other. But if words and pictures themselves continue to be considered as standing in formal opposition, performing essential and dichotomizing functions, then we carry all those other articulations—as they have been conceptualized but also represented in the pages of comics—along with them.

And when we can so cleanly hold these terms apart, (as David Carrier asserts in his book considering how words and pictures work together in comics) "breaking down seemingly essential boundaries is often thought to be unnatural, and so morally pernicious" (70) because

> we expect the world to fit our preconceived stable categories, and so what falls between is easily felt, depending on our temperament and politics, to be either exciting or menacing. Hence the fascination with, and fear of, cross-dressing, androgyny, people of "mixed-race," comics, and other forms of in-betweenness. (70–71)

■

> *Not surprisingly, Wertham objects also to another kind of what might be called inbetweenness encouraged, so he thinks, by comics—homosexuality. (Carrier 69)*

In our place and time, then, the history of words and pictures and comics I have just presented helps make sense of the retrospective construction of identity that is Alison Bechdel's memoiristic graphic novel, *Fun Home: A Family Tragicomic*. Because of the articulations of words and pictures we've inherited, and because the mix of words and pictures in comics has been used to signify what hasn't been considered serious or proper, Bechdel can construct identities not by dissolving dichotomies but by working across them, stirring up their previous articulations.

On one page in *Fun Home*, Bechdel uses word captions to describe how her father's shame inhabited our house as pervasively and invisibly as the aromatic musk of aging mahogany. In fact, the meticulous, period interiors were expressly designed to conceal it. Mirrors, distracting bronzes, multiple doorways. Visitors often got lost upstairs. (20)

In this graphic novel, Bechdel reconstructs her growing up as though it were a re-enactment of the myth of Icarus and Daedalus. The house that her father so carefully restored becomes his labyrinth, the place where he can hide himself, "a maze of passages and rooms opening endlessly into one another . . . and from which, as stray youths and maidens discovered to their peril . . . escape was impossible" (12). Underneath the last three words, however, Bechdel draws herself as a child running out the house's front door, evading her father's anger after she accidentally broke something.

In an article on the work of several comic artists, Frank L. Cioffi argues that comic artists can arrange words and pictures together to create different disjunctive effects. For example, Cioffi argues, R. Crumb sets words and pictures to "work at absolute cross purposes" (112) in a "continual assault on middle class values" (111); with his use of cartoon animals to tell a Holocaust story, Art Spiegelman "sets up something like a cognitive or emotional dissonance within readers" (116–117). In *Fun Home*, however, it is dissonance that the father is working so hard to hide: "He used his skillful artifice not to make things, but to make things appear what they were not. He appeared to be an ideal husband and father, for example. But would an ideal husband and father have sex with teenage boys?" (17). Within its own labyrinthine temporal structure, the book retells how Bechdel came to know about her father's life and its connections to her own sexuality, and in the process the book hides nothing. On the pages of this book, words and pictures (and, along with them, the often-hidden matters of gender and sex and families) are made visible in their articulations—but dissonance is not the point of it. If the words and pictures suggest opposing possibilities—as they do in the frame sequence I described above in which the child escapes the house—it is not to show conflict but rather to make visible certain identities that can only be lived across the clean boundaries that separate the dichotomies I discussed several pages back.

Toward the middle of the book, just before the book's only two-paged spread that holds a single frame, Bechdel writes that

Proust refers to his explicitly homosexual characters as "inverts." I've always been fond of this antiquated clinical term. It's imprecise and insufficient, defining the homosexual person whose gender expression is at odds with his or her sex. But in the admittedly limited sample comprising my father and me, perhaps it is sufficient. (97)

and

While I was trying to compensate for something unmanly in him . . .
He was attempting to express something feminine through me. (98)

But it is also the book *Fun Home* itself that is an inversion of the father's
life—as well as of the mother's. The book, hand drawn but mass produced
and highly public, describes the child's attachment to reading and art,
learned from her parents, and makes visible—and visibly claimed—her

own sexuality and her own artistic abilities. In *Fun Home*, words and visual display are the devices through which her parents both understand but also reshape and so obscure their desires (one reviewer calls the book "a comment on the architecture and ornament of emotional obfuscation" [Bellafante]): her father has the house and garden, her mother the local theater productions, they write letters (her mother a master's thesis), and they read, and they read, in many drawings. The family goes on one trip to Europe together, when Alison is young:

> It was a thrilling trip. In Switzerland I talked my parents into buying me hiking boots. In Cannes, I argued compellingly for the right to exchange my tank suit for a pair of shorts. Such freedom from convention was intoxicating. But while our travels widened my scope, I suspect my parents felt their own dwindling. Perhaps this was when I cemented the unspoken compact with them that I would never get married, that I would carry on to live the artist's life they had each abdicated. (73)

As in the panel I placed at this chapter's beginning, Bechdel draws herself as a child who doubted her abilities to think through writing. She shows the writing system she devised to question all her thinking, a system that eventually almost blots out her diary's words, and she shows how she followed algebraic convention to refer to her menstrual period so she wouldn't have to name it. But then she describes learning about orgasms while drawing, describes her own coming out (drawing herself looking up *lesbian* in a dictionary and finding relevant books in different libraries), and draws panels of herself masturbating (while reading) and having sex with other women (sometimes also while reading).

In *Fun Home*, the fraught household is described as resulting from the tensions of people trying to live as though "male" and "female" were cleanly defined by lists of dichotomous qualities like those I quoted some pages back. In the logic of the book, then, if the dichotomies are to be dissolved, words and pictures cannot be aligned with male or female or with thought and emotion, internal and external, time and space. Instead, male and female or thought and emotion come to be *across* words and pictures—and the words and pictures get complex as a result.

In *Fun Home*, the few frames that do not have a caption lettered above them have word boxes inside of them, often serving as labels to name or further explain what is pictured—and there are a considerable number of frames in which words are what's pictured: newspapers, magazines, and novel covers; graffiti; the pages of novels, dictionaries, police reports, passports, childcare manuals, calendars, and bird identification guides; memos; memorial stones and markers; letters both typed and handwritten;

diaries. There are also labeled maps and drawings of televisions showing movies and the news. Words function multiply in this book, in other words, and so these variously reproduced bits of paper and pages—in addition to suggesting that these events did indeed take place, as various commenters and Bechdel herself have argued—make visible how the lives in the book are composed from many bits and pieces, are visible from many perspectives but not from any single or simple list.

The pictures in the book are straightforwardly drawn in what Bechdel calls her "regular cartoony style" (Chute 1009) that makes visible the careful action of a drawing hand. Carefully redrawn photographs open each chapter and are placed within chapters, including one large enough to be the subject of the only two-page spread in the book. Most panels showing people are presented as though the reader/viewer were looking on from a middle distance, a framing device Bruce Block, in a book on the aesthetics of visual texts, describes as potentially encouraging reflection; the panels showing the pages of writing and type or photographs are drawn at close viewing distance, as though a reader/viewer were holding them. This viewing movement from middle to close distance keeps readers close, moving more or less closely in and out of the emotion and thought of the book. And, as with the preceding paragraph, what needs to be noted is that the pictures show how hard the word "picture" (or "image") has to work if we are to make it stand for all that can be pictured: the photographs, television screens, book pages, maps—everything else listed above—show that, in this book, there is no single visual representation, or kind of visual representation, capable of holding the complexity of identity the book constructs.

Overall, the book's pages show no regular pattern to how words and pictures can be connected. The visual field of the pages, as one scans over them, shows none of the regularity of (for example) the 3x3 grid of evenly sized panels that characterizes Moore and Gibbons's *Watchmen* or of the four-panel spreads that characterizes Barry's *One! Hundred! Demons!* Every page in *Fun Home* has its own arrangement of captions, labels, and drawings held together within the overall constraints of the page margins. The possible relationships of words and drawings in this book are also multiplied, not endlessly but well beyond the restraint of what word and picture or male and female can be in the lists from the beginning of this paper.

I want to be clear, however, that the identity Bechdel makes visible in this book is possible only because of those earlier lists. Like us all, Bechdel inherited an understanding of word and picture that separates them out and articulates them as in those lists. The identity that comes-to-be in this book, across word, picture, gender, and sex, might cross those lists, and complicate them, but is still in response to them.

■

The creators of these characters are in the vanguard of artists who are exploring the forms and conventions associated with comics as a means of revisiting and revising the conventional narratives that inscribe one's political, social, and gendered roles. (Tensuan 951)

In black graphic narratives, characters' negotiations of the complexities of racial categories also engender a self-reflexivity whereby they comment on the very form they inhabit as a means of openly challenging both narrative conventions and social norms. (Ryan 924)

The comics form is forever troubled by that which cannot be reconciled, synthesized, unified, contained within the frame; but it is in being so troubled that the form defines itself. (Gardner 801–2)

Word and picture can't be arbitrarily yanked out of the lists with which I began this essay. What makes it possible for Bechdel to construct the identity-to-be-tested in *Fun Home*—just as what makes possible the narratives told by Howard Cruse about growing up gay in Civil Rights era Alabama, by Phoebe Gloeckner about childhood sexual abuse, or by the contributors to *McSweeney's Thirteen* about sexual melancholy—is that comics and graphic novels come out of a history of attempted holding on to the keep-your-place positions in the dichotomous lists about and histories of words and pictures, male and female, high and low.

As comics and graphic novels take on such topics—precisely because they can, given their history—what new (potentially normalized) relations are being established between and among the terms of the dichotomies? How are the dichotomies being questioned and pummeled?

How, too, might we encourage people in our classes to work across words and pictures in order that they too might question the identities available to them? How might we encourage people in our classes to work across words and pictures in order that they too might engage with new mediations and hence new embodiments?

2 PAUSING TO REFLECT
Mass Observation, Blogs, and Composing Everyday Life

Paul Walker

How dreary to be somebody!
How public, like a frog
To tell your name the livelong day
To an admiring bog!
> — Emily Dickinson, "I'm Nobody, Who are you?"

Once
I tried to write invisibly,
but all lifetime is a candle.
> — Richard Kenney, "*Coda*"

What is it about a blog that prompts a consistent commitment to writing, and how do bloggers find time to be so involved in real or imagined conversations? I realize that many blogs don't last beyond the first few posts, but even if the contributions don't last, the many abandoned blogs (I've left two behind myself) still indicate a powerful initial desire to record ideas or random thoughts. This, of course, is what generates enthusiasm about new media—the ability of these technologies to facilitate communication between a writer/speaker and an audience without traditional gatekeepers.

Yet, in that enthusiasm, the abilities of new media can overshadow what may be a fundamental desire to be heard that factors into the motivation for the creation and use of any writing technology. Those of us who study writing insist that any technology used for writing be examined critically to encourage and enable writers to understand its use and significance. We know we must be careful about overenthusiastic social narratives "linking technological change to social change" ("Lest We" 293) as Cynthia Selfe has described, and we have learned to avoid too much emphasis on the "technology itself." Attentive exploration of technology's cultural, material, and historical aspects, according to Christina Haas, protects us from the supposition that technology is either all powerful and revolutionary or transparent and benign (31). Haas contends that by recognizing the "inextricable" relationship between writing and the material world, we will identify technologies that for centuries have facilitated writing as "language made material" (3). Thus, understanding the "multiple dimensions" (Selfe, "Lest We"

322) of technology, not simply "its consequences," helps us remember that technical facilitation, writing, and the content for writing have a long history and complex "infrastructure" (DeVoss et al. 37), which should temper and guide any overeager praise of "new" technologies.

Noting that all communicative technology was "once-new," Nancy K. Baym describes how research of digital technologies is "too often plagued by the notion that everything is new." Continuing, she states that "our focus on 'new media' should not blind us to which things we ascribe to particular technologies are better attributed to novelty and the ways in which cultures project their concerns onto technology." Likewise, Wiebe E. Bijker warns against placing inordinate importance on technology without understanding the social roots:

> One should never take the meaning of a technical artifact or technological system as residing in the technology itself. Instead, one must study how technologies are shaped and acquire their meanings in the heterogeneity of social interactions. (6)

A study of new media, then, should address historical patterns that illustrate how literacy practices, rooted in cultural events and everyday life, are enabled by various social and technical factors. People not only project themselves through technology, but as Baym identifies, they "project their concerns" upon technology, reminding us that meaning remains within the humans that build and use technical systems. Thus, according to Baym, "we need to link our theory, framing, research inquiries and findings to the history on which the production, reception, adoption and everyday use of technologies rests."

Responding to such a call, this chapter centers on a historical example of writing—mass observation—to show how notions of blogging's literate and technological power can be situated within the historical and myriad social factors that shape and are shaped by any emerging technology. Mass observation (MO), a 1930s anthropological project involving the writing of ordinary citizens of England, illustrates how any technology may have the capability to increase everyday life's influence on collective knowledge. Further, MO addresses how writing may form a transcendent move from an ordinary individual to a legitimized author. The validation of a perceived audience contributes to the continuing development of technology towards increased individual access to public debates and conversations. MO is not, of course, the oldest or most profound facilitator of such literacy, but in significant ways, its process and participants anticipated today's blogs as a circuit for the "productive power" of writing everyday life.

Founded by three members of Britain's middle class, MO recruited observers to conduct an ethnographic study of working-class populations, and solicited volunteer "correspondents" from the working classes to submit day diaries and responses to directives inquiring about issues and major events mainly during World War II. MO enabled large numbers of these "ordinary" persons to lend their voices to national issues, and thus provided the "masses" with the opportunity, through publication, to sense the symbolic and real power of writing words strangers might read. By framing MO alongside blogs, I hope to show that new media are not exclusive in the facilitation of networked writing and that a personal sense of satisfaction may accompany projecting one's self, through writing, beyond body and spatial boundaries. Although discussions involving individual identity and desire have inherently speculative elements, writing undoubtedly plays a complicated role in constructing our "personhood" and individual contribution to society. Through the words of selected MO participants and bloggers, this chapter illustrates that MO's example as a social and literacy practice—addressed fully by Dorothy Sheridan, Brian Street, and David Bloome—also provides insight into internal and external motivations for writing via everyday life and technology.

MASS OBSERVATION IN ENGLAND

In late 1936, an increased interest in understanding contemporary culture in England led Charles Madge, Humphrey Jennings, and Tom Harrisson to embark on "anthropology at home" by inviting the cooperation of voluntary observers (Madge and Harrisson "Letter"). Those voluntary observers were intended to be secondary to paid investigators who conducted lengthy ethnographic research in working-class areas of England—but the work of the paid investigators was eventually overshadowed by the words of volunteer observers, who were asked to keep a diary of their own everyday experiences as well as comment on "directives" of national import. The volunteers' words fulfilled the founders' desires for contemporary anthropological study and publications, and were also of use to the government and other organizations in understanding war-time feelings and views of the populace.

The first "day diary" directive was sent out to volunteers in January 1937, instructing them to keep a diary of what they did on February 12, 1937. They repeated the process on the 12th of March, the 12th of April, and throughout the year, which included May 12, 1937, the day of George VI's coronation following Edward VIII's abdication of the throne—a major cultural event that testified to how major events interrupt, and cause reflection on, everyday life. On the coronation day, MO sent observers into the crowd to record behavior and sent out questionnaires asking "Where were you on May 12th?" In the published work of that day, *May the Twelfth*, the day diaries of the volunteer writers prevailed (Sheridan et al. 28), illustrating the appeal of an ordinary perspective. Perhaps because of the perspectives that volunteer writers contributed beyond their day diaries, Madge, Harrisson, and Jennings became more interested in the "directive" work of the volunteer writers. Collecting these directives, they said,

> immediately puts us in touch with a section of people in the population who were at one and the same time ordinary, hardworking folk and also intelligent and interesting enough to want to help us. We did not regard these people as being themselves scientists studying the mass, nor did we consider them as being a random sample of public opinion. Their position was something different. They were observers, untrained but shrewd, placed at vantage points for seeing and describing in their own simple language what life looks like in the various environments which go to make up England. ("They Speak" 3)

The language used by Madge and Harrisson to describe their volunteers as ordinary, simple, and interesting enough led some to criticize MO as being "a middle-class adventure at the expense of the working class" (Gurney, quoted in Sheridan et al. 27). Yet MO volunteers were genuinely "without access to more public channels of communication" and therefore "a relatively 'voiceless' group in pre-war Britain" (Sheridan et al. 33). In the words of Madge and Harrisson, the collection of "what life looks like in various environments" by volunteers became "a camera with no distortion[, telling] us not what society is like, but what it looks like to them" (*First-Year's Work* 66). The metaphor of the camera was significant, according to Nick Hubble, who, referencing Freud, argues that Madge and Jennings "set out by collecting images from their trained volunteer observers to consciously create the conditions for unfamiliar associations that would allow the opportunity for expression than would otherwise 'naturally' occur and so accelerate social transformation" (13).

Such a reading of MO's intentions illustrates how everyday life's power through the ordinary can originate from both a personal and a political agenda. If provided the opportunity to be "liberated from externally imposed sense associations" through written response to "unnatural associations," one can make use of the "productive" notion concerned with how power can be transformed, not simply accessed or resisted (Sheridan et al. 241). MO's invitation and publication of ordinary people's opinions on national topics provided broad "symbolic capital" (Bourdieu) that allowed untapped cultural capital of "intelligent and interesting enough" observations to be heard. Thus, the "apparently mundane, 'everyday' writing and literacy practices of the Mass-Observation correspondents" reflect how "writing opens up and transforms the social positions occupied and available to be occupied" (Sheridan et al. 241).

The original mass observation was, alas, short lived. Jennings left the project in 1939, just two years after its inception, and Madge left in 1940 because of conflicts with Harrisson in their approaches. MO operated in various forms during the war, but "without its founders, Mass-Observation gradually lost its subversive eccentricity; in 1949, it was incorporated as a market-research firm" (Crain). In the 1960s the archives were discovered in a basement by two historians and were given a place at the University of Sussex. In 1981, the directives from MO began again, and the project continues to recruit correspondents, issue directives, and invite academic research today. The exemplary process through which MO garnered information, as Sheridan et al. illustrate in their connection of MO to literacy, is as important as the actual words of the volunteers and observers. As Madge posited, the observer's task was "not to raise to the level of his own consciousness aspects of humanity hitherto concealed or only guessed at, but he has to raise the level of consciousness collectively of the whole mass[;] he has to induce self-realization on a mass scale" (Hubble 113). By soliciting volunteers from classes outside the media and academic gates, MO demonstrated the public urge to write, and the enabling, authenticating power of writing the everyday in forming collective knowledge.

THE "PRODUCTIVE POWER" OF EVERYDAY LIFE

The sociologist Rita Felski notes that women and men are "embodied, embedded subjects, who live, for the most part, repetitive, familiar and ordinary lives" (31), and "unless a specific problem emerges to demand our attention, we rarely pause to reflect upon the mundane ritualized practices around which much of our everyday life is organized" (29). The results and methods of MO provided data for the anthropologically curious interested in looking over the shoulders, so to speak, of their ordinary neighbors. MO participants were directed to, in essence, "pause to reflect" on those mundane and repetitive everyday practices. Like the MO founders, participants recognized that the "ordinary" voice was missing from "establishment" discussions, and they agreed that government or scientific experts could not accurately speak for them. Their on-the-ground insights challenged the observation-based anthropological study of everyday life by exemplifying first-hand the notion of "liberation" from within the mundane spaces of physical existence.

Over half a century later, blogging software, among its other uses, allows individuals to likewise record conventional, habitual, and occasionally insightful aspects of their everyday lives. Blogs are recent renditions of what anthropologists at MO's time recognized in the words of MO's respondents: manifestations of a perceived authenticity wherein individuals grasp the "exotic" power of everyday life and the possibility for elevation from the ordinary to the extraordinary (de Certeau; Firth; Goffman; Malinkowski). In fact, for theorists such as Henri LeFebvre and Michael Gardiner, studying the commonplaces of everyday life is essential to discovering the "power concealed in everyday life's apparent banality" (LeFebvre, *Everyday Life* 37) and to "unlock the extraordinary potential that is hidden in its prosaic routines" (Gardiner 6). Jürgen Habermas also believed that the "lifeworld" holds "emancipatory potential in relation to the prevailing systems of power" (qtd. in Bennett and Watson xv). Implicit in these lofty notions of everyday life's power is the transportation of the person to less ordinary realms—the projection of one's identity. Habermas believed that we cannot construct an identity independently of the identifications others make of us (107), and according to Lev Vygotsky, writing and language are among the tools that mediate our individual and cultural development. Writing, then, can make us who we are, yet it can also facilitate development or change in that identity, depending on the amount of "productive power" we hold—the means and ability to voice one's "ordinary" thoughts (see Kress, *Learning*; Street). In order to realize the "emancipatory potential" of everyday life, one has to somehow transcend the everyday so as to discover and unlock its power. Thus, while everyday life's grounding theoretically provides the potential for authenticity and transformation, in Felski's terms, authenticity and transformation cannot occur until one can stop daily tasks enough to record them so as to reflect on them, which ultimately requires time and technical facilitation, or writing technologies (C. Haas).

The realization and extension of everyday life's power, then, relies on writing technologies, time to pause, and reason to reflect. But we have to acknowledge that this power in everyday life may include a false consciousness of that power's value. Technological tools, time, and purpose are means that broaden the "productive power" of individuals, but "individual literacy exists only as part of larger material systems, systems that on the one hand enable acts of reading or writing and on the other hand confer their value" (Brandt 1). Despite the supposed limitlessness of the internet, writing for the internet maintains a resemblance to print publishing because it consists of aspects agreed on and built by individuals within existing systems of power and influence, which may determine the ultimate power and real, not perceived, authenticity of its technical facilitation.

The popularity of blogs and other internet-based technologies thus complicates the convergence of the ordinary and the authentic. If we are interested in contributing to the cultural conversation but not affiliated with a multimodal news organization, the blog can cause us to believe we are part of that collective society that before was beyond our "personal lifeworld"— or, in Habermas's words, beyond the bounds "of all possible experiences and actions that can be attributed to the individual in his exchange with his social environment" (111). However, the sheer number of such communications, along with the retentive gatekeeping of the (old) media, may inhibit our actual reach and thus the extent of actual power gained through blogging, because that collective identity we are after doesn't actually *need* us. As Habermas states, "Only *a certain segment* of the culture and action system is important for the identity of a collective—namely the taken-for-granted, consensual, basic values and institutions that enjoy a kind of fundamental validity in the group" (111; emphasis in original).

Nevertheless, Habermas posits that projecting our identities beyond our personal lifeworlds leads to a reflective form of identity formation, wherein the "projection mechanism"—such as a writing technology—creates in us a "knowledge that to a certain extent individuals and societies themselves establish their identities" (116). While there are bloggers who have established themselves as "fundamentally valid" to one group or another, the majority are simply extending their lifeworld by projecting their ordinarily embodied selves beyond it. The increasing number and quality of personal blogs, which resemble public diaries of ordinary lives, support Habermas: communicating the everyday to a potential audience may provide elevating satisfaction through the establishment and projection of one's identity.

Within Habermas's frame, we can identify blogging as part of a historical and social progression of projection: the blog capability is not neutral because of its wide use, nor is it novel because of its technology. Rather, like a printed book, the blog is a normative structure, a multimodal genre with surprisingly staid conventions. Because of their immediacy, blogs are indeed effective enablers of the historical enthusiasm for projecting ourselves beyond our circumstances, but they are not creators or indicators of a new desire to share our mundane lives with the world or to contribute to the collective understanding of our culture as part of identity development. Mass observation enabled a similar desire, and its example helps us understand our embodiment in the everyday and our attitudes toward writing technologies as a means of literacy and the (virtual) dissemination of discourse.

REASONS TO "PAUSE TO REFLECT"

In relative terms, the notion of public opinion is a recent historical phenomenon brought about by increased printing technology in the nineteenth century so that "widespread expression and discussion of private opinions was collectively manifested" (Hubble 22). Although literacy in the populace has steadily increased, the access to public dissemination in the last two centuries has tended to decrease. As described by Habermas, representative democracy ironically allowed government to move away from a "critically debating public" (136). The means to reach a large potential audience is typically available to a limited number of individuals, and even these individuals' thoughts are vetted by fewer individuals (editors, publishers) by whom the dissemination is controlled. The professional filtering of information provides levels of officialism, and in the famous words of John Stuart Mill, an escape from the "tyranny of prevailing opinion." But as media grow inseparable from the political and economical interests of a relative few, the ability of filtered information to express the opinions and understanding of the individual members of the populace is severely restricted. Hence the enthusiasm of MO participants to disclose thoughts on their lives and issues of their time.

MO gave respondents a reason to reflect and a technical means for the dissemination of their ideas, and they made the time to contribute. The "everyday" aspect of their responses could be unusually mundane. For example, one respondent in 1945 provides an unexpected inventory of personal feelings and actions in spite of significant historical news:

> When the first newsflash came through the radio announcing the surrender of the German forces in north-west Germany, I was in bed mopping my ears . . . . It looks as though I shall spend the day and days following in close, solitary seclusion. My ears are a most revolting sight and even Dr. B is baffled. I am worried and tired and do not want to go out or meet anyone . . . . My friends are sympathetic and anxious but I feel rather a leper and imagine all strangers to be goggling at me . . . . I bought lettuce, radishes, beetroot and mustard and cress, came home, prepared salad, Hovis and butter, glass of milk, honey and an orange, and got into bed and ate it there. (Garfield)

Despite her reluctance to go out in public for fear of "strangers goggling at me," that same hesitation is not in her writing, although she knows she will send this detailed glimpse of her day to strangers. The fascinating part of this response is how the momentous is immediately reduced to everyday particulars. She makes no comments on the end of the war, choosing rather to explain in great detail her health concerns and grocery list at the time of the announcement. Another respondent, during this same period, provides an unappreciative take on an art exhibit he attended while waiting to hear in person the official announcement of the war's end. Again, the focus is on the immediate concerns—comfort and hunger—rather than on the momentous atmosphere of world history or the representation of art:

> I put a pencil mark in the catalogue against the exhibits that were able to keep me in front of them for more than five seconds. No. 31: "Girl Resting" by A.R. Middleton. She is naked, but it was the position of her left foot that caught my eye and I wondered how she could pose in that position without getting

cramp . . . . No. 184: "Still Life" by Frederick Elwell. There is a cold ham with a nice wide cut in the middle showing the inside lean part, and a pork pie with a couple of bottles of spirit alongside. It made me feel hungry, and I remembered that I had a sausage roll in my pocket, but I could not eat sausage roll in the Royal Academy. (Garfield)

The above responses do not indicate immense thought regarding the day or event they were directed to relate in writing. But that was the point. Diaries, according to Menand, have an "absolute fidelity to the present," meaning the absence of elongated perspective or reflection. Thus, one of the appeals for the ordinary people of MO was being a part of something larger without compromising their own personal in-the-moment perspective, as described by Ken Barrow, a British sociologist:

> The history of ordinary people has to be written while it's happening as there is no surviving source material otherwise . . . . I think the whole point of M-O is that it is the individual's own particular view. The ordinary voice. (Sheridan et al. 158)

In this way, MO was revolutionary, because as noted by Dorothy E. Smith, the study of everyday life is incomplete because "sociology is part of the ruling apparatus" (8). The only way for an equal representation of women and men in the sociology of everyday life, according to Smith, is for everyday life to become a "problematic, . . . an explicit discursive formulation of an actual property of the organization of the everyday world . . . —a reality as it arises for those who live it" (9). The power of everyday life will not come about through a sociological discovery but through its being expressed by those living it, wherein "writing opens up and transforms the social positions occupied and available to be occupied" (Sheridan, et al. 241). Deliberate reflection and perspective were not absent from MO, as evidenced by certain responses. One respondent explained, in an interview about the directive process, how much he thought about the directives:

> My mind fills up with the directive, and as I start on it my mind will whirl around with all the ideas that they're asking questions about. My ideas are formulated, every time I see anything, so all I've to do is write it down . . . . I want to get right on to the nub of it, grasp it properly, what they're asking, and work it all out. It'd take awhile, I'd keep thinking about it. It'd go for days. And then once I'd got writing, it all flows through. (Sheridan et al. 205)

Exponentially, blogs facilitate "pausing to reflect" in order to make public the ideas and experiences of private individuals. Echoing the "whirling around" of the MO participant above, this blogger describes how he/she handles the idea-driven blogosphere:

As a writer, thanks to blogs I'm more intellectually stimulated than I've ever been in my life. I can't get to sleep because I have ideas I want to respond to or that I want to instigate. I bolt out of bed in the morning to get in a little more time thinking out loud and thinking together. The water's boiling with our ideas. ("Why Do We Blog?)

The technical means for releasing these ideas forms an important part of the circulation process, yet it seems the main difference is immediacy. The MO participant deliberately thought about the directive until he was ready to write, and the words "flowed"; the blogger's thoughts interrupted sleep and he or she was satisfied only when his/her thoughts were communal via the blog. But whether the "directive" was received by the MO volunteer or grasped by the blogger, a rhetorical situation existed to drive the production of communication. The technology, in both cases, is essential to delivery once they've been given a reason to pause to reflect.

Currently, anyone with internet access can create a blog or join a social networking site and "critically debate." We know that a very small percentage of the world's millions of blogs contribute significantly to public policy or collective knowledge, but that very potential is a powerful, if statistically unrealistic, motivator. As shown by MO participants' and bloggers' reasons for participating in their respective mediums, the actual audience may be less important than the perception of that audience.

WRITING FOR GAIN

My use of transcendence in this chapter is limited to the sense that writing under the impression of a potential audience leads to perceived or real validation/authentication beyond one's ordinary life. This transcendent satisfaction of writing can only be recognized by the individual, and must be formed outside the act of writing that leads to its conception. In other words, without MO participants and bloggers expressing such sentiments outside their day-to-day or issue-related writing activities, this discussion would be moot. Fortunately, the MO founders inquired of several of their volunteer day diarists to ask (1) Why did you join mass observation? (2) What do you think it is for? (3) What do you yourself most hope to gain from it? and (4) What suggestions have you for work that it should undertake? (Madge and Harrisson, *First Year's Work*). In this section I sample from their responses to questions 1, 2, and 3 because those questions align with archived blog queries that ask "Why do we blog?" and "Who do you blog for?" In the sampled responses, I am intrigued by those who mention the degree of personal value they gain or do not gain in writing for a potential public.

First, here are some responses by MO participants that express the self-satisfaction occurring through the project, both in terms of the act of writing and writing for a wider and unknown audience:

Assisting (although in a minor way) a worth while movement such as mass observation gives me a real sense of satisfaction. This is what I most hope to gain from it, as long as I am permitted to help. Also I should like the thrill of seeing something I have written in print. (*First Year's Work* 74)

. . .

I only hope to gain from [MO] the recreation of writing, and the pleasure of knowing (and hoping) that I am doing something definitely USEFUL for the future of society. (*Wartime Women* 21)

. . .

I hope to gain . . . some knowledge of the vast undercurrents of modern life which I hold will be of immense interest to Sociologists of the future who will write of the twentieth century. Then there is an added interest, and anything that makes life fuller makes it happier, also a sense of usefulness to the community other than just looking after a house and my family, a sense that is wider I think. (*Wartime Women* 19)

These participants relate that writing can provide satisfaction from recreational and active perspectives, as well as a method for gaining new knowledge. But the "added interest" for them was the hope that their words would be printed or otherwise distributed to benefit a "wider" society than the one in which they operated, with reference to increased happiness. Other participants hoped for "immortality in print" (Sheridan et al. 182) or a sense of assistance in "accelerating the rate of evolution" (*First Year's Work* 75). Some participants, however, were less hopeful of the personal benefits of writing for MO, placing the value of their observations completely outside themselves:

I do not expect any immediate gain as it will most likely be some time before results are available to benefit me in a public sense. (*First Year's Work* 71)

. . .

I lose nothing by giving information to mass observation, and they apparently place value on my humble observations. (*First Year's Work* 73)

. . .

The studies of daily lives with every little detail should be very interesting to posterity in the way the Samuel Pepys diary is . . . . [However,] I do not hope to gain anything from it personally, though I am interested to read the bulletins and hope to read the books produced later. (*Wartime Women* 18)

Placing writing's benefits upon posterity, not themselves, suggests their sense of "gain" is outside their perceived identities. In fact, the man who said he lost nothing by contributing wrote that to expect a gain from writing for MO was like insisting on payment for giving directions on the street. Further, the knowledge of the possibility for "books produced later" represents a deferred knowledge benefit, but unlike other respondents, this writer ignores a validating, transcendent hope/realization that her words could be included in a public document. While modesty foregrounds MO's "apparent" interest in the "humble" observations of individuals, I sense that these respondents are viewing "gain" as the public validation that one should not seek. This speculation is based on similar sentiments given by bloggers who likewise want to separate themselves from the "shallowness" of the hope for external validation:

> I started blogging some years ago largely to pass time and share experiences. A small part of me, however, was selfishly hoping for admiration and affirmation; a shallow attitude I've long abandoned. (Hozschlag)

> ...

> I'm absolutely certain that I blog for myself. My blog is the all-me, all-the-time station. That's its purpose, and if zero, ten, or ten thousand people read or stopped reading, it wouldn't matter. I'd blog to an empty house or a full one. My desire to please people suggests, at times, that maybe I should let my audience drive my content. But my instinct demands that I stay true to what and who I am, not what others want. (Hozschlag)

The idea that the audience does not matter, mentioned also by several of Hozschlag's 131 respondents, illustrates a paradox identified by Walter J. Ong: the more personal writing is intended to be, he suggests, the more fictionalized the audience ("The Writer's Audience" 73). MO enabled some diarists to attain internal satisfaction from the knowledge that there were others like them and their words might someday reach a "public" beyond MO's investigators. A blog's imagined audience likewise embeds the writer into the technology and mediates that individual's personal satisfaction and audience validation. The audience of a diary is complex, for addressing oneself in "full sentences and paragraphs" is not an easy task, generally resulting in the revised intention of writing diaries for "posterity" (Menand)—a switch from internal inherence to external expedience. Thus, according to Ong, if the history of diaries was written, "it will have to be a history of the fictionalizing of readers" ("The Writer's Audience" 73). The MO participants' knowledge that their words could be printed and bloggers' knowledge that anyone on the internet can read their words are examples of Ong's fictionalization of readers, because the writer makes changes to include a perceived audience, even without directly addressing an audience. The MO movement and blogging thus fit Lisa Ede and Andrea Lunsford's premise that writing "is a means of *making* meaning for writer and reader" (82; emphasis added).

Many writers hesitate to take on such authority, resulting in an unsure approach to audience, confirming Ong's points. The "high road" among sampled bloggers seems to be writing for oneself first and writing for the readers (called "punditry" by one blogger) second; doing both should emerge from the self, not the audience. A proud sense of ordinariness prevails among the blog query responses, and to presume to be important to others before being true to one's self is to seek false authenticity and identity. Yet writing technology inherently creates a potential audience, and the intervention of that audience, even if temporarily forgotten or consciously ignored, complicates meaning, as illustrated by this MO participant:

> The most difficult aspect of writing for me—its heart of darkness—is the sense of an audience. I tend to take an "I write as I please" approach. No harm in that, I suppose, as long as it doesn't lead you into the self-indulgence and obscurity of a purely internal address. But, though I claim no special integrity as an author and certainly have no message for the world, I would find it impossible to write in sheer bad faith to an external formula. (Sheridan et al. 196–7)

The personal self-indulgence of writing complicates the "shallowness" of writing for others. The notion among my sample of bloggers that writing for the audience is secondary to writing for one's self removes writing's role in Habermas's two-way identity-defining process. The complicated response by the MO respondent above, along with bloggers who recognize the way the audience confuses and enhances their own writing, illustrates the identity confusion inherent in making words public:

> I blog for me, and would continue to blog if I lost all of my faithful visitors, but at the same time I know that the frequency of my entries and the way I write them is purely aimed at the visitor. (Hozschlag)

> ...

> I blog because it extends me in a way that affirms who I am. The affirmation comes from knowing I can be myself and not be alone in my thoughts, dreams, and fears. (Hozschlag)

The purposeful and meaningful use of *blog* as a verb in the above responses provides a twist to Ede and Lunsford's idea that "the writing process is not complete unless another person, someone other than the writer, reads the text also" (93). For some bloggers, it seems, blogging produces affirmation and then produces connection—"knowing I can be myself and not be alone." Using existing technology for writing, we exchange sovereignty for an audience, yet the idea of that audience can affirm our projected identity. MO volunteers were aware of other volunteers, and knew that someone was reading their diaries, and they thus felt a part of something larger than themselves, just as these bloggers are "affirmed" by the knowledge that their "visitors" are reading what they have projected to that larger sphere.

"IT'S OUR NEIGHBORHOOD"

For many, "Weblogging is the only place for an amateur writer to be real and be read" ("Why Do We Blog?"). However, as shown here, MO also proved to be a significant place for an "amateur" to express a written opinion in 1930s Britain. Beyond the poignant linguistic similarity in the combination of the terms to *be real* and *be read*, the similarities between MO and blogs suggest that authenticity and legitimacy are unlikely to be attained without a sense of validation from others in a community or network. Whether it involves a quest to transcend or evolves simply as a byproduct of writing, moving beyond our perceived "ordinariness" relies on technology's evoked audience in order for our identity to be shaped by the identification of ourselves by others:

> Why blog? Because it's our neighborhood. It's where we live. We create ourselves and we spend much of our time in some online mode. It's just an extension of who we are and how we spend our time.

For many, the metaphorical blog neighborhood and the actual online neighborhoods (Second Life, Sims) as real locations for our virtuality mark a distinct re-envisioning of everyday life. But such a view of virtual community is not unique to the digital age. One MO participant viewed MO as a way to presumably escape the company of immediate neighbors who did not share enthusiasm for discussing national issues: he sought a new "neighborhood" through MO, writing that "I most hope to gain from it: more information in all these matters, and contact with other people to whom these things matter" (*First Year's Work* 75). Whether this individual ever had direct "contact" with fellow participants, he expected to be part of a virtual neighborhood of thinkers.

Interestingly, MO diaries also illustrate the nonvirtuality of existence— one's embodiment in a physical neighborhood that is, nevertheless, a construction of social interactions. During the Blitz, diaries of the morning after detailed which houses in the neighborhood were hit, or described conversations about which neighborhoods were supposedly hit or spared. An MO volunteer from the town of Coventry, following an unexpected bombing of the area instead of London, lamented that "the size of the town meant that nearly everyone knew someone who was killed or missing. The dislocation is so total that people easily feel that the town itself is finished" ("The Blitz"). Without the connections that each individual forms for the whole neighborhood, virtual or actual, the community, and its power, cannot exist.

Central to MO was a transformative power that, through collective individual effort, enabled and harnessed "human potential and creative energy" rather than continuing the roles "disciplinary and coercive forms of power have taken on in modern society" (Sheridan et al. 241). Rather than gaining access to the power that was held by dominant institutions, MO correspondents "challenged and redefined relations of authority over knowledge between dominant institutions on one hand and 'ordinary' people on the other" (290). The productivity of writing's transformative power for MO's volunteers was based on the ability to "act on" the literacy practices that surrounded them precisely because MO demonstrated "a space in which ordinary people can make and do with literacy practices available in this society" (289).

On a broader scale, the technology of blogs also provides that space wherein writers make astonishingly visible the ways in which they make meaning from and transform the information and materials from dominant institutions. The shared ordinariness of everyday life and opinions preclude the validity and influence of online communications. That commonality creates a "neighborhood," or in digital terms, a network—defined by Jeff Rice as a "space of connectivity" ("Networks" 128). Just as Sheridan et al. illustrate how MO created a literacy space outside a constructed system and filled it with those lacking a location to make meaning (289), Rice posits that networks "are ideological as well as technological spaces generated by various forms of new media that allow information, people, places, and other items to establish a variety of relationships that previous spaces or ideologies of space (print being the dominant model) did not allow" ("Networks" 128).

In our current multimodal and online environment, it is easy to agree with Rice's last phrase because we are overwhelmingly aware of the forms and relationships that are created so quickly through online technologies. But as suggested earlier, new media are not the only creators of networks, nor especially are they creators of the drive to connect. MO, likewise, was an enabler—a significant technological, sociological, and psychological endeavor that complicates how we situate networking notions of "new" media. Madge, Harrisson, and Jennings facilitated a network that connected people across social positions and geography to form a common bond among writers who acted individually to form a collective. Writing a blog indeed keeps writers "connected to information in ways the space on the page does not allow," but the online space does not necessarily eliminate completely the limitation that "the space on the page keeps bodies of information (and, thus, bodies) separate" (Rice, "Networks" 130). The virtual connection of online writers is no more ideologically powerful than the embodied virtual connection among MO correspondents, who realized their contribution to historical record as both an individual and collective entity, despite not being in direct contact with other observers.

On the surface, one real difference between MO's enabling ability and the enabling ability of blogs seems to be that the availability of MO's collective identity was limited and controlled by the organization in order to give voice to a specific social group. However, while the technology of "new media" is available to several layers of privilege, from the high school student to the executive, and despite the millions of blogs, the inherent constrictions of internet access still subvert an unknown and unvoiced population. Bijker illustrates how it is nearly impossible to track all of the factors and individuals that contributed to the design or use of a given technology, and this, he notes, leads to the idea that a study of sociotechnical change can set free those who are socially subservient to the dominant culture. But, since "all relevant social groups contribute to the social construction of technology and all relevant artifacts contribute to the construction of social relations" (288), all individuals should be made aware of the "social and micropolitical" structures that enable effective use of those artifacts, for whatever purpose. The power that one obtains through writing everyday life is always available to, and mostly determined by, the dominant culture. Therefore, while recognizing the opaque yet enabling components of technology, our educational authority in using these technologies should be carefully modulated. If we extend an unmitigated construction of the socially empowering abilities of technology, tomorrow's (and today's) bloggers may overlook the reality that technologies are designed within social and cultural constraints of power and access that are not too unlike the class system to which MO responded.

Accordingly, we must recognize new media as enablers with political limits. Composing ourselves, through expressing our habits of everyday life, is a literacy practice enabled by, and embodied in, current technological and social innovation. To view blogs and other new media without the perspective of previous technological and social enablers of "ordinary" people is to place too much emphasis on the all-powerful myth of technology. Our habits and their interconnectedness with the physical and informational environments that surround us create the impetus to compose and express ourselves, while technological progression represents (only) the development of the means to do so. If not grounded in social relationships, historical perspectives, and habits of everyday life, technology can encourage "easy attention for adding nothing" ("College Essay")—Dickinson's croaking frog.

Thus, "the need for MO's founding vision of a transformed participatory mass society based on a dialectical combination of collective independence and individual agency is now greater than ever" (Hubble 225) because technical facilitation of that agency has escalated far beyond the vision of MO's founders. In the study of mass observation as it relates to current technology, the historical connections of reflective and observatory writing show that "mass participatory" transformation within ourselves can indeed occur when technical facilitation empowers us. The key element is the perception of audience; whether it is ourselves or the rest of the world, the knowledge that our ideas and habits matter to someone seems to excite us to share them by whatever means are at our disposal. The quick rise and exponential growth of new media so powerfully facilitate writing and literacy as to require us to pause; to remind ourselves that technology can prevent our recognition of the social and cultural processes that lead to technical advances. New media challenge us to compose ourselves meaningfully, balancing how we embody everyday practices, power, literacy, want of attention, culture, and identity. This challenge connects us with writers like M-O volunteers and others in history who, by their reflection and our knowledge of their words, achieved a degree of authorship and validity by consciously, even enthusiastically, projecting their everyday life—and its infrastructure—during their "ordinary" lifetimes.

3 AUTHORING AVATARS
Gaming, Reading, and Writing Identities

Matthew S. S. Johnson

To claim that exploring identity—our own and that of others—is a common focus in the composition classroom would be absurd. Not because it isn't so but because identity exploration has become so pervasive that making such a claim would amount to prosaic reporting of conventional wisdom for those even remotely familiar with contemporary pedagogical theory. We have even come to accept that identity is comprised of multiple selves (or, if we prefer, the self is comprised of multiple identities, whichever term we may wish to privilege), and that a single "self" may simultaneously occupy numerous subject positions.

John Trimbur succinctly captures this focus on identity in his textbook *The Call to Write*: "Writing," he says, "should belong to everyone in the various roles people play" (xxxvi). And even in *Writing from Sources*—I say "even" only because its title arguably indicates that the book focuses on something other than the inward self—Brenda Spatt informs students that "most of the knowledge and many of the ideas that you express to others originate outside of yourself" and "you simply go about your activities, communicating with others and making decisions based on your acquired knowledge" (ix). Both claims do, ultimately, center on the self and its agency: what we know, how we know it, the roles we perform based on that knowledge, and how those performances shape what we do and say. Myriad other writing textbooks make similar claims, implicitly or explicitly, to the effect that identity exploration is a crucial activity for rhetorical invention and for learning in general.

Exploration of the self can lead to an exploration of the world that one inhabits, and simultaneously how world and self affect one another, are influenced by one another, are even formed by one another. Such exploration is often (rightly, I think) cited as one primary goal of academic or scholarly writing. Consider the preface to *Writing Analytically*—indeed its opening lines—in which David Rosenwasser and Jill Stephen introduce the focus of their text: "This book argues that analysis, rather than dissecting information, fosters an exploratory attitude toward experience" (xv). What's more, "Writers are like scientists," Rise B. Axelrod and Charles R. Cooper claim in *The St. Martin's Guide to Writing*, "they ask questions, systematically inquiring about how things work, what they are, where they occur, and how more information can be learned about them" (569). Identity and experience exploration and experimentation help to foster an inquisitive spirit, one that is a prerequisite to effective analysis.

In practice, as composition scholars and teachers, we tend to ask students not merely to examine their own identities and those of others but to do more: we ask students to create identities and be conscious about their design. A first-year composition course, as the single remaining course required of students on many university campuses, is often used to introduce students to "college life" or "college learning." To focus on the development of a productive attitude toward college is implicitly to ask students to recognize and acknowledge a subject position they already occupy or are already given: they are students. In fact, their identities as students often intrude upon their developing authorial roles, as when statements such as the jarring "For this assignment, I chose to write about" appear in their essays. And while, I would venture to say, all of them already write as students, the college composition course asks them to create a second, nonstudent identity to be used in the academic community, an identity that may at first feel distinctly unreal, foreign, or even transgressive. Common queries such as "You mean we can use 'I' in our papers?" and "Should we express our opinions in our arguments?" indicate their discomfort with assuming the authoritative roles we ask them to fill—that is, the anxiety they feel acting through an identity they may not feel qualified to fully possess.

Ultimately what we are asking students to do is to become writers (not just people who happen to write sometimes), to form authorial identities. And we often do this by asking them to explore—the self, the perspectives of others, the subjectivities that society constructs for us and those we create for ourselves to occupy—and to be conscious and even self-reflective about that exploration. While we unconsciously switch from subject position to subject position regularly, or to use Spatt's phrase, "simply go about [our] activities" (for example, responding to different individuals in different environments, such as a teacher in a classroom as opposed to a roommate in a dorm room), the conscious creation of an identity is comparatively rare. And while I would argue that Trimbur, Spatt, Rosenwasser and Stephen, and Axelrod and Cooper herald this creative (that is, having to do with an act of creation) activity in their academic texts, we can also glimpse such an endeavor in an unlikely place: computer role-playing games.

Computer games in general and role-playing games in particular have long provided their players the opportunity to explore various identities, especially through the sophisticated player-character creation processes (to which I return, below) during which gamers must define the character that they are to inhabit for the gameplay experience. While the game itself enables gamers to conduct identity explorations and even experimentations, the game manuals, like the writing textbooks from which we teach, ask gamers to be conscious of the identities they construct, and to investigate the implications of the subject positions their player-characters are to operate within, paralleling the sort of identity awareness we often try to encourage in the composition classroom.

Consider the echo of Trimbur's "roles people play" and Rosenwasser and Stephen's "exploratory attitude" in the *Neverwinter Nights* manual (a *Dungeons and Dragons* style computer game):

> Before you can play Neverwinter Nights, you first have to decide what type of character you want to play. There is a great deal of room for customization, so this may seem a little intimidating at first. It is best to remember that there are no good or bad characters, and different people appreciate different aspects of the game. You can create any number of characters, so feel free to experiment. (Knowles et al. 38)

In this sense, games are more "open" than composition, where, rhetorically speaking, there are certain qualities that need to be ethically expressed. In academic writing, there are "bad"—or at least completely ineffective—identities. In gaming, the manual clearly indicates that the game will not allow players to construct characters that simply will not work, even if creating characters is still "intimidating"; it is only within the game's framework that "free play" is allowed. Composition students, however, must be wary of expressing identities that are ignorant, prejudiced, naïve—or at least they think they must be wary, even if the comparative safety of a first-year composition course is a prime place to address such concerns. In either case, then, whether one is creating a character or trying on an academic persona, feelings of anxiety are common. Carefully considering audience is in part a way to alleviate these anxieties: writers do so in order to determine effective appeals and strategies, and game manuals ask gamers to analyze their experiences so that they might benefit from the knowledge such analysis provides during gameplay, thus increasing the gamers' level of enjoyment.

Composition textbooks and computer role-playing game manuals ask much the same of their readers: to examine (experiment with/in and explore) the world, the self, others, and the relationships between them in order to make sense of experience. They ask them to discover a "meaningful pattern" (Rosenwasser and Stephen xv) that can be used to make knowledge and shape experience. Analysis of experience—one's own and that of others—can be aided by systematic experimentation, which can help one to reach significant findings. In essence, the various subjectivities that writers experience and that identity exploration reveals through gaming or writing-as-a-way-of-thinking (another essential element of numerous writing texts) serve as cornerstones of identity itself. Both academic worlds and game worlds, and writing and gaming, demonstrate the odd fact that an entirely constructed identity is not necessarily a false one, and both reveal that such constructed identities have the potential to become, with time and use, as much a part of the self as any other naturally occurring or socially assigned identity.

READING AND GAMING

Not only do our writing assignments ask students implicitly or explicitly to construct identities but our classroom readings also reveal that the spotlight is trained squarely on identity. As merely one of numerous texts that can serve as representative examples, consider Andrea A. Lunsford, John J. Ruszkiewicz, and Keith Walters's *Everything's an Argument with Readings*, whose chapters "Who's the Fairest of Them All?" (about body image), "How Does the Media Stereotype You?" (not only about stereotype as a particular method of identification, but also about how that method influences you—the primary self), and "What Does Language Say about Your Identity?" (no comment necessary, methinks), among others, focus predominantly on identity. Indeed many of the readings in such texts are intended to help students understand the significance of various subject positions through vicarious experience.

While they may be overlooked in composition classroom and scholarship, a careful look at computer game manuals reveals that the texts accompanying games ask players sophisticated and complex questions about their identity formation—their own and the player-character's—through the "lens" that the character-creation process provides. If identity exploration, resulting from character creation and development, is enabled by games as many game scholars have argued, game manuals specifically call for it. These manuals, while often seen as an extraneous part of the game, are not only necessary if one is to extract a full experience of the game, but can be seen as works of literary art in their own right.

GAMING MANUALS—BEYOND HOW TO PLAY

As increasingly complex characters and storylines have been introduced to games, enabled by advancing computer technology and changes in play venues, so too has reading become more important to gameplay, both in terms of reading game manuals (as opposed to merely referring to them as instructional reference material) and reading-as-analysis that the manuals specifically ask gamers to do. There is a certain amount of "this key does this" and "this key does that" in nearly all gaming manuals. There should be. The first goal of a computer game manual, after all, is to help the gamer play the game. Literacy theorist James Paul Gee supports this view, commenting in an interview that "if you play the game, what you do with the manual is use it as a reference to look up stuff that you need to know to get better or to understand something in the game that you don't think you fully understand" ("Grading"). This use-value of instructional manuals is certainly accurate, but represents only part of the whole picture, or at least focuses on only a particular type of gaming manual. What's more, this perspective defines the conventional wisdom of what a manual's function is, preventing us, in part, from considering manuals in a more complex ways, for instance as texts that potentially inspire inquiry about the objects they introduce. I am interested here in what more the manuals communicate to players, what they ask gamers to do in addition to manipulating game controls. As it turns out, they provide and suggest a lot more than keyboard/mouse operation and explanations of particular menus and icons.

Many game manuals, and especially those for role-playing games, offer back story—sometimes quite vivid and absorbing descriptions of the gaming world and its history. And the manuals relate this information in myriad ways. Some, like the *Neverwinter Nights* manual, are straightforward. Its introduction to the world of the game reads like entries in any cultural dictionary, delivering the information clearly and concisely. For example, under the heading "The City of Neverwinter," the manual reads, "This is a cultured city where most of Faerûn's civilized races live in peace with each other . . . . In recent months, a terrible plague has forced the once-vital city into quarantine" (Knowles et al. 29). Other manuals are more creative in their deliveries. The *Baldur's Gate* manual is separated into two major sections: gameplay (5–34) and "Volo's Guide to Baldur's Gate" (35–133), a guidebook written by the fictional adventurer Volothamp Geddarm, who opens his guide (in a suitable script font, no less, lending visual authenticity), "This guidebook is one of the very finest in my ongoing tour of the Realms—I can guarantee that you'll find no more diligent guide than your humble servant, Volothamp Geddarm." After Volo's commentary, a different voice—the famous Wizard Elminster's—appears in a different script, reading, "Volo? Aye (sigh). I've spoken to ye before about his 'accuracy,' but he is getting a little better. Maybe that makes his writing more tolerable. Perhaps" (Muzyka, Kristjanson, and Ohlen 36). Interestingly enough, Elminster comments explicitly on Volo's text, calling readers' attention directly to the prose; in other words, the gaming manual includes rudimentary rhetorical commentary, some self-reflective meta-analysis not of the content of the writing but the writing itself. While this is not as common an occurrence in gaming manuals as calls for identity exploration, to be certain, nevertheless it is an example of a practice commonly suggested in composition textbooks that appears in an unlikely place.

The Arcanum: Of Steamworks & Magick Obscura manual takes this creative touch a step further, representing itself as a compilation of the works of various fictional scholars from the world of Arcanum: the foreword is said to have been written by "Dr. Julius M. Crenshaw, Department of History, Tarant University," a location the player-character can visit in the game. The first chapter begins, "The following is excerpted from the *Principia Technologica*, re-printed here with permission of the publisher, Tarant University Press, and the author. © 1876 all rights reserved." The chapter is titled, "Principia Technologica, Being the Collected Lectures of Sir Harris Guffingford" and its first section is headed, "On the Eternal Conflict Between Natural and Supernatural Forces" (Philips et al. 3). I offer a flavor of these manuals to indicate not only that they serve as much more than instructional manuals—that they can be creative, clever, well written, hyper-conscious of rhetoric-with-purpose—but that they implicitly and explicitly ask their readers to dedicate themselves to more than just gameplay. Gamers need to consider how history and culture and identity, regardless of being imaginatively invented, shape experience and ways of knowing.

The *Baldur's Gate* and *Neverwinter Nights* manuals are even quite explicit about what is not necessary to read in order to play the game, but is necessary for a fuller experience: "Many of these things are not absolutely essential to know in order to play, but knowing them may help you to get more enjoyment out of the game" (Muzyka, Kristjanson, and Ohlen 4) and "This background information is not essential to playing Neverwinter Nights, but may help you understand the world of the Forgotten Realms" (Knowles et al. 3). In other words, the manual authors recognize that some gamers will just want to hop to it, while others are more interested in an immersive experience, not unlike the two sets of *World of Warcraft* participants whose needs are provided for by separate game servers. To accommodate them, the manuals' authors consciously ask players to examine the way they might engage the game and from what perspectives before gameplay has commenced. And frequently, a game manual will ask its readers to think about material not even directly related to gameplay. It is somewhat ironic that the vast majority of these gaming manuals' pages are not dedicated to how to play the game, arguably the manuals' primary purpose.

Consider, for example, the first chapter of the *Arcanum* manual, which explains the scientific developments of the inclined plane, the swinging pendulum, and the electric circuit (Philips et al. 3–7)—not generally the explanatory material that one would expect to find in a game manual. Arcanum is a traditional fantasy world, complete with the necessary regalia of magical spells and mythical creatures, but the game is also about the conflict beginning to develop between old magic and new mechanical technology. The manual provides explanations of the same scientific developments that accompanied the conflict between religion and science, for instance, in our own history. These are connections that gamers are to take seriously. But so as not to lose focus on the spirit of entertainment, the manual ends with a recipe for "Grandma Cookhill's Three Bowl Bread." While the manual playfully claims that it comes from a "halfling recipe" and that the resulting bread "is wholly appropriate fare to offer elven visitors" (Philips et al. 189), it is a bona fide recipe for banana bread.

These instances demonstrate not only the generic complexity of many game manuals, but also that the players are, upon reading the manual, primed to move beyond the boundaries of "mere" gameplay. While of course the manuals' authors recognize their readers as players who need to learn the rules of the game, they are also introducing the world's culture—its artifacts, characters, stories, history—that will provide a richer environment when the players begin to interact with that world through their avatars. The authors recognize that the identities of the avatars are, in addition to the decisions the players will make about them, shaped by the worlds they inhabit. "So in summary," the *Neverwinter Nights* manual invites, "Play, explore, and create. Play and enjoy the game we have created for you, explore the tools, and create your own worlds of adventure. Finally, you can venture forth on the internet to explore the worlds other individuals like yourself have created" (Knowles et al. 2). Asking gamers to explore, rather than just play (although playing is certainly part of the experience as well), is to motivate them to consider more carefully what it is they are doing.

Conducting a close reading of the manuals reveals that their authors are consciously creating a text and not just teaching a gamer to play. That is, they are priming gamers for potentially immersive gameplay by writing about history, culture, philosophy, religion, and other aspects of gaming worlds. But more importantly, they are calling for gamers to become active readers of the manual, the game, and the gaming experience—indeed, they are asking for cocreators who will design characters who interact productively with the game world. The writers recommend strategies for creating player-characters—through the same process I discussed above—offering suggestions to players for how to progress through the admittedly complex procedure. Once again, the process begins by thinking, not clicking:

> One way to navigate the character creation process is to start with a character concept. Many roleplayers enjoy mimicking figures from history, myth, or popular culture. Those who enjoy a challenge sometimes construct a flawed character, perhaps one who is sickly or a bit of a buffoon. Perhaps they might take a classical stereotype and play it in a new and refreshing manner. (Knowles et al. 38–39)

The writers could have said, "First, click the character-creation button." But they didn't. They opted for a more intellectual approach that, in addition to enhancing the gaming experience, also demonstrates their recognition of the gamer as an active thinker and gaming as a critically engaged activity. Asking the players to adopt personae from history or myth assumes that they know some. Suggesting that players consider a "flawed character" suggests a certain degree of literary knowledge. Likewise, referring to "classical stereotypes" assumes familiarity with them. And looking at such stereotypes with some new, creative twist is not dissimilar to exercises I have asked my own students to do in class, and parallels Rosenwasser and Stephen's suggestion to "challenge a commonly held view" as an "opening gambit" to begin an analytical essay (198). These suggestions encourage the gamer/student not only to create an identity, but to seize authority; the creation of an identity is a productive initial step, but to author, to develop an authoritative identity is the key aim.

Consider the type of exploratory thinking undertaken by the gamers I have described as compared to Diana George and John Trimbur's explanation of their goals for their writing course reader:

> In *Reading Culture*, we ask students to look at culture as a way of life that organizes social experience and shapes the identities of individuals and groups. We will be using the term culture in this textbook to talk about how people make sense of their worlds and about the values, beliefs, and practices in which they invest their energies and allegiances. (xxii)

Further defining one of their key terms, they say that "culture means all the familiar pursuits and pleasure that shape people's identities and that enable and constrain what they do and what they might become" (3). Ultimately, George and Trimbur ask students to explore the "real world" much in the same way that game manual writers ask gamers to explore Faerûn or Arcanum, both of which are stocked with individuals and groups with different systems of "values, beliefs, and practices" that are sometimes harmonious, often discordant, but always steeped in tradition and motivated by reason that makes sense, at least from a particular cultural perspective or tradition. All of these features unfold as the gamers explore virtual worlds. Furthermore, the gamers do so from various perspectives, which the *Neverwinter Nights* manual reminds us: "Remember, much of the fun of *Dungeons & Dragons* [on which *Neverwinter Nights* is based] is in watching your character grow and change" (Knowles et al. 39). The goal of these sophisticated role-playing games is not simply to win. Rather, it is to explore a world and talk with its inhabitants, uncovering their motivations, needs, desires, histories, and generally how their individual subject positions operate within the larger cultural sphere, and in relation to the avatar's own subject positions. Only by embarking on these tasks will the avatars be successful in completing their goals in the game and the gamers be able to maximize their overall experience.

GAMING, READING, AND WRITING IDENTITIES

The writing textbooks I mention here incorporate analyses of identity, a practice that has become important to composition studies, as—and I assume I'm preaching to the choir here—learning to write a coherent sentence is not enough for authors; nor is simple pointing-and-clicking the whole experience for gamers. Of course focusing on analysis of identity helps students develop something to say; it offers them a framework for critical thinking, where they can see their own subjectivities existing and operating in a larger sphere. Contemporary composition studies attempts to get students to recognize the interconnectedness of written and visual texts to each other and to a wider culture, and to the authors and readers—and players—of it. The game manuals call for gamers to become active readers of the manual, the game, the gaming experience, and by extension, themselves. This activity enables gamers to examine and author their own subjectivities by investigating the choices they make in character creation, the ways characters in the game react to their player-characters based on those choices, and the decisions they are compelled to make in multilinear gameplay (all of which have consequences in how the story unfolds).

Academic discourse is akin to role-playing games, in this respect. That is, their generic definitions each demand the construction of an alternate (additional) self—or selves—and help to govern the newly formed identity's trajectory: the game, through its guidelines, also defines the expectations assigned to different characters, much in the same way teachers should help to define the expectations scholarly readers have of authors. The "rules" governing various character types (thereby preventing them from acting in inappropriate ways, as I mentioned earlier) are not unlike the unspoken "rules" of academic writing by which authors' experience, expertise, and membership in the scholarly community are assessed. While gamers must play the role of avatars, so too must students play the role of academics.

I have largely been drawing parallels between role-playing game manuals and composition textbooks. These connections themselves are inherently significant, revealing the power of identity exploration to inspire critical thinking, active investigation, and reflection upon the experiences that result. In composition studies, the identity exploration we foster in our classes ideally prompts students to write, or at least to invent, which is a vital component of writing processes. And the writing our students do is squarely focused on work. The conventional wisdom is either that they develop academic discourse (create their own scholarly identities) in order to help them throughout their education—that their writing courses have direct applicability to their other classes—or that they write because "any profession requires writing," or that writing will help them be competitive in the professional market, or some other nebulous, vague indication that sometime in the future our students will see the value in what they learn in undergraduate writing courses (however accurate we may, in fact, believe those claims to be). A little less conventionally, we argue that students need to write out of political necessity, which is where identity exploration is of the utmost importance, as it helps students to develop ethos, to recognize the importance of audience (in order to persuade and to avoid getting hoodwinked), to be able to see from multiple perspectives, to accept and celebrate difference in an increasingly global society, to become active and productive citizens. One point at which the formation of the avatar diverges from the formation of the scholarly identity is found in the motivation behind such creation. The *World of Warcraft* role players who specifically demanded that Blizzard dedicate servers to actual role play reveal that in addition to being necessary, educational, or politically expedient, as writing teachers claim, identity exploration can be inherently pleasurable. Experiencing another's perspective can be fun.

The recognition of the parallels between gaming and writing, and especially the motivations that their accompanying instructional guides—game manuals or composition textbooks—illuminate, is productive: it is, I hope, comforting for teachers, constructive for students, and revealing to both, to discover that the sort of analysis we do in the classroom does, in fact, appear in nonacademic venues. One of the primary goals I set for my writing students, and I hope it is both unsurprising and commonplace, is to work against conventional wisdom, to prompt students to recognize, and then inspire them to interrogate, those ideas that they believe to be their own, but that ultimately originate elsewhere. I do not want to read papers about how advertising objectifies women as sexual objects (yes, we can clearly see that), how holidays have become overly commercialized (well, yeah), or how electronic technology has reshaped traditional family life (yep, it has). Claims like these, no matter how well executed in writing, however seemingly "new" they are to students, still do not ask students to move beyond what is familiar, but rather bring to the surface those latent arguments on which mainstream media loves to report: celebrity worship leads to eating disorders, and violence in video games leads to school shootings. Such claims are, ultimately, mere reiterations. Serious interrogation—exploration—of the subject positions we occupy and how they shape the various roles we play, though, can help students reach beyond their comfort zones, try on not "just" a different discourse, but a different frame of mind.

Motivated by the exploration game manuals ask them to do and by complex gameplay, gamers create player-character identities so immersive that they enable the exploring of subject positions that, while disconnected from their biological selves, nevertheless can have a strong influence on their reading, writing, and thinking. Game designers manage to make this activity—one that involves time, work, and frustration, as any gamer knows—into not only a productive practice, but a desirable one. Given the not dissimilar activities we, as professors of composition, ask our students to do, it is not beyond the realm of possibility that we can harness the pleasure gamers experience and recreate it in our classrooms. Recently, one of my first-year writing students submitted an intriguing analysis in which she argued that increased divorce rates are a result not of some foggy change in family values (which was a major component of the original "argument"), but rather of the acceptability of divorce, of the simple introduction of divorce as a viable option, and how options really are the mark of a strong, free society. In essence, she was associating a seemingly "bad" phenomenon (rising divorce rates) with a seemingly "good" one (freedom of choice); in so doing, she realized that a short marriage does not mean an unhappy one, and that an arranged marriage or marriage of convenience can be productive, even as those circumstances seemed to work against what she thought she knew. The email that accompanied her digitally submitted paper read, "Just for the record, I don't actually believe anything I put in this paper." And yet the argument was a fine one—narrowly focused and coherent, but also exploratory, reaching beyond the conventional. The success of the argument was due, in part, to her willingness to explore a different frame of mind, a subjectivity that did not immediately reflect her own beliefs: in essence, she explored an alternative identity and consciously reflected upon that experience.

There is a parallel phenomenon occurring in two seemingly disparate fields that indicates they are not, in fact, so different in the ways they motivate their potential practitioners. Perhaps recognizing where playing a game and practicing academic discourse (a binary in many of our students' minds if there ever was one) intersect—in consciously formulating and exploring identities and/or various manifestations of the "self"—we can re-evaluate a stagnant set of ideals for which both audiences (teachers and students) have traditionally privileged the one over the other. Experiencing alternative identities, consciously playing with their various personae, may cause the alternative *I* we would like to see appear in our students' papers, the one that initially makes them so uncomfortable, seem not so inaccessible.

FURTHER READING

Companies are listed by Publisher/Developer:

Arcanum: of Steamworks & Magick Obscura. CD-ROM (PC). Sierra Entertainment/Troika Games, 20 August 2001.

Baldur's Gate. CD-ROM (PC). Interplay/Bioware, 30 November 1998.

Doom. Downloadable (PC). id Software, 10 December 1993.

The Elder Scrolls IV: Oblivion. DVD-ROM (PC). Bethesda Game Studios/Bethesda Softworks, Inc., 20 March 2006.

Fallout 3. DVD-ROM (PC). Bethesda Softworks/Bethesda Softworks, 28 October 2008.

Neverwinter Nights. CD-ROM (PC). Atari/Bioware, 16 June 2002.

Spacewar! Programmed Data Processor-1 (PDP-1) at the Massachusetts Institute of Technology. Steve Russell, 1962.

Star Wars: Knights of the Old Republic. CD-ROM (PC). LucasArts/Bioware, 18 November 2003.

World of Warcraft. Massively multiplayer online role-playing game (PC). Blizzard. Entertainment/Blizzard Entertainment, 3 November 2004.

4 HOW BILLIE JEAN KING BECAME THE CENTER OF THE UNIVERSE

David Parry

While I do not want to paint too broad a picture, I think it is safe to say that the early reception of *Wikipedia* by the academy was characterized by glib dismissal, followed by open disdain. A few exceptions not withstanding, many academics and institutions ignored the early stages of its development, maintaining a healthy skepticism of an encyclopedia that "anyone could edit." But as *Wikipedia* continued to develop, becoming one of the web's most trafficked sites, so grew the attacks on the value of an internet encyclopedia edited and composed by millions. As it became clear that *Wikipedia* was developing into a central—and in many places primary—place students would turn to gather information, academics and institutions responded with increasingly alarmed rhetoric, leading at times to the outright banning of *Wikipedia* by professors and institutions.[1] But, as *Wikipedia* has matured and developed into one of the "backbone" sites that organize the internet, the academic climate surrounding it has moved from heavy resistance to a perhaps begrudging acceptance, where *Wikipedia* itself has become an object of serious academic inquiry.

Much of the early research and commentary on *Wikipedia* has attempted to compare it to print encyclopedias by measuring traditional criteria, for example article length, number of entries, and method of composition (multiple authors versus a single accredited expert). But, these conventional analytic methods have failed to capture the unique nature of this digital formatted and networked encyclopedia.[2] Accordingly, analysis has begun to switch from measuring the size of any one node to measuring its relation to other nodes in the network.

1. This response has always struck me as particularly ridiculous. The propriety of students using *Wikipedia* as a source and citing it in papers should have nothing to do with its status as an internet encyclopedia, but rather its status as a secondary source. Students should no more cite *Wikipedia* than they should *Brittanica*. Rather, the issue here is the appropriate use of an encyclopedia as a source rather than the particular instance of *Wikipedia*.

2. The now somewhat famous study in *Nature* serves here as the pre·eminent example. In December of 2005 researchers found in forty-two tested entries relatively little difference between from measuring the size or content of any individual article towards measuring its connectivity; *Wikipedia* and *Britannica* in terms of accuracy. This article gained so much attention that it promoted a response by *Britannica*, which, in a letter to the journal, contested the legitimacy of the study.

Recently, Stephen Dolan, a student at Trinity College in Dublin, authored a computer program to measure the network size of *Wikipedia*. Unlike prior network analytic tools, Dolan's program did not measure the distance between the two furthest *Wikipedia* articles (in order to find the articles which constitute the endpoints and thus determine the project scope). Instead, Dolan's program looked for which articles are most "central" to *Wikipedia*. It sought articles from which is it easiest to reach the others. In other words, Dolan was looking to determine which articles served as the most robust hubs, rather than looking to measure the scope of the entire network of articles.[3] One can think of Dolan's approach as the "six degrees of *Wikipedia*," if you will, modeled after the "six degrees of Kevin Bacon" game in which players attempt in six links to connect Kevin Bacon to any other actor or actress. In other words, the program tracked the fewest number of clicks required to get to any other article. For example, it takes an average of 3.98 clicks to get from Kevin Bacon to any other article on *Wikipedia* (not just any other Hollywood personality).[4]

Not surprisingly, high on Dolan's list were dates and category lists—entries such as the year 2007, which has links to all the major events that occured during that calendar year. These list-style entries, lists of dates, or even focused organizational lists such as "Presidents of the United States" dominate the top of the list of entries with the lowest average click count.[5] But for the sake of intellectual exploration and the analysis of networked encyclopedias, let us remove these articles that catalog and index and instead look at what "real articles" are actually at the center.[6]

---

3. Dolan's research can be accessed online via a site he maintains: <http://www.netsoc.tcd.ie/-mu/wiki/>. This site contains not only an explanation of his work (the code he used) but also allows one to download the entire list, as well as input two entries to find the shortest path between the two.

4. Or at least this number was accurate as of the time Dolan's program ran. One of the dificulties in writing about *Wikipedia* is distinguishing which *Wikipedia* one is speaking about. Should all attributions of *Wikipedia* contain the past tense as opposed to the present (e.g. *Wikipedia* "said" vs. *Wikipedia* "says")? The convention is to refer to the content within an article as currently articulating such a position, as in *Britannica* "says." It is assumed that the encyclopedia to which one is referring is a relatively stable object, yet in the case of *Wikipedia*, the continuance of utterance presumably provided by the stability of print and authentication is absent.

5. Notably, not all of these high-ranking list articles are years, dates, or ones we might think of as being central hubs. The list is populated by entries such as "Deaths in 2004," "1990s," "List of Treaties," "List of the first female holders of political offices," but also other seemingly more trivial lists such as "List of QI episodes (B series)," "List of C-130 Hercules crashes," "List of IMAC Venues," and "Skyteam Destinations."

6. In some regard, the dominance of lists is telling, indicating that catalogs and indexes serve central roles in network connectivity, and while indexes in the codex encyclopedia are crucial for locating desired information, in the case of the networked work, the locational function is served by the search bar. These indexing articles serve a different organizational role, helping to manage the signal-to-noise ratio in a markedly different way than in the codex encyclopedia.

Highest on this focused list is the United Kingdom. Given *Wikipedia's* Western cultural bias, and that this main "United Kingdom" article links to extensive historical entries throughout different periods, its position as a hub in the network is predictable. In the third position on the list is the United States, for similar reasons: the United States article is, not surprisingly, well developed and links to a number of other equally developed articles about the US. Furthermore, given the particular American cultural bias of *Wikipedia*, the only thing that is surprising is that it is not higher (although considering the relative short history of the United States, the article's subordinate position to the United Kingdom entry is predictable). The difference between the first and third positions is ultimately not that large, as the average click number for the main United Kingdom entry is 3.67 and that of the US is only slightly higher at 3.69. What is surprising, however, and noticeably different from the other top entries, is the second entry in the list, one with a click count of 3.68. Given the title of this article, the astute reader undoubtedly would have guessed that this priviliged second position is held by Billie Jean King. Billie Jean King outranks major historical figures such as Ghandi, or Franklin Delano Roosevelt, manifesting a lower link count even than other, perhaps more prominent, popular culture figures such as Kevin Bacon or Madonna.

Upon close examination of the *Wikipedia* article on Billie Jean King one discovers a thoroughly written entry, covering her personal life, tennis career with full statistics, information about the famous "battle of the sexes," her sexual orientation, and, indeed, even a reference to the fact that "King appeared as a judge on *Law & Order*, one of her favorite television shows, on April 27, 2007." In many respects this article fulfills the *Wikipedia* vision of an ideal entry: "well-written, balanced, neutral, and encyclopedic, containing comprehensive, notable, verifiable knowledge."[7] But, at 17,000 words, the article surpasses mere encyclopedic quality and borders on a minibiography. Jesus only gets 11,000 words and Shakespeare less than 7,000.

In this respect we might say that *Wikipedia*, as illustrated here by the case of Billie Jean King, reproduces the impulses laid out by the *Enlightenment Encyclopedia*. The *Wikipedia* article is an attempt to capture all of the relevant and important information about one subject, to record and present it for others to consult—the "complete" picture of Billie Jean King in a transparent readable format. And, further, despite *Wikipedia's* presentation in the digital medium, it is to a large extent conservative archival form, at least on the level of presentation and governing ideology (if not on the level of

---

7. The "About_Wikipedia" page lays out its governing philosophy, explaining the ideal articles should strive towards, the criteria for inclusion and deletion, as well as a section on the advantages and disadvantages of *Wikipedia* when compared to traditional encyclopedias.

composition), one we might easily recognize as informed by an enlightenment tradition of archivization.

Wikipedia in this respect is a librocentric archive. It embodies ideologies
present within the codex print form—think libraries and encyclopedias—
but not necessarily intrinsic to analog formats. Librocentricism, however, is
not coterminous or even necessarily correlated to print material structures;
rather it is an outgrowth of a specific metaphysical perspective towards the
ability to capture, fix, and fully present knowledge. What librocentricism
culturally accomplishes, or at least tries to stand in as a metaphor for, is a
certain stability of knowledge. One sees this most prominently in the physical form of the book: a beginning, middle, and end, a linear arrangement
that when traversed, promises to deliver on a specific subject. Whether that
knowledge is of a specified subject matter, such as a non-fiction encyclopedia entry on Victorian England, or a fictional narrative, *Pride and Prejudice*,
is immaterial. In both cases, the idea is that by consuming all of the pages
in linear order, one acquires the complete picture of the information contained within the specified pages. Movement from page to page produces a
sense of progress wherein the reader is presented with causal links leading
to the final eschatological page that delivers the complete picture, wherein
the book is made complete, knowledge transmission guaranteed. Both the
encyclopedia and the library re-enforce this librocentric thinking, gathering together in one place everything of relevance to saturate the context
and provide an end, ensuring stability.

What I want to emphasize here is that to understand the "book" as an
archival format (and by extension the encyclopedia and library associated
with this format), we need to separate the ideological imports of this structure from the simply material ones. What has been called the *Gutenberg
Galaxy* is more correctly, as Tom Pettitt points out, the *Gutenberg Parenthesis*.
Within this parenthesis, certain ideologies and prejudices were associated with the idea of archivization, ones which transfered to the book, but
which are not dependent on its material structure. We can see how this is
the case from the way in which the word *book* circulates separate from the
actual physical existence of a particular volume or set of printed pages
bound together by cardboard: the *Book of Love*, the *Book of Nature*, to throw
the "book" at someone. In each of these phrases "book" represents the idea
of a completeness of knowledge—a metaphor for a type of communication
and knowledge presentation rather than its material form—in other words,
the entirety of a certain matter codified into physical form for the sake of
knowledge transmission. And, in this sense, the *Wikipedia* article on Billie
Jean King is the "book" on Billie Jean King.

Despite the fact that most writing takes place first in the digital, that the
first material support is so often the screen and pixel, this "new" digital age

is still haunted by, determined by, the librocentric trappings of the book. Our writing machines and archival formats still respect this figure of the book. Despite claims of the liberating potential of hypertext or the internet, there is little to suggest that these structures of archivization have escaped this infatuation with the book as the ideal format for knowledge transmission. (The Billie Jean King article is just one such example, where a digital archive serves as a resource to collect "all of the essential information" about a specific subject matter.) So much of what is written on digital archivization, as Derrida notes,

> re-creates the temptation that is figured by the World Wide Web as the ubiquitous Book finally reconstituted, the book of God, the great book of nature, or the *World Book,* finally achieved in its onto-theological dream, even though what it does is to repeat the end of that book as to-come.(15)

Despite the idea that digital support structures supposedly free the archival formats from the restrictions of the analog codex forms, a digital networked structure such as *Wikipedia* is valued precisely because it fulfills librocentric criteria. That is, rather than constitute new possibilities for archivization and knowledge transmission, these new forms adopt the criteria of the prior, staking their worth not on their supposed newness or revolutionary form, but rather as the logical evolution of their predecessor.

The digital seems to overcome the limiting paradox of physical archives: the librocentric mandate to simultaneously gather and disperse.[8] And, along these lines, it becomes easy to see how the internet is seen as the logical progression of the librocentric archive; the digital is even more book than the book. In other words, the digital networked archive is not something radically new that threatens to overturn our prior knowledge formats but something that, at least up until now, very much fits within the criteria and values of knowledge formation and dissemination laid out by the librocentric archive. In this respect the digital archive is not that which brings about the end of the book. It is just the logical extension of librocentricism.

Digital archivization, especially with respect to *Wikipedia,* has yet to escape these librocentric criteria. It attempts to fulfill this Enlightenment vision, saturating context, gathering all of human knowledge in one location to preserve meaning without the threat of dispersal. This reproduction of librocentric values in the digital archive would not be limited to

---

8. As Derrida explains, it is this paradox that structures the codex archive, and even the book itself. A library, for example, on the one hand must operate by collecting books in one location, gathering them together to preserve them. But it has value only insomuch as individuals can consult the archive by ungathering what the library has preserved: removing the book from the shelf, checking it out. And thus the library always gathers to prevent the threat of dispersal, the very thing it was designed to enhance.

Wikipedia, one could also include other projects such as the *Hurricane Katrina Digital Memory Bank,* or the *William Blake Archive,* both of which attempt to preserve "all" of the content surrounding specific historical events or individuals, to serve as the definitive account and repository for these matters. In this regard, those who critique *Wikipedia,* seeing it either as the utopic fulfillment of the Enlightenment project of universal knowledge or the dystopic declination of the pursuit of truth, are not arguing about the value or role of a digital archive, but merely disagreeing about the extent to which something like *Wikipedia* fulfills this role. Andrew Keen and Andrew Lih are ideologically closer than either would like to admit.[9]

Wikipedia is little more than a fulfillment of the logic of librocentric thinking, the final eschatological promise of the book of the world. Whereas books are limited by space, digital archives are not; whereas books are costly to produce and transmit, digital archives are relatively cheap; whereas a book can be read by only one person at a time, the digital archive provides access to multiple readers; whereas a book is threatened by its material form (it can be lost, damaged, burnt), the digital archive resists any localized environmental threat. Whereas in a library the text is limited to a singular dispersal (in the sense that only one person can check out a work at any given time), digital works seem to transcend this physical limitation, allowing for dispersal to an infinite number of viewers without undermining their being gathered at a particular locale. Not limited by space, and seemingly free from physical danger, however, *Wikipedia* fulfills the vision of the library of Alexandria, sans threat of fire. As Jerome McGann observes in *Radiant Textualities,* "The library as a model underlying the invention of the internet resists the way of distinguishing digital and paper based textualities" (25). Indeed Jimmy Wales, the founder of *Wikipedia,* is fond of saying that he is "very much an Enlightenment kind of guy," and he consistently articulates his vision of *Wikipedia* as an instrument for fulfilling the Enlightenment project of universal knowledge. One of *Wikipedia*'s goals seems to be to fulfill the librocentric goal of the encyclopedia in a way that *Britannica* or any other codex work could never do: to collect in one location all of human knowledge for universal dissemination.

Billie Jean's inclusion then seems entirely normal, even if her entry is longer than average. For what use would an encyclopedia be if it did not contain information on her tennis career and political, public, and private life? Furthermore, this is where critics of *Wikipedia* fall short in their

9. Andrew Keen made a name for himself as a "digital curmedgon" when he wrote *The Cult of the Amateur,* a book that claims that the internet destroys culture. Throughout the book *Wikipedia* figures as a prominent example. Andrew Lih, the author of *The Wikipedia Revolution,* defends *Wikipedia* as an example of the positive changes the web can bring to knowledge archivization and dissemination.

critique when referring to the "List of 500 Pokemon Characters." It might seem odd that an encyclopedia would contain extensive lists of characters from a fictional universe. Yet, clearly Pokemon represents part of human knowledge, and if the goal of the encyclopedia is to collect "all of human knowledge," then it must necessarily contain reference not only to the "Knights of the Round Table" but "Pokemon Fire Red" and "Professor Oak" as well.[10] While any source that contains an article on chess boxing—three clicks away from Billie Jean King and an article which, although only 750 words in length, is still longer than the entry for Amos Tutola, which is 500 words and three clicks away from Billie Jean King—is an encyclopedia that is clearly an ideological reference, it is hard to discount *Wikipedia* because it includes articles, or places certain ones at positions of power relative to others, as hubs in the network (as is the case with Billie Jean King). What *Wikipedia* is actually chronicling is which places are sites of human knowledge, what articles are of interest to the public that uses them.

Wikipedia's impetus is still informed by that very enlightenment ideal of producing the "book of the world" that explains the entirety of human knowledge and that would be used by a fully engaged literate public. *Wikipedia* claims to "acquire knowledge," and "share knowledge," in a "fair and balanced" manner. But perhaps the clearest instance of how *Wikipedia* sees itself as the fulfillment of Enlightenment ideals is in what *Wikipedia*ns call the neutral point of view or NPOV: "The ideal Wiki article is balanced, neutral, and encyclopedic." As Roy Rosenzwieg has aptly articulated, *Wikipedia* attempts to mimic the neutral rhetorical tone of the codex encyclopedia. In fact, the "achilles heel" of *Wikipedia*, its drab writing, is as much an effect of being composed by several authors as an effect of a composition that favors neutrality—privileging the presentation of facts over interpretation. Indeed, in some sense *Wikipedia* is simply the logic of data collection—encyclopedic universal knowledge—carried to the extreme: an attempt to present just the facts, and all of them.

Not surprisingly one sees this reflected within the articles that often read rhetorically as lists of fact, which is why *Wikipedia* seems to excel in the scientific entries over those in the humanities. Because of the dominance of the NPOV and the goal of presenting facts, *Wikipedia* articles often tend towards annulling narrative logic, and they often slide towards presenting information with simple sentence structures and in an outline format. But this is simply the logical outcome of the Enlightenment quest to create the

---

10. The ongoing debate between the deletionists, those who want to establish conservative criteria for an article's inclusion, and the inclusionists, those who have much more liberal criteria, characterizes one of the, if not *the*, essential current debate by *Wikipedia*ns, and how this question is settled, as Mark Pesce notes, will to a large degree determine the future of *Wikipedia*.

world book, an absolutely transparent collection of facts. In this sense, I would suggest that *Wikipedia* is not a radical archival structure, some alien force, but is rather the monstrous progeny of the librocentric archive.

Perhaps one could object here and argue that poststructuralism has done much to call into question the Enlightenment ideologies pursued in the librocentric archive by demonstrating how these governing ideologies have always been a fiction. I agree that these theories have done much to expose the inadequacy of the idea of the book as complete, whole, guaranteed communication. Yet to a large extent these governing fictions of librocentricism still inform the pursuit, collection, and archivization of knowledge in the digital networked era, and in this respect we have done little to escape the Gutenberg parenthesis. We have expanded on its principles, not overthrown them altogether. And so for many of those who critique *Wikipedia* (both those who see its utopian possibilities and those who see its dystopic qualities), its value comes precisely from the way in which it fulfills the hope of the Enlightenment codex encyclopedia by capturing and preserving all of human knowledge, making it freely available to all those who have access to the internet.

But *Wikipedia* is not entirely a librocentric archive. Indeed, there are significant ways in which it breaks with prior archival formats. And it is by paying attention to the ways in which *Wikipedia* differs that we gain insight not only into how it is that Billie Jean King came to be at the center of the universe, but also how digital networked archives manifest a new archival format. Crucial in this analysis is tracking how relations develop not along the traditional criteria of an article's worth (inclusion in the work, final presentation, number of words), but around links and network influence. Now in one respect, this is nothing particularly new, for encyclopedias have always contained internal links as a way to organize and signify relations between articles—the "see also" within an entry, or even the indexes which serve as giant lists of relevant material. But the link in the digital networked space has become the central organizing principle, not the supplemental feature added to aid in navigation.

In *Targets of Opportunity*, Samuel Weber makes the rather provocative, and I think useful, claim that when we turn to analyzing networks, it is not the net that matters but rather the work, as a great deal of "work" goes into the process of turning a net into a network. While we could choose to focus on the nodes in the net, the sites where content is held or made manifest, the more important question seems to be how one adds work into those nodes, turning a net into a network. In modernity, work is more closely associated with oeuvre, the notion of a deliberately created unit; *work* is thus used as a noun, as in a piece of art work, or a specific article entry in an encyclopedia, the product of the aim and intent of one individual. In the digital era the noun sense of the word *work* recedes as the verb sense takes on greater significance:

nodes (net) + work = netWork

There is indeed a great deal of effort that must go into maintaining the structures that produce a distributed network of information. Where a network gains purchase is in the elaborate set of connections, via the narratives that form across the nodes. The nodes have meaning, if you will, only insomuch as they are worked into the net. And thus the ability and power to narrate and focus these connections to disseminate, transmit, rework these narratives is ever more important. Unlike prior archival formats, the work that goes into this work must be constantly maintained, updated, and cared for. *Wikipedia* becomes a substantially different and diminished object without its bandwidth, incoming links, or Google ranking.

As Albert-László Barabeasi explains in *Linked*, we often treat networks as flat spaces, distributed collections of nodes wherein it is possible to travel from any node to any other single node, with links randomly distributed in an egalitarian space. However, networks are anything but spaces of equanimity. Links between nodes develop over time, with some nodes developing more links and a higher rate of connectivity. Thus these hubs become powerful places in the network distribution as they play the important role of connecting otherwise unconnected nodes. As Barabasi explains: "[Hubs] dominate the structure of all networks in which they are present, making them look like small worlds. Indeed, with links to anunusually large number of nodes, hubs create short paths between any two nodes in a system" (64).

Thus it is difficult to judge a *Wikipedia* entry based on the criterion of accuracy, or the authority and credibility of a particular author, for even if we suppose that a particular entry was written by an expert and is flawless, the article must link to other articles within *Wikipedia*, and other nodes across the internet, in order to have meaning. (This is entirely different from the prior archival model where an "expert" on Billie Jean King would present the definitive interpretation of her biography.) This would hold in a temporal sense as well, for the article must be open to edits to go on working into the future (rather than establishing itself as a definitive singular work). Hence one cannot analyze *Wikipedia* separate from its use, from its workings in the network of information. While this is to some extent true of any book—its contextual uses inform meaning—in the case of *Wikipedia*, the speed at which it works and its open relation to an unpredictable future make it hyperbolically true. And in this respect it is very much not a traditional archive, for its edges and borders can never be neatly and artificially contained by the work of a book binder.

Thus I would suggest that we need to understand *Wikipedia* as a technical organism rather than a static archive. Consider, for instance, that every second, *Wikipedia* is updated between two and three times. This means that while particular articles might be relatively stable, the whole of *Wikipedia* is in a constant state of flux. This feature of *Wikipedia* is aptly demonstrated by "time lapse" screen captures of specific *Wikipedia* articles that chronicle the evolution of a particular entry; examples are the heavy metal umlaut video, which shows how this seeming piece of minutiae developed into a well-developed article, or the video of the *Wikipedia* entry of the London bombings, which demonstrates how that particular article became a repository of information of this event, updated with both true and false information faster than any individual journalism source.

More importantly, consider how *Wikipedia* is now monitored by hundreds of volunteers who spend hundreds of hours maintaining it against the onslaught of new information, or attempts to spam, graffiti or otherwise maliciously alter its contents, a process further complicated by the fact that there are now "bats," computer programs that run throughout *Wikipedia*, autocorrecting, formatting, and deleting information added to particular entries in conjunction and negotiation with human users. This analysis increases in complexity and importance as we realize how prevalent *Wikipedia* is, how much it serves as one of the organizational backbones of the internet, and how increasingly other institutions and organizations are using wikis to archive material.

Ultimately, I think we miss the point of digital networked archival structures like *Wikipedia* if we analyze the object alone, treating it as a text to be read that would be subject to the same hermeneutic analysis we as scholars leverage against other static works. *Wikipedia* is not a static object that is written, a closed object that one consults. It is instead more analogous to a living organism that is maintained and kept healthy. Indeed, those who contribute to *Wikipedia* often speak of their role in such "caretaker" terms. The author function of a particular article or bit of text is replaced by a curatorial function in which an encyclopedia serves as a place where knowledge is communally stored, produced, and accessed, requiring constant observation and maintance. For *Wikipedia* is nothing without the community of users who work on it, keep on working on it. One can copy the entire data structure that comprises the text—it is relatively small (133 GB give or take)—and port it to anywhere (the license allows this). Yet, you would not be porting *Wikipedia*, not only because there is a great deal of network capital tied to the particular internet address associated with *Wikipedia*, but also and more importantly because you would not be porting the community of users. Here is where *Wikipedia* substantially differs from prior archival models that have both a longer and a shorter lifespan than it does. These spans are shorter in the sense that the information in a codex volume quickly becomes outdated, whereas *Wikipedia* is constantly kept up to date. But this "up to dateness" also means the lifespan of *Wikipedia* is shorter, connected to the community; if the community disappears and ceases to maintain the archive, the archive's value's is rendered null. *Wikipedia*'s archival format does not fix the knowledge it presents; while print encyclopedias strive to produce a finished work, *Wikipedia* is not only "open" in the sense of allowing outsiders to edit, but "open" in the sense that its material is always open to future discursive productions, to a future that is not controlled, an openness that is a threat to its very existence. We should probably think of *Wikipedia* and its archival cousins as continually maintained processes rather than final products. This view is a substantial shift from the librocentric prejudice that governs the *Gutenberg Galaxy* and still to a large part informs current thinking in the humanities.

Rather than the case of the codex encyclopedia presenting information as "truth," *Wikipedia* preserves the discursive formation of the article, where as I indicated, the standard for inclusion is not "truth" but verifiability. That is, can the particular claims be linked to, connected to, other places where those claims are made?[11] And although the previously stated goals of *Wikipedia* seem to mimic the librocentric—that is, collecting in one place the transparent truth about subjects—this network approach shows how this goal is already, from the beginning, impossible, for "truth" is subject to particular structures of power, some democratic—voting on what changes should take place—and others not—the intervention of an administrator. Regardless, the formation of the archived information in *Wikipedia* is made part of the archive, and it is in this sense too that *Wikipedia* is more "open" than the prior codex model. The discursive practices that produce the analog archives often took place within the closed walls of the university, publisher, or library; what counted enough to appear as part of the archive, what was saved, if you will, was decided in a closed manner. In the case of *Wikipedia* such decisions are folded into the archive itself.

Each article page is the result of a discursive process that is preserved within the pages of the archive itself. Indeed, we are perhaps reading *Wikipedia* backwards, for unlike *Britannica* or other codex form encyclopedias, *Wikipedia* preserves not only its current iteration but all prior iterations. In this respect, if we only look at the current article on the Billie Jean King page, despite its rather thorough and lengthy nature, it is difficult to understand how it became the center, or at least number two, on the link

---

11. This, as Axel Bruns notes in *Blogs, Wikipedia, Second Life & Beyond,* is in part what distinguishes *Wikipedia* from a codex encyclopedia like *Britannica. Wikipedia* does not claim to be presenting facts about the world, but rather it claims to present representations about facts that are claimed and explained in other places (115).

ranking. The key to uncovering the peculiar network value of the Billie Jean King article is in looking at the discussions pages, the places where the discourse about the discursive production is recorded.

The more intriguing aspects of *Wikipedia* are stored on the discussion pages, where contributors argue, negotiate, and ponder about not only the content of any given article, but the particular wording used in it. Thus any particular entry is only a small, narrowly framed text representing the current formation of a much longer, more elaborate process. As Clay Shirky observes, a *Wikipedia* article "is the product not of collectivism but of unending argumentation. The articles grow not from harmonious thought but constant scrutiny and emendation" (139). This is precisely the case with the Billie Jean King article, where several editors heavily invested in having certain information about Billie Jean King displayed persistently argue about the scope of the article. Proposed cuts to text on either her tennis career, or her personal life, are met with resistance by editors determined to have those pieces of information included in the article. And although several suggestions have been made to resolve this conflict—for example, splitting the article into a main Billie Jean King article and a second Billie Jean King tennis career article—as of the writing of this article, no such agreement about dividing the entry has been met. (Such an action would, of course, lower the average click rating.)

Indeed, by reading the discussion page carefully, we can see how the Billie Jean King article become a locus of debate among different groups and editors. At the bottom of each *Wikipedia* article is a list of categories to which each entry belongs; one can think of these as the folksonomies users have created to help organize *Wikipedia*. For example, Abraham Lincoln contains links to 1809 births, presidents of the United States, Illinois lawyers, and even small pox survivors. In the case of Abraham Lincoln, his groups are relatively consistent, containing what we could describe as a high rate of "bonding capital" that ties together groups we might intuitively associate with each other. But in the case of Billie Jean King, her categories cut across groups, displaying a higher rate of what we could describe as "bridging capital": American feminists, 1943 births, living people, LGBT people from the United States, American vegetarians, American tennis players. Thus, while many would argue that Abraham Lincoln is a more important "historical" figure, Billie Jean King is more important (or at least the article is) in establishing connections between different knowledge clusters.

As long as we continue to evaluate *Wikipedia* with librocentric criteria, we will miss recognizing what is unique about this archival format. If we were only talking about *Wikipedia* here, the danger from ignoring these archival changes might be minimal, but *Wikipedia* is merely one node in the entire network—granted, it is a large node, but it is still only one node. What *Wikipedia* offers us though is a particularly instructive place of critique from which to understand how this digital networked archive affords new possibilities for knowledge formation and archivization. However, the future here is by no means guaranteed. *Wikipedia*, and its archival cousins, might grow increasingly bureaucratic and hierarchical, and indeed the recent history of *Wikipedia* suggests precisely this trend: an effort to pursue librocentric goals at the expense of leaving the structure more open and organic. What is clear though is that as these digital networked archival formats grow in both size and influence, we will need to pay careful attention to the possible restructuring of values they bring.

5 INFORMATION CARTOGRAPHY
Visualizations of Internet Spatiality and Information Flows

Jason Farman

The term *cyberspace* has evoked the process of navigating and embodying the spatiality of the internet since the word was coined by William Gibson in his cyberpunk fiction. In spatial terms, cyberspace has also been understood as an emerging "frontier space" that users are able to construct freely to fit their particular needs. It is a space of exploration, of possibility, and of social connection on a global scale. While most internet users identify with the notion of "navigating" this space, the process by which this navigation occurs bears little resemblance to the ways we chart and move through material space. The physical world has historically navigated and understood the world around it by charting it with maps. In fact, maps have even defined the space at points (see, for example, Hartley's discussion of the symbolic ownership of an area by an empire through designating it on a map). Instead, users navigate the internet typically using a web browser, search engines, and hyperlinks. One link leads to another, and the user is wandering the internet in a situationist-style dérive with no clearly charted route or destination. Such a process of navigation is attributed to the massive tangle of links (attributed to another metaphor of the web).

This study aims to identify the possible uses of internet maps, what such visual representations might look like, and how they might serve the purpose of representing the inequalities present in the transmission of information on a global scale. Drawing from several internet maps with differing approaches to information visualization, this paper analyzes the problems facing the mapping of information flows and how internet cartography can address these problems through visualizing information not as raw data but as a lived social space experienced in a situated and embodied way. Ultimately, I demonstrate that the creation of an internet map must always account for the visual and data limitations of maps in general. (As Monmonier's studies argue, all maps "lie"). As we seek to theorize what a useful user map might look like, we must address how users engage cyberspace on multiple levels and in diverse ways to create visualizations suited to their specific goals.

THE SPACE OF CYBERSPACE

In her study of embodiment in mediated spaces (and technology as pros-thesis), Stone argued that "what was being sent back and forth over the wires wasn't just information, it was bodies" (176; emphasis in original). While it may seem commonsense to argue for the internet as an embod-ied space, many cyberpunk writers, cyborg artists, and technology theorists have argued that the body is obsolete in the digital age (such as Moravec's *Mind Children*, STELARC's homepage that welcomes visitors with a banner that reads "THE BODY IS OBSOLETE," and Kroker's thought that we are transcending the body through digital technologies). The assumption that there can be a cyberspace without bodies overlooks a central component of the production of space. Space, as Lefebvre argued in *The Production of Space*, is not simply a container into which we place objects and peo-ple; instead, space is coproduced with bodies and objects. Lefebvre writes, "Each living body is space and has space: it produces itself in space and it also produces that space" (170; emphasis in original). Space is depen-dent upon bodies and bodies upon space. If users understand a sense of movement through the internet, then they are experiencing the embod-ied space of cyberspace. Movement and navigation require space and con-ceived space requires bodies.

The internet is not an easily charted space the way material space can be. The objects that make up this landscape not only function in extreme-ly diverse ways (from HTML, Flash, and VRML web pages, to videos, imag-es, music, currency, data of all types, the list is seemingly endless), but these objects are in constant motion. As Dodge and Kitchin write,

> Whilst some aspects of telecommunications infrastructure and cyberspace are relatively easy to map, such as plotting the networks of service providers onto conventional topographic maps . . ., other aspects are very difficult. This is because the spatial geometries of cyberspace are very complex, often fast-chang-ing, and socially produced. Cyberspace offers worlds that, at first, often seem contiguous with geographic space, yet on further inspection it becomes clear that the space-time laws of physics have little meaning online. This is because space in cyberspace is purely relational. (2–3)

Echoing this notion that internet space is constantly in movement, Jahshan cites Lévy's notion that the form and content of cyberspace are "still par-tially undetermined" and that "the mobile maps of these fluctuating spac-es belong to terra incognita, adding, with Massumi, that even if cyber-nauts were able to achieve the immobility required to get more precise bearings, the virtual landscape itself would continue to flow, to swirl, and to transform the gazer" (26). Jahshan compares Lévy's concept of social mapping of the internet to Massumi's topology of cyberspace. He writes that Massumi's

> new concept of mapping, better adapted to the new virtual spaces [, is] based on a topographical vision of cyberspace. Defining topology as 'the science of self-varying deformation,' he concedes that since a topological unity is multiple (because in constant deformation), it is theoretically impossible to actually diagram and follow every step in a topographical transformation." Lévy's cartography, on the other hand, "short of being a topographical attempt, is content to map a 'space of knowledge,' a sort of 'anthropological cartography.' (26)

These notions offer insights into the subject's conception of lived space in the internet and how such a space is mapped. One problem confronted when creating a usable map of the internet is the issue of directionality. Unless charting the global connections or material infrastructure of the internet onto a geographic map, compass points do not have bearings in cyberspace. Instead, we encounter the space through our direction of purpose or through social proprioception. The first option is encountered through individual wanderings through the internet, in which direction is continually changing based on the user's movements and moment-by-moment objectives. Writing about this sort of wandering, Sobchack writes, "When I was a child, I always thought north was the way I was facing. Sure then in my purposeful direction, there was a compelling logic to this phenomenological assumption. Bringing into convergence flesh and sign, north conflated in my child's consciousness the design of my body and the design of an atlas page" (13). Sobchack's childhood assumption that north was the direction aligned with the first-person point of view mirrors the phenomenology of internet wandering. North is associated with the privileged perspective of the individual and serves a creation of internet space that, rather than being developed out of the social, remains locked into the "personal" computer.

In contrast to the privileging of the individual construction of internet spatiality, theorists like Castells argue that the mapping of these networked societies—always more of a process than a place—is dependent not on geographic locale but on digital connectivity. While proximity is no longer a prerequisite for social interaction, according to Castells, with the move of the internet onto mobile devices that can log on and place the user at specific GPS coordinates, proximity is being reasserted into the online interactions in which people engage (such as utilizing an iPhone app that can tell the user "who's here" within a specific radius). The utilization of the internet on mobile devices takes the user's proprioceptive engagement with cyberspace beyond the individual's "direction of purpose" on the screen and places it onto a physical landscape that is coproduced with social interaction. While these mobile devices that connect to the internet can be plotted geographically with GPS coordinates, they are always in movement (in contrast to the personal home computer) and any attempt to "ground" them with a cartographic representation will be immediately out of date. As Jahshan writes, "Most of the maps [of the internet] are time-bound, i.e., they are either historical, depicting some network state dating a few years back or, on the contrary, so 'current' that they are only valid the moment they are produced. What is more serious is that when they are printed they are already outdated." He continues by noting, "The issue of fore-casting is also problematic: how can one accurately predict network move-ments? . . . The very changeability of networked technologies renders the above mapping attempts at best a precarious endeavor" (24). So, given the ever-changing landscape that refuses to be grounded through cartographic techniques, why would we attempt to map the internet in these ways? What use could an internet map actually serve and could an internet map actu-ally become a useful tool for the internet user?

INFORMATION VISUALIZATION AND EVERYDAY INTERNET USE

Many internet users turn to a search engine to guide their journey through cyberspace, entering a query and letting the text-based results direct them to relevant web pages. However, such interactions with the web offer only a glimpse into the scale of this dynamic space. Addressing the scale and potential of the internet and communicating that to the everyday user is where the field of information visualization is useful. As Card, MacKinlay, and Schneiderman write,

> Current methods of access leave much to be desired and do not adequately exploit this immense resource. Information visualization could play a substan-tial, even enabling, role here in helping users find information faster, under-stand the structure of the space, find patches of interesting information for greater examination, or make the space more learnable. (465)

Information visualizations offer a view into a structure that cannot be eas-ily understood outside of some form of graphic representation (either because the structure is far too complex to be represented in textual form or because the structure's scale cannot be sufficiently represented in other ways). As Dodge and Kitchin explain, "In essence, maps and spatializa-tions exploit the mind's ability to more readily see complex relationships in images, providing a clear understanding of a phenomenon, reducing search time, and revealing relationships that may otherwise not have been noticed. As a consequence, they form an integral part of how we under-stand and explain the world" (2).

Since internet space is fluid and changing, any sort of visualization would have to address this characteristic. Since we have often used metaphors to start understanding our interactions with the internet, visualizations have often employed these metaphors to help us navigate this space. Card, MacKinlay, and Schneiderman point out that the User Interface Research Group at Xerox PARC classified these metaphors into four categories: "(1) the digital library metaphor, (2) electronic mail metaphor, (3) the electronic marketplace metaphor, and (4) the digital worlds metaphor" (465). Just as these metaphors address how we interact with the internet, visualizations can thus not only meet the current understandings of how we perceive cyberspace but can also teach us how to think about cyberspace.

Dodge and Kitchin emphasize that such visualizations, while being useful in helping us understand the internet, must also never attempt to be exhaustive. The nature of mapping visualizations is that they must always be selective in the scope and purpose of the information they display. Dodge and Kitchin write,

> In many cases, maps or spatializations of cyberspace are designed to change the way we interact with cyberspace. A key question is thus to ask to what extent a mapping is successful in these aims: does a map or spatialization change the way we think about cyberspace, and do those that seek to offer new modes of interaction offer viable spatial interfaces that could replace or supplement current methods of data management and navigation? In other words, do the maps or spatializations achieve their aims, whether that be improving comprehension, providing new means of navigation or interaction, or selling a service? (4)

Thus, when approaching how we can create a map of the internet, it is illusory to think a single map can meet the needs of users and adequately represent the nature of the internet. A map must address a specific aim and purpose rather that attempting to be exhaustive. This notion is skillfully argued by Monmonier in his book, *How to Lie With Maps*. As his title suggests, a map (as a singular representation) traditionally presented a limited point of view dedicated to its particular purpose. He writes,

> A good map tells a multitude of little white lies; it suppresses truth to help the user see what needs to be seen. Reality is three-dimensional, rich in detail, and far too factual to allow a complete yet uncluttered two-dimensional graphic scale model. Indeed, a map that did not generalize would be useless. But the value of a map depends on how well its generalized geometry and generalized content reflect a chosen aspect of reality (25).

He goes on to note that the medium on which a map is presented in conjunction with the limitations of the human eye will always restrict the amount of data that can be presented on a map without causing so much distortion as to lead to illegibility. Similarly, the limits of what a map conveys are often not simply issues of the technological or physical limitations but rather choices on the part of the cartographer. Harpold writes that "details are commonly eliminated, falsified, or distorted so as to improve a map's efficacy toward a particular end, resulting in the misrepresentation or exclusion of information, which may serve other ends or reveal inconsistencies" (11). Since mapping the internet often deals with flows of information and retrievable data, it is often assumed that representations of these flows and statistics are objective rather than subjective—but, as Monmonier and Harpold point out (in conjunction with cultural geographers such as Soja, Wood and Fels, Harley, Edney, and Pinder), maps are never objective and grounded signifiers of an ontological reality. Instead they are perspectives that are always situated.

ATTEMPTS AT INTERNET MAPPING

As has been argued up to this point in my study, mapping the internet faces many challenges. From its constantly moving and flexible nature, to the limitations of information visualization to exhaustively display such complex data, the internet has resisted being mapped in a way that has connected with the everyday uses of this space. While such maps have not been thoroughly successful, many maps (for different purposes) have used information visualization techniques to display some compelling representations of the internet that reveal many important characteristics of the internet.

Maps have been connected to the internet since its inception. The ARPANET served as the basic structural foundation for the internet as we know it today, initially linking UCLA to Stanford in 1969. The following maps (fig 1 and fig 2) show this first node and the subsequent growth of ARPANET to include several other nodes across the United States.

These geographically specific nodes of the internet can reveal the pervasiveness of internet use and access worldwide. A similar approach to this type of mapping was implemented by Matthew Zook in his 2007 Google Earth overlay (fig 3), showing the global connections between internet hosts and the locations and sizes of domain names registered in each country.

What Zook's internet map demonstrates, in an interactive 3D map, is the global unevenness of information flows. Maps of these lived information flows—as they are associated with geographic locales—demonstrate in a profound way the inequality of information transmission on the global scale. Thus, visual representations of the internet and the transmission of information serve the larger purpose of signifying the need to address issues of the digital divide between those who have access and those who

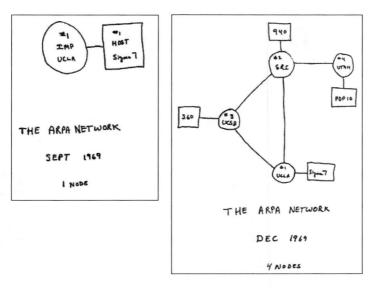

Figure 1: The first maps of ARPANET. Accessed from http://personalpages.
manchester.ac.uk/staff/m.dodge/cybergeography/atlas/historical.html

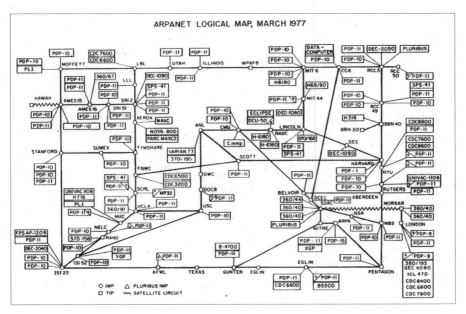

Figure 2: A 1977 map of ARPANET showing its growth across the United States. Accessed
from http://personalpages.manchester.ac.uk/staff/m.dodge/cybergeography/atlas/historical.html

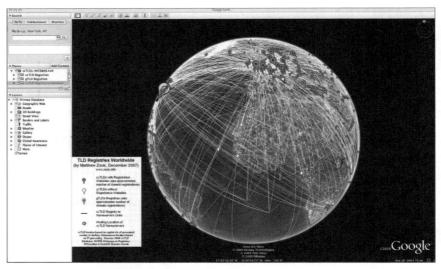

Figure 3: Matthew Zook's Google Earth overlay showing global internet connectivity. Google Earth screen capture used by permission.

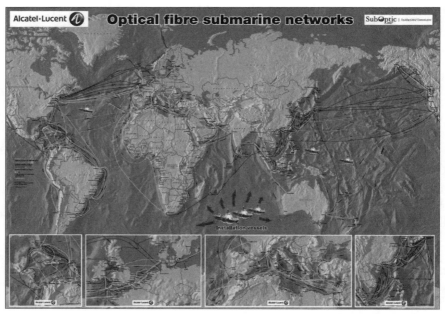

Figure 4: A 2007 map of the global internet infrastructure. Accessed from http://www1.alcatel-lucent.com/submarine/refs/World_Map_2007_LR.pdf

Figure 5: "Arc map" showing worldwide internet traffic during a two-hour period. Accessed from: http://personalpages.manchester.ac.uk/staff/m.dodge/cybergeography/atlas/geographic. html

do not in the Information Age. While the internet may be a "lived space" for many in developed countries, maps like Zook's Google Earth overlay show that the large majority of people on the planet are not inhabitants of this cyberspace. According to the March 2009 statistics published by internetworldstats.com, only 23.8% of the world's population are internet users. As visualized in Zook's internet map, only 5.6% of the people in Africa are internet users.

Part of the problem of access is the distribution of internet infrastructure. Since this structure is more stable than the content of the internet, it is more easily mapped, as demonstrated by the maps produced by Alcatel Submarine Systems (fig 4), a major manufacturer of telecommunications systems. These maps chart the cables that connect users worldwide to the internet and reveal that the inequality in information distribution online is directly (and obviously) connected to the distribution of infrastructure.

A similar geographic visualization was created in 1996 by Stephen G. Eick and his colleagues at Bell Labs (fig 5) showing the flow of internet traffic in a two-hour period.

Harpold persuasively critiques visualizations like the Arc map, noting that (along the lines of the cultural geographers) such maps seems to simply present objective data in visual form. Such mapped data is often misunderstood as existing outside the realm of critique. He writes,

> These and similar cartographic representations of the internet [are interrogated] as a first step in a critique of the complicity of techniques of scientific

visualization with the contrasting invisibility of political and economic formations. I propose that these depictions of network activity are embedded in unacknowledged and pernicious metageographies—sign systems that organize
geographical knowledge into visual schemes that seem straightforward (how
else to illustrate global internet traffic if not on images of . . . the globe?), but
which depend on historically—and politically—inflected misrepresentation of
underlying material conditions.

By noting the Arc map's use of light and dark, presence and absence, on
or off, Harpold can point to the visualization's significant political messages. He argues, "Viewed with an eye to their unacknowledged political
valences, these images of the wired world (that is, of the mostly unwired
world) draw, I will argue, on visual discourses of identity and negated identity that echo those of the European maps of colonized and colonizable
space of nearly a century ago." This resonates with Edney's concern that
"Imperialism and mapmaking intersect in the most basic manner. Both are
fundamentally concerned with territory and knowledge. . . . Maps came
to define the empire itself, to give it territorial integrity and its basic existence. The empire exists because it can be mapped, the meaning of empire
is inscribed into each map" (1–2).

internet maps that connect information flows and infrastructure to a
geographic visualization are only a small portion of the maps that have
been created of cyberspace. Others have sought to chart out the interconnected nature of the internet in more abstract visualizations. Drawing from
the approach that Castells encourages—that mapping cyberspace is more
about social connections than about geographic space—these maps seek to
chart the ways information links across the internet. For example, the 2000
map created by Hal Burch and Bill Cheswick (fig 6) creates a fractal map of
the core of the internet, charting over 100,000 ISPs and color-coding them.

One final example of an attempt at internet mapping is the 1999 charting of the interconnected websites owned by the international publishing
firm, Verlagsgruppe Georg von Holtzbrinck (fig 7). The map seeks to show
how the sites are connected, who runs them, and what content they hold.
This visualization is color-coded and arranged to prevent overlap and visual distortion, with lines connecting the sites and a thumbnail screen capture inside the circles representing the site.

MAPPING THE INTERNET FOR USER NAVIGATION

While most of these maps can offer very useful insights into the scale, interconnectedness, or political ideologies that surround the internet, none of
them address the issue of the user's process of everyday navigation through
cyberspace. Instead, as previously mentioned, most users simply chart their

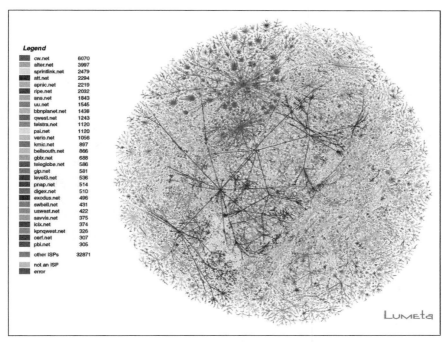

Legend		
	cw.net	6070
	alter.net	3997
	sprintlink.net	2479
	att.net	2294
	apnic.net	2219
	ripe.net	2032
	ans.net	1843
	uu.net	1545
	bbnplanet.net	1438
	qwest.net	1243
	telstra.net	1120
	psi.net	1120
	verio.net	1056
	kmic.net	897
	bellsouth.net	866
	gblx.net	688
	teleglobe.net	586
	gip.net	581
	level3.net	536
	pnap.net	514
	digex.net	510
	exodus.net	496
	swbell.net	431
	uswest.net	422
	savvis.net	375
	icix.net	374
	kpnqwest.net	326
	cerf.net	307
	pbi.net	305
	other ISPs	32871
	not an ISP	
	error	

Figure 6: Hal Burch and Bill Cheswick's 2000 map of the "core of the internet" charting over 100,000 color-coded ISPs. Screen capture from Dodge and Kitchin (43).

course utilizing search engines or links that are not organized visually in a way that can help to make sense of the scale, content, or interconnected nature of the sites we encounter. Most of the internet maps discussed in this study tend to emphasize the data rather than the user's connection to that data (and how we as internet users can connect to and interact with it). There is no entry point for embodied interaction that resembles the user's process of navigation.

Certain digital media have used maps for user navigation in ways that can offer some insight into approaches for charting usable internet maps. From the 1995 Eastgate Systems map of the electronic literature piece *Patchwork Girl* by Shelly Jackson to the in-world map in VRML social networks like Second Life, mapping connections across thematic content and social networks has benefited users of large digital spaces. As previously mentioned, usable maps must be understood to address particular needs and objectives rather than as seeking to be exhaustive. A map demonstrating the interconnectedness of a network of friends across online social networks would serve to visually render these connections in the social space of the internet. As it is currently laid out on the homepage for sites like

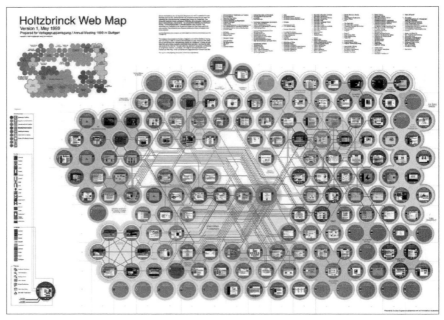

Figure 7: The 1999 map charting all public websites owned by Verlagsgruppe Georg von Holtzbrinck. Screen capture from Dodge and Kitchin (95).

Facebook, the flat HTML layout of the page does little to visualize this social network as a lived space and active environment. New, usable approaches would better serve the already prevalent notion that the social network is a lived space, embodied and produced by its users. For the likes of Phillip Rosedale, the founder of Second Life, our interactions with cyberspace will continue to turn away from 2D representations and take advantage of the graphics and broadband capabilities of our current systems, moving toward lived-in, 3D environments in which people from around the globe can interact and alter virtual objects in a more dynamic way. As these spaces offer users a visual representation of the material space they navigate on a daily basis, perhaps the maps of these spaces will also take advantage of the sense of depth and movement that 3D offers and that is ultimately the very nature of the internet.

6 MULTIMODAL METHODS FOR MULTIMODAL LITERACIES
Establishing A Technofeminist Research Identity

Jen Almjeld and Kristine Blair

Jen Almjeld and Kristine Blair

WHAT'S IN A NAME?

"But this isn't research."

Dissertation director Kris Blair cringed when she heard these words from the graduate-college-appointed outside reader, a male faculty member from the college of technology and presumably someone amenable to doctoral candidate Jen Almjeld's proposed dissertation topic on the rhetorical processes of identity construction within female users' MySpace profiles. The outside reader's skepticism was similar to what Blair experienced working with another graduate student, Christine Tulley, on her dissertation, which also employed a feminist methodology and a collaborative research study. (This experience is chronicled by Blair and Tulley in "Whose Research Is It Anyway?"). Although Christine's and Jen's dissertations were written six years apart, the concerns raised were similar in that the dissenting committee members foregrounded the objective aspects of the study—data collection, methodology, and positive results—at the expense of feminist political goals that value women's texts and contexts and seek to conduct research that benefits women as a whole. In this essay, then, we share the story of Jen's research project and the misunderstanding and resistance common to such feminist research methodologies and propose researcher positionality through autobiography as a way to counter such resistance.

Jen's dissertation proposal described her intentions to enact feminist political goals by situating the digital practices of female MySpace users within a rhetorical and historical context. Her proposed study sought to document and connect the online rhetorical practices of women with practices from other women-centered genres—such as commonplace books and scrapbooks—in order to establish a continuum of feminist rhetorical practices consistent across genres and media. Through the analysis of young women's MySpace profiles, Jen planned to highlight women-centered discourse and the spaces in which such discourse flourishes. These genres, as seen in Gannet's discussion of diaries in *Gender and the Journal*, for example, are often dismissed because of their status as trivial and non-academic; work like Jen's would thus problematize not only the way in which MySpace users construct their digital identities but also the way in which the ideological presumptions behind the genre construct female users. In spite of recognition by many scholars regarding this sort of work to reclaim multiple and often marginalized voices, not only did the outside member protest, but another male committee member queried whether the project could be executed without the "feminist stuff," again suggesting a lack of understanding about the importance of a feminist theoretical and methodological framework.

Given Jen's status as feminist teacher and researcher, and the project's careful consideration of a wide range of interdisciplinary research about women's rhetorical space and cyberfeminist practice, the proposal at its core seemed well justified, and it had support from women in the audience and on the committee—yet the outside representative preferred a study that hypothesized a number of features about women's MySpace profiles and relied on a quantitative analysis to determine which of those features were common enough to warrant discussion. To some extent, Jen's study did rely upon the coding of profiles to determine a range of features that could represent identity construction, but it also included a theoretical analysis of the assumptions about gender that may have influenced profile development as well as the aspects of that development that could nevertheless prove empowering for women. It was clear that the outside committee member had some knowledge of research methodologies; in his objections, he kept referring to the oft-cited Lincoln and Guba book *Naturalistic Inquiry,* indicating a familiarity with less-positivistic approaches, yet he was unwilling to validate the triangulated approach of grounding the discussion of MySpace within a historical trajectory of women's public and private discourse while also relying on textual analysis and theoretical/feminist calls for situating the researcher. Nor was he willing to accept the technofeminist agenda central to Jen's project, one that sought to validate the use of MySpace in the literate lives of young women. While he was open to the idea of textually analyzing MySpace profiles, the frameworks used to conduct such an analysis were what, for him, diminished a potentially viable "objective" study. Judging from the resistance the project received, it seemed the desire to focus on validating feminist writings historically and theoretically was the correct one.

Although the external reader's presumptions of what a valid research study of MySpace should entail was consistent with a range of appropriate methodological concerns regarding subject selection and the validity of data-collection processes in relation to research questions, more feminist aspects of reflection and acknowledgement of sociopolitical action were seen as insignificant and inappropriate, things to be eliminated from the study in order for the project to be "research." Certainly, as feminist teacher-scholars, we should have to explain our methodologies, grounding them in current interdisciplinary dialogues that influence rhetoric and composition, computers and writing, and new media research. Such articulation is important, as Patricia Webb notes, in expanding our understanding of what constitutes acceptable research and in moving to more multimodal approaches to research to "open up new areas for us to research as well as expanding the kinds of answers and results we can achieve" (473). Webb's argument is compelling but may be a bit more problematic than she expects, especially, as Jen experienced, for young scholars in the field seeking initial publications and attempting to traverse the rigorous terrain of the dissertation. To further feminist and technofeminist goals for awareness of researcher positionality and debunking the myth of true objectivity, this essay offers techno-biography as one model for enacting such research transparency.

In addition, the shift toward new media creates further challenges regarding ways researcher identity is created and how that identity impacts both how we approach questions in the field and what we are willing to question. Indeed, for many scholars investigating new media texts—utilizing new multimodal research methodologies—the task may be complicated by bias from colleagues unaware of the need for a range of methodologies when studying digital writing. While the call for multimodality in composition research is not a new one (see Lauer), our recent experience with Jen's dissertation (an intersection of feminism, technology, and seemingly nonacademic literacies) revealed to us that all research methodologies are not created equal and that blending methodologies continues to cause controversy in the academic community.

Just as technology complicates the understanding of what composition is or can be, we must complicate and explicate what it means to conduct feminist research in technological spaces. Within this chapter, therefore, we outline a range of performative practices that not only align methodology with context but also reshape the identity of the researcher and respond to criticisms like those expressed in Jen's proposal meeting that feminist and technofeminist methods are less rigorous or valid than alternative research methodologies. Part of this process also involves documenting Jen's virtual identity development not only as a feminist teacher-researcher but also as a woman, in order to articulate how technology remediates both feminist methodology and the intellectual questions that govern the analysis of new media spaces.

THE POLITICS OF FEMINIST METHODOLOGY

In their recent chapter, Kris Blair and Christine Tulley stress that digital writing researchers need to align themselves with theories and practices that call for increased multimedia and multivocal delivery and access to scholarship that will inevitably foster broader definitions of research. While rhetoric and composition has, as a field, struggled to legitimate its disciplinary practices within departments of English, and while qualitative approaches across the disciplines have themselves been legitimized as modes of inquiry equal to seemingly more objective, quantifiable methods, Blair and Tulley shared the difficulties within and outside the discipline in legitimating feminist research in technological spaces. Part of this difficulty is one of labeling: What is feminist research, how does such research methodology redefine the roles and boundaries between researchers and subjects, and what are its intellectual questions? Our goal is not to summarize the rich body of feminist research and the key theorists (Sandra Harding; Shulamit Reinharz and Lynn Davidman) who have addressed these issues. Rather, we wish to foreground several tenets of feminist research we feel are applicable to and inform the process of new media composition, both inside and outside the academy.

At the same time that we advocate and delineate this applicability, however, we believe that new media researchers must continually rearticulate and contextualize research around spaces, technologies, and identities not only for our larger community of scholarly peers in the field of computers and writing but also for our colleagues with whom we interact on a daily basis. Within our own context of Bowling Green State University, we find that the question "What is feminist research?" is one we must continually address for those who question the rigor of what we do, precisely because of an inability to recognize or label the rich triangulations of methods, sites, and participants that enhance our field's understanding of technological literacy acquisition. And within the more specific context of dissertation research taking place in our doctoral program in rhetoric and writing, Jen and Kris, not unlike Christine and Kris several years earlier, have felt the need to define, legitimate, and ultimately show a balance between feminist tenets of reflexivity and reciprocity and objectivist attention to rigor and results.

At its core, feminist research has concerned itself not only with method but also with politics, with "explicit attention to the social relations manifest in women's everyday activities" (Naples 94), and also with capturing "women's lived experiences in a respective manner that legitimates women's voices as a source of knowledge" (Campbell and Wasco), when both culturally and academically such voices have only recently been heard within. This project of marking formerly forgotten female texts and voices as worthy of academic study is not confined to feminist studies, but has clearly found a foothold in both composition and literacy studies as well. With texts that include Cheryl Glenn's 1997 *Rhetoric Retold*, rhetoricians

have "regendered" and reclaimed texts previously considered unimport-
ant either because of content or authorial status (Foss, Foss, and Griffin;
Ritchie and Roland), or because of the private space or form of the genre,
as shown with Finders's research on adolescent girls' hidden literacies in
school-based settings. Such scholars find both rhetorical and anthropological worth in these everyday writings and artifacts and have set about,
through both explicit research agendas and multimodal methodologies, to
capture the voices of those long ignored.

Embedded within this dialogic and potentially empowering process,
many feminist researchers have acknowledged the need to establish and
articulate our positionality, with self-reflexivity as a traditional model that
"acknowledges the positions the researchers occupy in relation to his or
her participants" (Deutsch 891). This reflexivity typically acknowledges the limits of findings based on our status as insiders or outsiders and
our inability to eliminate the inevitable power imbalances between the
researcher and the researched. Despite limitations, feminist research methodology, not unlike other theories that disrupt static notions of subjectivity, representation, and knowledge, aims at reciprocity between researchers
and subjects, privileging participant voices in ways that, if not providing a
direct benefit to the individuals we study and the spaces we jointly occupy,
allow them to shape more precisely the representation of research and the
knowledge resulting from it. Instead of othering our subjects and objec-
tively presuming separation, feminist methods have privileged the commonality and, ideally, the reciprocal benefits of research in ways that potentially break down insider/outsider binaries and establish shared experiences among women within local and global sociopolitical frameworks.
Ultimately, as Nancy Deutsch suggests, "We must continue to mine the fault
line between feminist and researcher, woman, and academic, and uncover
the ways in which our work can both emancipate and enlighten ourselves
and our society" (900).

WHAT'S TECH GOT TO DO WITH IT?

How might the feminist goals we outline manifest themselves in new media
contexts? How does technology remediate reflexivity and reciprocity, along
with researcher and subject identity? In other words, in what ways do new
media spaces and communities demand feminist research methodological approaches? Certainly, an abundance of research exists across the disciplines chronicling the impact of technology on women's lives. From the
earliest work of Cheris Kramarae in her collection *Technology and Women's
Voices*, feminist scholars have questioned the extent to which a range of
technologies—workplace, household, reproductive, and communication
based—have both empowered and disenfranchised the women who use

and are used by them. Not unlike research within the computers and writing field, early discussions of life online stressed community, empowerment and a freedom to escape gendered hierarchies (Cherny and Weise; Turkle), even as some researchers soon began to foreground technology's role in women's oppression (Spender). Within the writing of the computers and writing community itself, Hawisher and Selfe chronicled the early rhetorics of technology, from technomanic egalitarianism to a whole host of technophobic concerns about virtual violation that have been mirrored in the larger culture then and now. More recently, in *Cyborg Lives: Women's Technobiographies*, academic women from the University of London's Department of Innovation Studies blend personal narrative and critical theory to explore Haraway's cyborg metaphor "for its potential and problems in helping us to make sense of our experiences through the telling of stories" (Henwood, Kennedy, and Miller 13). The editors rationalize the choice of technobiography as a way of capturing a sense of pluralism and diversity of experience. While within our own discipline, technorhetoricians (Kitalong, Bridgeford, Moore, and Selfe) have also relied on technobiographies, the goals of both sets of scholars are similar: to rely on narrative and biography to neither celebrate nor scapegoat technology, but instead to theorize how our relationships to technology have been influenced by material conditions that are simultaneously gendered, sexed, raced, classed, and aged. Applying feminist research methodologies to new media spaces thus requires us to be explicit about our own positions as researchers writing and through the new media spaces we study.

The ability of media to influence and be influenced by users is not unique to modern technologies, however, and how we see ourselves and how others see us is and always has been remediated by media we consume and produce (Bolter and Grusin; Manovich). Just as handwriting, the printing press, and eventually the personal computer have changed our world and the ways we communicate, new media has an indisputable impact on our identities and knowledge production. Thus, researchers producing new knowledges and those consuming the knowledges are affected by both the physical and political facets of the new media environments they populate. An important component of feminist new media research involves analysis of the ways women in particular use technology to represent themselves and the limits of various digital tools to construct such representations. And just as composition studies has addressed its natural fit with qualitative methods as viable modes of inquiry in academic and professional writing spaces (Bishop), technofeminists have explored the extent to which hypertext and other multimodal environments are natural fits for blending the personal and political (Sullivan "Wired Women"). Equally important, but admittedly less well articulated, are the ways in which women are simultaneously complicit with or resistant to the traditionally gendered construction of identity as well as gendered patterns of communication in new media contexts, something Jen's study of MySpace addresses specifically.

Within a feminist methodological framework, researchers are not exempt from this identity construction process. As we grapple with insider/outsider status in both real and virtual locations, one crucial element to establishing a connection with subjects involves the extent to which we actually inhabit the spaces we research. Initially, professional and personal online identities were more limited, constrained by the words on the screen as users joined listprocs, newsgroups, IRCs, and MOOs. Today, "keeping in touch" (as Kramarae subtitled her original 1988 collection) is a much more multimodal process, involving participation in blogs and microblogs, social-networking software, gaming environments, text and instant messaging, pod- and vodcasting. Granted, it is difficult for a researcher to keep in touch with technologies, let alone keep up with the technological innovations that are inherently more rapid than either pedagogical or methodological innovations. While faculty are using e-mail, course management systems such as Blackboard, or even class blogs or wikis, our students are using Facebook, MySpace, or Second Life, or even newer spaces such as Twitter, and relying on instant messaging and status updates to communicate in ways that don't seem to make their way into our traditional academic spaces, either real time or virtual. While researchers such as James Gee and Mark Prensky have highlighted this divide between students as digital natives and teachers as digital immigrants, we, as technorhetoricians, naturally have felt obligated to bridge this gap within our own classes and work to "keep up" with the wide range of Web 2.0 tools. new media researchers, then, are obliged to stay current with trends by participating in and discussing that participation in online spaces and communities.

Indeed, new media researchers who neither keep in touch nor keep up with digital tools and the social contexts in which they are utilized run the risk of reinscribing outsider status. As several studies indicate, digital practices can create a range of communication gaps; for instance, Lynn Clark chronicles the insider/outsider relationship that cell phone use and instant messaging can establish between adolescents and their parents. Because such insider/outsider relationships apply to research subjects and those who study them, it is important to question how researcher experimentation with new media not only impacts researcher identity but also bridges the gap between researchers and participants. Inevitably, researcher identity construction is an inherent part of the technological spaces we study, as we must be able to function in such spaces in order to understand communication processes and establish credibility with subjects. We also must be able to enact and articulate for readers our own identities as techno-feminist researchers both inhabiting and interrogating new media spaces.

By troubling researcher identities—as remediated through new media texts and practices—technofeminist researchers are able to discuss the range of questions the larger field of composition studies should be asking in regards to what we recognize as viable research. These include questions about the role of self-reflexivity in research, the false insider/outsider dichotomy, new media's place in the rhetorical tradition, and the role of digital tools in developing researcher and subject identities. Consistent with feminist methodological approaches, particularly involving technology, Jen's own narrative not only provides a reflexive component to such work but also demonstrates the ways in which online identity construction is complicated by the digital tools researchers use to develop a digital presence and what such tools presume about gender, race, and sexuality. Sharing Jen's technobiography, here, and in part in her dissertation, enacts technofeminist research methodologies and might begin to address concerns of balancing scholarly rigor and sociopolitical agenda.

JEN AND MYSPACE

Understanding that feminist and particularly technofeminist approaches are not readily accepted by all scholars, Jen devoted 8 $1/2$ pages of a 166-page dissertation project to "Revealing the Researcher." This section described Jen as a researcher influenced by the likes of Kirsch, Sullivan, and Webb, and thus aware of her position of power. This section also expressed the hope that Jen's "experience as a woman using MySpace allowed [her] to interrogate rhetorical moves made by other females online" (Almjeld 88) while recognizing that her "work as a woman, academic, feminist, and MySpace user influenced this work" (89).

Jen's interest in new media research began with her first dabblings as a cybercitizen. Throughout her education and career she utilized computers and other technologies for a variety of reasons—research, photography, newspaper design during her undergraduate studies and early career as a journalist—but not until her doctoral studies did she really begin to use new media for entertainment and expression. Several of Jen's friends and colleagues were already MySpacers and eventually she joined in an effort to remain connected, especially during term breaks. Opening her first MySpace account—and eventual Facebook profile—was frightening to her: warnings about online predators, lost jobs due to personal postings, and countless hours logged "surfing" and posting aimlessly in such spaces echoed in Jen's head. But Jen's venture online did not reveal such an online space. Her endeavor was neither frightening nor costly (either in time or repercussions) despite the warnings, so Jen began to formulate research questions concerning online identity construction and the report-ed dangers of performing identities online.

Based on Jen's own misconceptions about social networking, gaming, text messaging, and other new media genres constantly under fire, she began to wonder if her experience was unique or if others faced similar fears, frustrations, and eventual joys online. Thus Jen focused on MySpace and girls' performance of gender for her dissertation proposal. While a technology focus seemed to please several of Jen's committee members, discussion of the appropriate rigor of her methodologies became an issue. How would she remain "objective" as a MySpace user herself? Jen sudden-ly felt a false separation in her own identity—a division between Jen as user and researcher, between lived online life and scholarly work. Jen faced and continued to negotiate the challenges of researching a community as an insider while retaining the objectivity of an outsider. Nancy Naples reminds us that this division is actually much less clear cut as "outsiderness and insiderness are not fixed or static positions," but instead are "ever-shifting and permeable social locations" (49). In Jen's work, she has found this flux, this blurry area, both beneficial and challenging. Early in her dissertation study Jen talked to a colleague about feeling a bit like a cyber stalker, or at the very least a voyeur, when it came to doing textual analysis of other peo-ple's profiles. The colleague, also a woman, said that Jen's work "doesn't feel creepy" because she is female and a MySpace user and "not just some dirty old man lurking online." Jen found this comment oddly comfort-ing and felt justified as both a woman and new media user to be making assumptions about ways other women were using this new media text. Her "insiderness" seemed to allow her both insight into the research proposi-tion and also safety and credibility as not a cyber lurker but as a technofem-inist researcher. Still, Jen's own experiences as a white, middle-class woman living and working in an online setting undoubtedly color the ways she per-ceived data, but without her own experiences, she may not have asked the questions in the first place. Deutsch agrees that "although the role of insid-er-outsider can be difficult to balance, it sometimes provides unique oppor-tunities for information gathering" (898). For new media researchers in particular, insider status may help to blur divisions between researcher and researched and between personal and scholarly knowledges. Similarly, Jen found being forced to question and defend the rigor of her technofeminist methodologies related to this project had a positive impact not only on her dissertation but also on her overall researcher identity.

What began as a private space for online communication and play has now become an important site for Jen's work. She is always aware of this split and of the implications her postings may have on current work and future employment. Nevertheless, Jen is mostly herself online, in the sense

Figure 1. Jen's MySpace
Profile Box.

that a cursory look at her profile information and attached pictures will
reveal Jen as single, white, well educated, and religious. The photographs
also show Jen with friends and, she hopes, convey a sense of humor. Still,
there are always limits regarding what she is willing to display and decisions
she must consciously make about her representations of self. For example,
for a few weeks the quote at the top of Jen's profile made reference to a
personal and somewhat risqué inside joke shared between her and friends,
but when she realized she needed screen shots of her online identity for
the dissertation she quickly changed back to a quote from feminist scholar Luce Irigaray (see fig 1). Despite Jen's willingness and even eagerness to
be pictured in a fake tiara and exaggerated feminine pose, she was unwilling to surrender her credibility completely and so clung to the currency of
the academy as seen in the words of a respected scholar. The dissertation
genre also shaped Jen's technology and researcher story as her technobiography in this article is much more personal than what she felt comfortable
including in her first major scholarly effort. Just as Jen struggles to balance
objectivity and insiderness, she also negotiates the gap between her personal identity and her researcher identity.

CONCLUSION: RESEARCHING NEW MEDIA AS A TECHNOFEMINIST

In her research at a youth club, Deutsch concludes that her ability to leave
the club and the research population influenced her status as insider/out-
sider (897), but it seems to have also influenced her private and public
selves. Researchers normally have the ability, which sometimes becomes an
obstacle, of distancing themselves from their research sites and subjects,
leaving us to question whether new media researchers ever fully abandon

their online identities. Can we ever shed our private online selves in favor of a public, research self utilizing new media as an uninterested scientist rather than a vested community member? And would an apparent willingness to do so satisfy the questions of those who desire objectivity over reflexivity? Being truly objective in research, as previous scholars have discussed (Harding), is an impossibility. Each time we choose a project or designate someone or something as worthy of study, we have made a subjective choice in some way validating that practice, artifact, or person. To be sure, striving for objectivity in data collection and analysis is a worthy goal, but it can best be obtained by admitting that it is impossible—by situating oneself as a researcher who is by definition biased in some way. Being so intimately involved in and defined by our own media usage impacts not only objectivity, but also researcher credibility

Embracing and enacting one's own online identity is a good beginning in building researcher ethos and an awareness of individual strengths and limitations. As Jen's online identity suggests, questions remain about how real one can be online and still hope to be taken seriously. Rebecca Lawthom writes that "it is difficult to be open and reflexive in a patriarchal academic environment" (536), but it is nearly impossible to avoid being open to at least some degree when using new media. Despite gained acceptance for feminist research methodologies, there still exists a very real danger in being too open or too personal in one's research or academic work. Ultimately, new media research may actually offer a way to diminish the stark division between personal self and public scholar, as we believe Jen's profile demonstrates. Because so many of us do so much living and working online, it seems inevitable that it would be difficult to so easily close off our private selves in favor of our scholarly personas.

Our experiences as researchers in new media—where personal and professional identities intersect—highlight both the problems and opportunities arising from new media research. For us, new media and feminist research methodologies have caused, at minimum, questioning, and on occasion outright resistance from other researchers and committee members. While such reactions are unpleasant, it seems this tension is a site for growth and expansion both as individual researchers and as a larger field. Perhaps the first step to fostering a deeper understanding and acceptance of various research approaches is to first consider the very real implications such methodologies have on researcher identity and to begin to pose some questions about the ways new media research in particular is remediating traditional notions of research and researcher:

- In what ways do new media artifacts remediate the rhetorical tradition? Just as feminist historiography reinvisions the rhetorical canon to include women's texts and contexts, so too should tech-nofeminist research. In what ways are women's new media artifacts similar to and different from the other types of "everyday" texts now considered viable sources of rhetorical analysis: quilting, art-work, scrapbooks, cookbooks, conduct manuals, sermons, speeches, and the like?

- To what extent do the features of various digital tools enable and/ or constrain the development of a professional and personal identi-ty for women? Do these tools allow for self-reflexivity for and about identity politics? What role do race, class, gender, and sexuality play in the development, access, and deployment of such identities for women, as well as for researchers?

- In what ways are women both complicit with and resistant to ideo-logical presumptions that the creators and designers of software have regarding the representation of women and girls?

- How do women actively work within technological spaces to con-struct a public identity? What rhetorical choices do they make and what rationale exists for these choices?

- How do technological environments bridge hierarchies between researchers and their subjects? Do various uses of technology create shared goals or experiences among online researchers and subjects?

- What role might new media research play in explicating "how sub-jects are constituted by social systems," as well as "how collective subjects are relatively autonomous from and capable of acting to subvert those same systems" (Weeks 92)? How might research sub-jects work collectively or individually use digital tools to subvert and transform gendered hierarchies?

- How do we learn to value other kinds of research and methodolo-gies and how do we educate others in our field and beyond about the value of the kind of work we as feminist new media scholars are doing? As Packard and Conway ask, "How might researchers who adopt different approaches . . . converse and engage . . . with oth-ers' literature?" (264)

As Rebecca Lawthom concludes, "Women who may be working as research-ers at the bottom of the research hierarchy have limited control over meth-od, methodology, and epistemology" (533). As a dissertation writer, Jen found herself seeking to reconcile her own research agenda with the need to please committee members and therefore complete her degree in the most expedient way possible. Inevitably, those being reviewed by tenure committees or seeking degrees are frequently "constrained by tradition-al genres such as the research article or the dissertation" (Blair and Tulley 308). Regardless, the attention the larger discipline gives to the intersection between writing and identity, and the ways these issues connect back to classical concepts of ethos and voice, warrant inclusion of new media texts, public and private and a blend of both, into the rhetorical canon. Such a call echoes those of feminist scholars who advocate for the inclusion of women's historical and contemporary texts and contexts to complicate the scope and definition of rhetoric, not to mention research. From our perspective, the widespread use of Web 2.0 and other tools among today's "digital youth" (Alexander, *Digital Youth*) further complicates connections between writing and identity, necessitating a range of practices that bridge the gap between academic and personal, public and private, researcher and subject, and print and new media. Contrary to the anecdote that began this chapter, such issues are not only vital to the relevance of undergraduate and graduate education in rhetoric and composition but also vital to the survival of a discipline devoted to writing, communication, and literacy practices—past, present, and future.

7 WRITING AGAINST NORMAL
Navigating a Corporeal Turn

Jay Dolmage

The dominant discourse surrounding the teaching of writing focuses on texts and thoughts, words and ideas, as though these entities existed apart from the bodies of teachers, writers, audiences, communities. As a discipline, broadly speaking, we in composition and rhetoric have not acknowledged that we have a body, bodies; we cannot admit that our prevailing metaphors and tropes should be read across the body, or that our work has material, corporeal bases, effects, and affects. Yet some recent attention to embodiment and to body politics in composition theory and research, and indeed the creation of a collection like this, suggest that we are beginning to recognize the corporeal entailments, foundations, and connections in the teaching of writing (see Couture, Fleckenstein, Hawhee, McRuer, Wilson and Lewiecki-Wilson). In this essay, I will build on this momentum as I argue that, in fact, ignoring the body has serious consequences. As we compose media, we must also—always—compose embodiment. I will also argue that we must be careful about which bodies we conceptualize. In this essay, I will critically investigate the ways embodied pedagogy can be developed without invoking normative models of embodiment. And I will make some modest suggestions about ways we can develop technologies and pedagogies for writing that not only affirm the body, but that affirm all bodies.

My theoretical background is in disability studies, and from this field I borrow a critical attention to bodily norms. When I use this word—*norm*— I refer to a complex social and cultural force. Norms can be "passive": a name for an ideal or standard; or the unexamined and privileged subject position of the supposedly (or temporarily) able-bodied individual. Norms are also very active: normalcy is used to control bodies; our normate culture continuously reinscribes the centrality, naturality, neutrality, and unquestionability of the normate position; our culture also marks out and marginalizes those bodies and minds that do not conform. Norms circulate, have cultural ubiquity, and ensure their own systemic enforcement. The normate subject is white, male, straight, upper middle class; the normal body is his, profoundly and impossibly unmarked and "able." On the page, this subject and his body translate as error free, straight, and logical prose; as a writing process that is a portfolio of progression towards perfection and away from all evidence of struggle and labor.

Because I feel both attuned to and distrustful of these norms, in the composition classroom I have often struggled to come up with alternative and non-normative means for engaging students in what we might call "embodied" writing—and I know I'm not alone. It may seem self-evident, but one key way to recalibrate composition to bodies is to foreground the fact that dominant pedagogies disembody, and to recognize that if a body is invoked, it is through a normative filter. The ways we police (or "coach") student writing shapes student bodily possibilities. Another way to say this is to assert that dominant pedagogies privilege those who can most easily ignore their bodies. Disability studies theorist Lennard Davis has written that "language usage, which is as much a physical function as any other somatic activity, has become subject to an enforcement of normalcy" ("Bodies of Difference" 100). He refers to not just writing, but also speech, and he argues that the ways we teach both are profoundly ableist: "[Signs and] utterances must all be able ones produced by conformed, ideal forms of humanity" (*Enforcing Normalcy* 72). He argues, then, that writing is based in a "normative linguistic modality" that has come to impose standards that reach beyond the page to the human body: "An economy of the body [dictates] our own metaphors about language and knowledge," and these metaphors in turn "support the illusion of the ideal body" (103). As we dictate that the word must bear no trace of the non-normative body, we grant the word (and the technologies that produce it) a normative imperative. Or, as James Wilson and Cynthia Lewiecki-Wilson have argued, language becomes an "address interpellating the body"; in other words, linguistic conditions, in part, shape the body normatively (2). Importantly, to impose linguistic standards, we define mistakes in terms of difference and divergence that are at once about writing "wrong" but also imply the nonnormalcy of the body of the writer. Davis suggests that ideals of "[bodily] normalcy and linguistic standardization (in English) begin at roughly the same time," and he argues that this is not a coincidence (*Enforcing Normalcy* 105). In this scheme, normative language was developed consonant with the fiction of the normal body. A linguistic mistake became a bodily aberration, and not just metaphorically.

We currently see this trend played out on the page through grammar and usage rules—which Sharon Crowley and Debra Hawhee suggest "are the conventions of written language that allow [people] to discriminate against one another" (23). But we also see normalcy imposed multitudinously through "surface features" like page layout and sentence length. We see normalcy interpellated through nebulous ideas like "clarity," which Trinh T. Minh Ha suggests "is a means of subjection" and "conformity to the norms of well-behaved writing" (16). "To write 'clearly,'" she argues, we are forced to "incessantly prune, eliminate, forbid, purge, purify; in other words, practice what may be called an 'ablution of language'" (17). These metaphors all reach from the page to the body. Think, as well, of the other words we use to describe good writing: it has voice, cohesion, flow, structure. Or, in opposition, it has awkwardness, modifiers are dangling, prose is constipated, turgid, convoluted. It is not fully developed. These are all metaphorical connections, in a way, asking us to recognize that how we shape writing on the page may indeed shape norms for the bodies that write these words. These metaphors, and the forms of academic discourse they produce, coincide and perhaps coproduce bodily attitudes, positions and postures. But a regime of bodily normalcy is also present, and perhaps even more insistent, in the writing process itself. As Davis argues, writing is a physical activity—as a process of somatic production, the economy of writing is always governed by the body. Despite this fact, few pedagogical approaches allow that the bodies engaged in this process should be viewed as diverse; to ignore the fact that our bodies all write differently is to superimpose a single bodily norm onto the writing process. Further, as Patricia Dunn and many others have suggested, "Editing and revising is a drama about power" (126). And these power dynamics, combined with an underappreciation of the difference of the bodies engaged in writing, bodies writing processes in normative and possibly hegemonic ways—an abstract, ideal, normate body shapes the bodily possibilities for all students.

In this essay, I will trouble the writing process, and highlight those aspects that are most tangled and intercorporeal. In my own writing, and in my experience as a teacher, I have come to see the process of revision as both a site of possibility, and as a fraught, dangerous exchange. In revision we can approach a greater awareness of our connection to others through peer review and discussion, and we can come to recognize our own rhetorical choices, their connection to our environment and our bodies, their translation across relationships, cultures, and interfaces. But in revision we also perform a drama of normativity, accommodating ourselves towards elusive standards, and thus towards what Davis calls "conformed, ideal [bodily] forms" (*Enforcing Normalcy* 72). As one step towards acknowledging this complexity, I have hoped to de-emphasize the common focus on error-free writing. I've tried to work against the assumption that writing is not a physical act. I've tried to recognize that, as disability studies and queer theorist Robert McRuer argues (echoing compositionists such as Lester Faigley and D. Diane Davis), "Composing is defined as the production of order" yet it is "experienced as the opposite." McRuer suggests that written composition is "focused on a fetishized final product" that is "straight" and that communicates mainstream competency, ability, sexuality, and culture (50). But he argues that we should in fact strive to focus on the messiness of writing, and embodied composition, to "keep attention on disruptive, inappropriate, composing bodies—bodies that invoke a future horizon beyond straight composition" (57). I think that, in many ways, in composition, both the focus on the product and the focus on the process push students towards something clean, and straight, and cohesive. The more that students can streamline or even hide evidence of labor, the more they are rewarded. Yet student expression and learning itself can happen in the gaps, in the sidesteps and the mistakes. As George Hillocks writes, paraphrasing Derrida, we compose in polysemous chains of meaning: "Every text is divided and fissured," and thus our experience of creating and interacting with texts is messy (7). The desire to elide this messiness is the desire to ignore the body, its attachments, enablements, and limitations. Peter Elbow has argued that "we think of the mind's natural capacity for chaos and disorganization as the problem in writing. . .but what a relief it is to realize that this capacity for ephemeral incoherence can be harnessed for insight and growth" ("The Shifting Relationships" 288). I would suggest that the same can be said of the composing body: its unpredictability and mutability, its difficulty and diversity, can be seen as a key element of our capacity for making meaning.

A BRIEF HISTORY OF MESSY COMPOSITION

Of course, my critique of standardization and of the hegemonic possibilities of pedagogy, and my argument for a more partial, messy understanding, only echo a consistent theme emerging from vastly different schools of thought in composition and rhetoric, from the current-traditional to the expressivist movement, to various process-based approaches (from cognitivism to social constructivism), to what we might call postprocess. For instance, some of the earliest research about the partiality and granularity of the composing process comes from cognitive science methodologies, which worked to invalidate views that divorced the meanings found on pages of student writing from students' meaning-making processes. For instance, in composition studies in the early 1970s, much was written about the "recursive" nature of writing. Lester Faigley later critiqued the use of this term, suggesting that it had been improperly defined and applied, yet he also acknowledged its popularity. The result was a directional-metaphorical shift. As Janet Emig wrote in "The Composing Processes of 12th Graders," composing "does not occur as a left-to-right, solid, uninterrupted activity with an even pace" (84). This perspective was somewhat revolutionary, and held great potential for disrupting the normative view of the inviolable, rational, proportionate character of the idealized text. Of course, such cognitive approaches can be rightly critiqued for simplifying complex processes into clean and discrete models, and have done more than perhaps any other trend in composition research to ignore and even denounce the body's involvement in the writing process. For instance, many cognitive models of the composing process ignored the role of the body as the key, ineluctable context for writing, centering the act of composition in the memory and in activities and interchanges that were posed as purely cerebral (see, for example, the Flower and Hayes model of composition). It is as though thought immediately jumps from brain to page. Yet the work of Emig, Flower and Hayes, and others did establish a sense of the loopiness of writing, as it focused attention on process, and away from product—even if it did reify the process as a sort of static and easily schematized, generalized, and thus somewhat normative transaction.

Other currents in the process movement, concurrent with the cognitivist turn, taking aim at current-traditional modes of textual analysis and criticism, suggested that writing teachers are "trained in the autopsy, we go out and are assigned to teach our students to write, to make language live," yet instead we "dissect and sometimes almost destroy" it (Murray 3). The argument was that process approaches could focus on the liveliness and unpredictablility of language. This focus appeared in expressivist approaches to pedagogy, but also found application in social-constructivist theories of composition, which likewise amplified attention to the partiality of any perspective or utterance and the prosthetic relationship between writers and readers, discourse communities, cultures, and society. In the eighties and nineties, postprocess or social-turn approaches then took aim, in particular, at the perceived naivete of expressivist teaching, arguing that no particular discourse can empower or liberate its practitioners. I suggest that embodied perspectives on composition, following these historical trends, can be postprocess approaches because they can critique how pedagogies have ignored the body (as they have ignored race, sex, sexuality, and class). Embodied composition approaches can also be expressivist in their championing of the body writing over the text written. And such approaches are also retroprocess, disorienting to the process lockstep and forward focus.

My own approaches to revision, as part of a complex process, are informed by these historical movements. Thus I acknowledge that revision can be a locus of cultural and physical forces that sometimes remove writing from its situation, its context, its bodies. Revision can be strictly about correctness, or about accommodating one's views uncritically to the audience—this could be a cultural and corporeal assimilation, a cosmetic surgery on the text and its author; it can also take writing out of the moment. We can't truly describe any writing process and then try to re-apply it to another context. In revision we can set aside, rather than revisit, the evolving mixture of the many overlapping positions of the personal, the cultural, the embodied, and the technological that go into writing. Recognizing such critiques, what I've tried to create, in designing environments and movements for revision, are multiple approaches to composition and critical thinking, allowing students to recognize within the "products" of writing the interplay of their own voices with others', of their words with the means of communicating them, of the politics of each and every writerly choice they make. This movement does not have to be about the creation of an ever-more-perfect text (or body).

As John Trimbur wrote in "Taking the Social Turn: Teaching Writing Post-Process," the 1980s social turn in composition was a "postprocess, postcognitivist theory and pedagogy that represents literacy as an ideological arena, and composing as a cultural activity by which writers position and reposition themselves in relation to their own and others' subjectivities, discourses, practices, and institutions" (109). I would suggest, following this trend, a corporeal turn—a theory and pedagogy that represents literacy as an ideological and embodied arena, and composing as a cultural and material activity by which writers position and reposition themselves in relation to their own and others' subjectivities, discourses, practices, institutions, and bodies. I believe that what is needed is an expansive approach to writing as well as to textuality. If there are ways to use revision not just to create a better product, but to lay bare, to resense, then we could realize the ways texts connect to one another, connect us to one another, the ways texts are embodied, and how such connections are never smooth but are rather tangled and strange, and result sometimes in noise and confusion, in something messy.

WIKIS

My experimentation with a differently embodied writing process began with writing I asked students to do on a wiki several years ago, when I was a graduate teaching assistant. A wiki—like the popular *Wikipedia*—is a website that allows users to create content, to write into the interface and produce its message, as on a message board or forum, but a wiki also allows any user to edit that content. A wiki's existence is revision—once redesign ends, it becomes a website, and no longer a wiki.

My approach was not that novel. I simply asked that "traditional" essays be written and revised on a wiki. The students accessed a sheltered wiki (programmed to ask for their university IDs before allowing them to read or edit on it) in a computer classroom. We moved or pasted papers onto the wiki (or drafted them in this medium, rather than moving them from a word processor). Each student was given their own page, and we linked the pages together through a menu page from which the class could jump to any of the other essays created by classmates.

One of the most useful aspects of *Wikipedia* and of the MediaWiki design I used in my class is the "history" function. In an article on *Wikipedia*, one can use the history function to see the many different versions of that article, from the time it was first defined to its most recent revision. One can choose two different versions from any point in time and compare them. Many of the changes or edits are also "claimed"—are designated by the name of the user who made them, so one can track the interactions, collaborations, and even the conflicts between the article's writers. Using this history function, students were offered the opportunity to look backwards and sideways through their work. This somewhat fractured textuality was novel to students in that it contrasted with their previous experiences of writing as a straight process towards finality. The wiki, which can reveal to a student a kind of flickering between ideas when we layer drafts upon one another and observe their changes, is also a deconstructive technology, calling attention to the choppiness and halting, rather than the flow, of invention.

On *Wikipedia*, people also end up writing together, cumulatively. And the ways research is incorporated can be both more explicitly noted and more immediately available, thanks to hyperlinks.

The wiki history function can be used to wafer a text not in order to dissect it and perform an autopsy but to deconstruct it so we might reanimate it. How students choose to reconstruct or personally narrate such a wafering or stuttering of the text can become a matter for discussion, through which much can be learned about the drama of revision. Does the wiki dynamize the writing process usefully, helping us see the frames and flows of writing? Does the movement back through drafts interrupt the obsession with progression that much process pedagogy fetishizes? Or does it push us towards standardization, ideality, and the marking of deviation? How do exactness, discreteness, and finality contrast with partiality and interaction?

In the writing classroom, wikis can be used for collaborative in-class writing. A wiki can also be used to allow students to edit their own papers, and the work of other students, online. Susan Loudermilk Garza and Tommy Hern argue that students function differently in a Wiki because it is an open environment. Closed environments, like the traditional classroom, "tend to recreate the teacher is in control of everything, I'm writing only for the teacher mentality." They note that "Wikis change the way knowledge circulates," showing students that "writing is messy; writing is a socially collaborative act; and wiki technology is a tool that enables writers to get into the mess and the social nature of writing." Analyzing this technology, we start to see what a wiki can do, but also what composition might always do: comment on the convergences and dissonances of collaborative work; interrogate interfaces and the movement between them; create transformative recursivities; call attention to the ways information morphs as it circulates among bodies, subjectivities and "machines"; instantiate within the body new patterns of movement/thought that might more closely resemble the fluid and fragmented processes of composition; lay out the many directional connections of composition by interrogating the history of an edited document, disturbing fraught boundaries within and between bodies, ideas, and products.

It might be suggested that all online navigation is invention, albeit a form of invention that troubles our need for tangible (paper-based) output. Put simply, there are more ways to create online than through the writing of code, and rolling through the web can be a creative act, even if it is often experienced as passive. Wiki navigation invites further invention, as we receive knowledge and immediately have the option to revise or speak back to it. Invited to reference and cite, play with space, and verbally perambulate, students invent as they navigate one another's work. Further, in a wiki, because of its "structure," a different movement is encouraged, is indeed necessary, to composition. You must move backwards and sideways, you must adapt the machine to your purposes, you must move between tools, you will (make) change(s). And because of the development of a more self-aware politics of textuality, the wiki is also a place where students and teachers might incorporate a critical modality, interrogating the crossing and crossing out of information in the midst of this generative process, asking us to question what is generated, how, and to what effect.

THE REVISION GALLERY

In one revision activity, I asked students to read one another's drafts on the wiki, and they made changes and imbedded comments. These changes and comments could be viewed by the students and then accepted or rejected. (This process is much like the Word "track changes" feature, and the comparison of drafts is also much like the Word "compare documents" function.) Students also could hyperlink to research materials (for research assignments), or to other students' work within the wiki, and they could do all of this work synchronously or asynchronously. They could work together in a computer classroom or at home, separately, over a weekend. I also tried to get them moving around a computer classroom, doing some reading and writing together, and then also having time to navigate independently and at their own pace, so that there were many different ways for them to sense the writing and engage in the process. I also encouraged them to alternate freely between revising their own work and providing feedback or revision suggestions for others.

I then followed up a class revision session, and an assignment to work on the wiki for homework, with an analog version of this interaction in the next class. I printed out four different draft versions of each student's writing using the "history" function, trying to capture the drafts when they were most busy with intertextual traffic. I taped these texts to the classroom walls, with each assortment of texts given its own space, and I introduced students to the environment as being like an art gallery. I encouraged them to circulate around the room and observe the artifacts. I asked students to give one another tours of their work, looking back at the decisions they made between drafts. I then asked students to—unlike in a traditional art gallery—start talking about each piece and writing back on them. Now, as students commented on one another's papers, they were paying attention to the writerly choices and negotiations that they had all made.

Students were literally repositioning their bodies around these dynamic texts, looping through our shared production with an eye on the revision process. Taking pen, pencil, or highlighter to these pages, we challenged the idea of a chronological, straight progression towards a final product as we moved backwards and evaluated choices rather than simply assuming that each revision brought us closer to closure, anything excised disconnected from what lay on the page when all was said and done.

In these ways, the wiki is a technology that holds great potential for connecting students to one another, and each to embodiment through writing. The activities I designed were nothing revolutionary, but they were one small way to respond to more normative composition pedagogy. Obviously, there are many other questions that could be asked about my use of the wiki—many of them critical of the limited ways I used the technology. Clearly, students need to be involved in the continued re-design and critique of this space and its tools. To begin with, this technology, like all others, needs to be assessed, repurposed, and revised based on its accessibility and usability. But this more open revision process, I hope, places students into a different series of relationships with their work, with one another, with the process, and with this complex textuality. Moving between computers and classmates, between ideas, approaching all of these things in a reflexive way, is the beginning of a looping, embodied approach to the act of writing, linked inexorably as it always is to revision—of text, embodied self, and society.

INTERTEXTUAL EXCHANGES

The first time I used the wiki was in a first-year writing-about-literature course that focused on the epistolary. Students were working on intertextual papers, analyzing the interdependent and complementary ways texts stand in relation to each other. Their work was not (just) to find relationships between brother-and-sister texts, but rather to suggest ways that reading and writing texts alongside one another, in relation to one another, creates varied perspectives on an issue. There were many amalgamations of texts, and though some students had chosen similar clusters of texts to analyze, by no means were their papers written discussing all of the same texts. The papers we worked with were also structured very differently. Several students decided to write their own intertextual papers in epistolary form, incorporating the different voices of people exchanging letters as they also analyzed the ways the different texts they discussed spoke to one another. Other papers took on an intertextual form explicitly by incorporating poetry, fiction, and elements of memoir. The hopping across genre within the papers, and the ways in which the intertextual essay assignment asked students to analyze relationships between texts, seemed to fit perfectly with the structure and the goals of the wiki environment—hopping across media and mediums, flowing between audiences, listening to different voices for guidance. One large group of students all chose to base their essays on an intertextual analysis of the poetry of Sylvia Plath, her letters to her mother, Ted Hughes's *Birthday Letters*, and the movie *Sylvia*—these texts in various figurations, and often augmented with other texts of the students' choice, for instance the poetry and letters of John Berryman or quantitative research on suicide and single mothers. Another group of students examined the movie *Last Letters Home* about the letters written by soldiers who passed away in the first Gulf War; excerpts from the book *Jarhead*, written by Anthony Swofford, a marine in Iraq, specifically sections where he writes about letters written by civilians to "Any Marine"; articles about the controversy over letters published in American newspapers from soldiers currently in Iraq that were later proven to be fabricated; and *Letters From Vietnam*, the classic book of letters home from that war. These texts were also variously re-arranged and augmented, for instance with lyrics from antiwar songs by the Dixie Chicks; examples of "Any Marine" letters students had written themselves in high school; personal stories about soldiers currently serving, including a funeral eulogy written by a student for a close friend; and so on. A third cluster of texts for analysis was organized around the movie *About Schmidt*, a movie that gains structure through its use of an epistolray exchange between an elderly American man and a fictional African "sponsored child"; advertisements for Childreach International; the short story "Dear Alexandros" by John Updike, which also is based on a letter to a "sponsored child"; and articles in the *New Internationalist* on the logistics and the politics of organizations which, like Childreach, allow Westerners to sponsor foreign children. These texts were augmented with outside research and with personal experiences, in one case with a correspondence between a student and her mother, who is a Childreach sponsor, and so on. Because the whole class had read, analyzed, and talked about all of these texts, we all had points of access to each of the intertextual essays that were written about the three clusters without there being very much overlap at all in the way students wrote about them, or even in those issues students focused on. In this way, the movements on the wiki, on the walls, and in the texts weren't just about getting "help" with editing a paper, they were about greatly enriching the conversations we had about these texts, respecting and developing the huge and emotional and complex ideas they conveyed, especially when put into conversation with one another.

Here are some examples of the exchanges that happened on the wiki. Short sections of student writing from the actual essays are in bold and in sentence case, while any of the comments we made within one another's work is in capitals. When I am commenting in caps, I sign my name. Students remain unnamed. My first example is pulled from the introduction to a paper about African aid organizations:

> I know you have been up late flipping through the channels and you happen to come across one of those commercials with the sickly African kids.
> THIS IS A POWERFUL OPENING. WILL YOU DIG INTO THE ATTITUDES THIS CREATES—PITY, PERHAPS EVEN A KIND OF RACISM? [name removed].

Here, I feel the reader used this opportunity to stop the author and question the impact of this statement. The comment seemed to ask the author, "Are you critiquing this representation or reproducing it?" Later, in a revision, and in a different section of the essay, the author addressed this comment directly. He went through a comparison of the claims of different aid organizations and critically read their websites in comparison to one another, focusing on this depiction of children as an appeal to emotion, but also commenting on how sponsors demanded accountability. He concluded, bluntly that

> if a program is using these innocent kids to make money it will come back to bite them in the ass in the end.

But perhaps just as importantly, when the paper was on the wall, this comment, and the author's decision not to focus too deeply on the attitudes that the images of "sickly African kids" create, but rather on the efficacy of the sponsorship programs themselves—their ability to get the money to the children with whom the sponsors exchange letters—led to a larger discussion. Students talked about how the commercials actually tried to prove, visually, that the programs worked, using gratuitous images of water, showing needles actually being injected (right into a child's buttock), food being eaten, and so on. What were the entailments of this visual argument?

This led to a discussion of the ways our university used pictures of African American students on its website—often students from the dorm in which the class was located, the "diversity" dorm. This discussion then led to talk about how the commercials tried to show sponsors of different races, but that students, even in a class that was predominantly African American, and in which the parents of some students actually did sponsor children, couldn't imagine a sponsor being anything but rich and white. How did this connect to our university's use of images of diversity, in spite of the low minority population? How do institutions and organizations create their "bodies"? How did African American students feel about being used as visual arguments?

Although the paper itself didn't fully address the loaded language of a specific image, it opened up the possibility for us all to do so in another venue. The result was a very useful mess for the class to dive into.

Next I'll look at an excerpt from a paper about Sylvia Plath:

> Having faced death but survived like Sylvia did in her failed attempts, an unhealable scar has been placed upon her heart—such unimaginable despair and aloneness felt in those moments, and then to still be thrown to the wolves, to life, without much help is a crime against the soul. HOW ABOUT LOOKING TO USE ONE OF SYLVIA'S OWN METAPHORS FOR THIS? DO TRY AND CHANNEL SOME OF HER POETRY IN HERE, SO YOUR READER CAN READ HER TOO [JAY]. To keep facing life, without any treatment must have felt like drowning in misery, and who could deny the want for peace? I don't think suicide is selfish because I understand the incomprehensible pain and aloneness one must be feeling to even have those thoughts. While I don't see it as selfish, I do not support it in any way shape or form, but never will I judge someone who acts on those thoughts, never. THIS IS ALL OPINION—TRY RESEARCHING SOME OF WHAT YOU HAVE FOUND TO BE TRUE SO THAT YOUR STATEMENTS ARE MORE CREDIBLE. MAYBE YOU COULD FIND A WEBSITE THAT DEALS WITH SUICIDE AND QUOTE THEM. I THINK YOU SHOULD STILL INCLUDE SOME OF YOUR OWN EXPERIENCE AS WELL SO THAT THE READER KNOWS THAT YOU'RE NOT WRITING IGNORANTLY. [name removed].

In this exchange, I'm the person who suggested incorporating some of Sylvia's poetry into the paper, and this suggestion is obviously different from the long comment provided by a student. We're both, perhaps in a veiled way, asking the author to get more intertextual. The author did choose to do more of this second kind of "research" and actually ended up drastically altering the paper. (Note that the author's ability to ignore my advice speaks to a disruption of traditional dynamics of authority.) What began as a very personal reflection on what Sylvia Plath may have felt in her final days became an essay with very "credible" research into the psychology of suicide. In a way, the student may have been moving further away from the affect of the issue, and may have been led there by peers. But this paper shows something else too—it shows that the wiki was a place where students could comment more freely on a topic that might be difficult to talk about face to face or in groups, with all of the benefits and drawbacks of this greater freedom. In a traditional peer workshop, there may have just been silence. As one student wrote on this author's paper,

> I THINK THIS IS A GOOD PAPER. IT PROVIDES A LOT OF INSIGHT ON A TOPIC THAT NOT MANY ARE COMFORTABLE TALKING ABOUT [name removed].

In another paper about Sylvia Plath, also looking into her suicidal feelings, the author concluded that what Sylvia had was a "deep connection with herself." A student commented: "I AM INTERESTED IN WHETHER OR NOT YOU THINK THAT DEEP CONNECTION WITH SELF IS A GOOD THING OR NOT" [name removed].

In a later revision, the author tackled this tough question:

> This connection to their inner emotions could be construed as a bad thing, but without their own sacrifice, the world might never have known what profound thoughts they actually had. Their beliefs and practices led them to a different kind of immortality than what most people seek.

Again, this revision shows how some of the key, complex thinking in the paper was generated out of a dialogue between students—something we could argue is always the case, but isn't always noticeable—or traceable, as it was because of this activity, across these mediums. And again, the result when we trace this complex thinking is not a clear line toward consensus. The "reviewer" is enabled to ask a question that rends the essay open. The writer is encouraged to locate ambivalence.

Susan Stan and Terence Collins have written that students revise more on screen when given the opportunity. While I wasn't interested in asking if this was indeed true in my class, or in asking if students commented on others' papers more, and I wasn't interested in asking any of the other quantitative questions we might ask of this wiki work, it was clear to me that students wrote differently here. In a paper that looked at letters from Iraq, but that also spoke very emotionally of the author's experience at a friend's recent funeral, a student wrote these summative comments:

> WOW I AM VERY GLAD YOU SHARED ABOUT YOUR LOSS, WHICH TOUCHED YOU PERSONALLY. THAT MUST HAVE TAKEN COURAGE ESPECIALLY SINCE THAT WAS SO RECENT. YOUR PAPER WAS EASY TO FOLLOW, AND THE ONLY REAL COMMENT I HAVE IS TO MAYBE INCLUDE ANOTHER EXAMPLE MAYBE OF THE WORDS OF ANOTHER PARENT WHO LOST THEIR SON OR DAUGHTER TO EMPHASIZE THAT

PAIN AND HOW SPECIFICALLY ONCE AGAIN THAT LOSS HITS HOME. THE DEATHS OF SOLDIERS ARE NOT JUST CASUALTY NUMBERS...THEY ARE REAL PEOPLE LIKE YOU AND ME. GREAT JOB :) [name removed].

I think the comments show that, in this case, the medium may have allowed for these students to exchange something important, for the commenting student to take care with his/her tone and to ensure (by encoding, by making rhetorical choices—perhaps even those things we'd see as "mistakes," like sentence fragments) that the message came off the way she wanted it to. What I recognize in this comment is an incredible mastery of this genre of so-called "informal" online writing, a genre that here allows the student to communicate her suggestions gently, as though the two writers are working together as an empathetic team to show how this loss hits home—a much different way to think about revision.

Finally, several days later, after—unfortunately—much of this dynamic interaction was ended, temporarily, by my need to assess their writing, I asked students to reflect on the entire process. Below are a few of the questions I asked:

1. We compared drafts of your paper in the in-class gallery. What thoughts have you had since then about the implied space, and work, and change, in between drafts? How did you feel seeing them alongside one another? What were your feelings about the typed comments on the essay, seen after you'd revised, and about those comments written on the papers during that class session?

2. In the computer classroom, online, and then in the gallery, how did you feel about the connections between you and your fellow students? Was your sense of ownership of the paper challenged? Did you feel a sense of collaboration?

3. Some students were frustrated by the format of the wiki, others seemed to have no complaints. How did you feel about using the technology? What could be improved? How did the wiki compare to working in Microsoft Word or another word processor? How did it compare to printing your paper out and bringing it in to class to workshop? What were the problems that arose as you tried to move around—in Word, in the wiki, in the gallery, between them all? What boundaries are there, what pathways? How might you have created or avoided them?

4. How do you now plan to revise your paper—or any of your work? Also, how would you revise the design of our class's use of the wiki, or of the wiki itself? Are there parallels between these revisions?

5. As I ask these questions, I am particularly interested in your physical feeling for the spaces in which we worked—how did you navigate around in the wiki, in your word processor, in the "gallery"—how did this affect your ability to write, to read, to think, to concentrate? Did you have a sense of your peers—where they were, what they were doing and thinking, as they read your work and wrote in your document?

6. Did moving around these spaces enable you to resee or rethink your positions in the paper?

Many of the student responses were generic and evaluative—the wiki was good, or it was bad, and little explanation was offered. But students also mentioned that they thought they could "see" their thought process between drafts when they brought different versions side by side, and that they could understand how peer comments led directly to rewriting. One student said she felt "more connected to her peers and freer to more honestly critique their papers" because she could "really see [her] growth and the growth prompted by peer comments" between drafts. My hope—and belief—is that this student saw growth not through the editing and perfecting of her prose, but through the critical process of introducing complexity and enriching the intertextual and intersubjective tangle. While some students felt alienated by problems with the technology, at least a few felt a connection through the wiki, and I think this means its use was justified. But it also suggests that even an activity as seemingly structured as this one is not repeatable, must be changed and altered according to context. Would it work as well, or better, had the students been writing something other than an intertextual analysis? The point, I suppose, is not to proscribe a process, but to find ways to emphasize the situatedness and partiality of communication, to draw attention to relationships and choices and the feeling for moving across ideas, genres, and mediums. My suggestion is that in paying attention to these things, we develop a feeling for our embodied composition.

OTHER BODIES

Disability studies theorist Rosemarie Garland-Thomson argues that our dominant culture encourages a gaze through which we each ignore our own body and its particularity and focus instead on the specter of Otherness and deviance. Through this gaze, there is a "privileged state of disembodiment . . . conferred upon spectators, however fraudulent" (Introduction 10). I began this essay by echoing this argument, suggesting as well that by ignoring the body, we may in fact be harming bodies. As

Vivian Sobchack argues, "The normative practices of our culture estrange us phenomenologically from our own bodies and the bodies of others. As a consequence, our comportment becomes inhibited and restrictive rather than a capacious system and style" (204). In these ways, a composition pedagogy that ignores the body might actually limit our ability to make meaning. I would argue, then, that to understand embodiment is to actually and centrally examine the body, the body image, the thinking of the body—not only as implied, normative inversions of a range of Other, wrong bodies, and not as a default ideal. To "compose" the body is to examine the shadows and scissions that differentially constitute embodiment. Likewise, if we want to truly understand embodied writing, perhaps what we need to most closely study are not ideal, complete texts, but the messy and recursive process of composing as we break our ideas apart through language. We need to see a polysemous writing process as that which allows for meaning to be made. I believe that if we see the body more peculiarly, we may in fact develop the tools to critically body the world, to embody discourse, and to develop embodied rhetorics and modes of composition. David Wills suggests that writing "makes explicit the very [lack and] break that constitutes the human body" (*Prosthesis* 246). If we see this "broken-ness" as central to our definition and embodied understanding of the self, then we should also see it as central to our understanding of the writing process.

I've already mentioned the ways I believe my work on the wiki begins to address disembodied composition. First of all, I think it is unique that the body—and body politics—were at the center of the students' discussion of one another's work, whether they were discussing mortality in surprisingly sensitive and philosophical ways, or whether they were discussing race and the manner in which their own bodies had been used by our institution for marketing purposes. Aside from the central importance of these topics, I also believe that the mediums and media through which we navigated shaped our interaction in important ways. I believe a particular politics and practice of embodied textuality can be facilitated by the use of technology such as the wiki. Further, traditional class activities can be layered onto these experiences in ways that reanimate the movement of bodies and ideas between texts. This was perhaps not a composing process centrally about embodiment, but it was a pedagogy directed sideways and backwards through practices I believe are critically embodied.

In composition and rhetoric we have, for too long, held onto classical generalizations that belittle the role of the body in thought and in the act of writing. And when the body has been invoked, it has been either as an impossible ideal, or as a baseline for discrimination. One solution is to seek to reconnect mind, body, and writing, and to do so focusing not on ideals, but on the body (and the text) as meaningfully messy and incomplete.

It might seem that the goal of such an embodied consciousness is counterproductive: that the teacher would reward progressively more "error"-filled work, and that the student would learn skills that would only "Other" them from the world of standard discourse. But the goal I am focused on here is not just better writing—whether this is measured through cleaner products, or through more smoothly incorporated practices. The goal of such pedagogy is a critical and reflexive thinking, the sort of thinking that perhaps writing can best allow when it is neither clean nor smooth. As we compose media and embodiment, we can refuse the forward march toward a perfectable text/body, and move instead through a recursive process via which gaps, erasures, mistakes and collaborations might be highlighted. This is the "corporeal turn" I've suggested. This is a critical turning away from traditional body meanings. This is a turn towards recognizing and enabling all bodies. Finally, this is a turn that asks you to revisit what I have argued for here, and perhaps to resist each of my conclusions, instead locating your own beginnings.

PART 1
ACTIVITIES

MEDIA = EMBODIMENT

Much motivates writing teachers to open their classroom activities to multiple media and communication technologies. Not only do newer technologies make multimodal composing easier than earlier technologies did, but the proliferation of multimodal texts in all areas of our shared lives suggests that our responsibilities to students should include considering how we compose and engage others with some broad range of the media available to us.

We have additional motivations in this book.

In our introduction, in our discussions of twentieth-century media theory grounded in nineteenth-century theories about production, we argued that an individual's production of media is about an individual's production of self—and of self in community. We believe we cannot be thinking, participating beings without individual abilities to produce usable and desirable objects, objects that circulate among others and so embed us into and with the lives of others—and into and within and sometimes against the structures and institutions of our lives.

We hope, that is, that we have made it clear, in our introduction and throughout the chapters of part 1, that the media we produce—and consume—embody us. Our media carry us out into the world when, in producing media, we feel ourselves to be individually expressing what matters. But our available and existing media also give us—and so limit us to becoming (until we find productive tactics to change or resist)—what makes sense among our various structures and institutions: each text we consume teaches us, usually not overtly, some way of being in the world.

Embodiment is therefore not theoretical (although it is certainly theorizable, as our works cited list shows). We experience relations between embodiment and media as we breathe, walk, talk, look, listen, sigh, read, write, and view. We feel our embodiment continually.

How can we not then make part of our teaching—and so of this book—activities that help us and those in our classes observe and question what it feels to be a body mediating and being mediated?

The following pages offer activities growing out of part 1's concern with how we are embodied in media. The activities ask students to consider the literacies and bodies encouraged by and required for media production and consumption.

ACTIVITY 1: (VISUAL) LITERACY NARRATIVE

Growing out of "Drawn Together," this assignment asks students to consider their own embodied literacy practices through the affordances of words and pictures.

Objectives

- Consider the differing affordances of photographs/illustrations and words for composing narratives.

- Articulate how we are represented through pictures.

- Describe how certain literacy practices and/or beliefs are shaped.

Considerations

- The narratives can be produced on paper, on the web (perhaps using web-based software such as Prezi or Wix), or in a slideshow format (such as PowerPoint or KeyNote).

- You can ask students to construct their narratives as slideshows or collages. Look at examples of collages and slideshows together to discuss with students differences between seeing many pictures all at once and seeing them in sequence.

- Consider assigning Scott McCloud's chapter "Show and Tell" from his book *Understanding Comics: The Invisible Art.* "Show and Tell" provides vocabulary for considering how pictures and words work together to shape readers' understandings. This vocabulary is formal and arhetorical; you will need to help students understand the rhetorical applications of the vocabulary.

Assignments

Overview

A literacy narrative tells a story about your relationship with reading and/or composing. It can be about a small moment of your relationship with texts (perhaps your early love of "choose your own adventure" books, or memories of your aunt reading to you, or the first time you made a video or a website) or it can be a larger story of how you came to be a reader, writer, designer, and/or composer. You will tell the rest of the class this story in two ways: through a sequence of photographs and/or illustrations alone and then through a sequence of photographs or illustrations mixed with words. You will then reflect on your visual and linguistic choices in a short reflection paper.

Part 1: Literacy Narrative, Photographs and/or Illustrations

Compose a narrative for the class about your relationship with reading and/or composing. The story can be positive or negative, but should illustrate how you have been and are being shaped as a literate person. You can consider literacy to mean reading and writing, but you might also consider your literacy practices with photographs, sounds, or video. Present your narrative through photographs or illustrations only. The number of photographs or illustrations is up to you: use as many as you need to convey your point.

Part 2: Literacy Narrative, Photographs and/or Illustrations + Words

Tell the same story but now use words as well as photographs/illustrations. You might consider composing your narrative in a comic-book style, but you might also find other ways of putting words and images together given your purposes. There is no limit on the number of words, so consider what you need to convey your purposes.

Part 3: Reflection Presentation

You will present your literacy narratives to the class in a five to ten minute presentation. In this presentation, you must

- share your narratives.

- describe why you chose the particular photographs or illustrations you did. Did they resonate with you in some way? What kind of understanding did you think the audience would glean from the photographs or illustrations? Why?

- describe whether you chose a story that you thought would be best told in this format or chose a story first and then found a way to tell the story in pictures (and words). How did this choice shape your storytelling?

- describe the reasons you used the words you did to tell the story. Consider how many words you felt were necessary, what types of words, and how they shape how a reader might understand your story.

ACTIVITY 2: MAPPING YOUR CONNECTIVITY

Drawing on the "Information Cartography" chapter, this assignment asks students to map their digital connections. This assignment can set up a research project that asks students to use the evidence of the maps to judge claims (in newspapers, popular magazines, and academic journals) about the digital lives of young people. Does class evidence show that other writers are making claims that are too large—or too small—about youth and online life? What adjustments would students recommend in the other readings?

Objectives

- Consider the definitions and mediations of "map."

- Explore various visual strategies for mapping information.

- Attend to how digital technologies weave into students' days.

Considerations

- Consider using class time to look at different types of maps, and ask students to define what constitutes a "map." Consider exploring the online Perry-Castañeda Library Map Collection at the University of Texas at Austin (www.lib.utexas.edu/maps), the website for the Hand Drawn Map Association (www.handmaps.org), or the *Strange Maps* blog (bigthink.com/blogs/strange-maps) as starting points. (Katharine Harmon's book, *You Are Here: Personal Geographies and Other Maps of the Imagination,* is also a rich resource.)

- While the assignment suggests connectivity types students can log, you may want to have a brainstorming session in which students list the digital technologies they use daily.

Assignments

Overview

You are going to choose one day during the coming week to log your phone and computer use. Your log will include what you did, where you did it, whom you contacted, and for how long; from your log you will compose a map to represent a day in the life of your connectivity. In composing this map, you will consider, first, how mapping represents your connectivity and, second, the varying ways and people with whom you connect.

Part 1: Logging your Connectivity

Pick a day in the coming week before our next class meeting. From the time you wake up until the time you go to sleep, note every time you use your phone or computer to connect with information or people. Consider every time you look up information, check Facebook, send or receive a text message or an e-mail, watch a *YouTube* video, play a video game, and so forth. Write down (1) the activity, (2) the time span in which it took place, (3) the person or organization with whom you connected, (4) where you were when you connected, and (5) the device you used (phone, laptop, computer lab computer).

Part 2: Composing a Map

Once you have your log, consider how best to map this information in order to convey to your audience what a day in the life of your connectivity looks like. You are not required to map every single instance, nor are you required to include all five areas from your log. What you must do is make visual choices that illustrate (1) how you use technology on an average day, (2) what you use technology for, and (3) where you are physically when you connect. How you present this information is up to you, and you can make this map using any media available to you—but others must be able to understand your map without your standing by to explain it.

Part 3: Justification Paper

When you turn in your map, include a short justification paper (one to two pages) that explains your visual choices. Describe how you chose the type of visual representation you did (why this type of map over another type of map?). Explain what parts of your log you chose to represent and why. Why did you exclude (or not) portions of your log? Finally, explain what you think the map helps illustrate to your audience. What does it say about your connectivity? How might your connectivity—and your relations with others—have looked through another kind of mapping?

Part 4: Comparison Paper

After you have looked at everyone else's maps in class, write a two to three page paper in which you analyze what the different maps encouraged you to understand about differing people's connectivity and relations with others. Also hypothesize about what these maps show you about your colleagues' uses of time and ways of relating to others. Finally, discuss the differing strategies others used to present their maps: What maps were easiest to understand, and why?

ACTIVITY 3: COMPOSING SELF AND COMMUNITY

Drawing on "Pausing to Reflect" as well as notions of media and embodiment raised throughout part 1, this activity engages students in the act of reading and entering online communities.

Objectives

- Consider how visual design shapes your sense of the author.

- Interrogate notions of community in online spaces.

- Practice entering a community based on genre conventions.

Considerations

- This assignment uses Tumblr, a microblogging platform that allows users to post text, photos, quotes, links, audio, and video. If you are unfamiliar with Tumblr, spend some time creating your own account and looking through the directory to see how various users work with a microblog (<http://www.tumblr.com/directory>). You might also read the short piece "Tumblr Makes Blogging Blissfully Easy" from the *New York Times* (<http://gadgetwise.blogs.nytimes. com/2009/03/13/tumblr-makes-blogging-blissfully-easy/>).

- Given how quickly various Web 2.0 sites come and go, if Tumblr is no longer popular, consider using any blogging or microblogging site, so long as it either has a directory or allows users to search blogs based on keywords. Students will need to find a community of bloggers who blog on a particular topic, so searching and/or directories are key.

- If students do not understand *genre*, introduce the concept to them—and then use the discussion of Tumblr below to help them develop their understanding of how genres are shaped by conventions. Discussing the blog they make will help them further understand the workings of genre.

In-Class Work

Introduce students to (or have students introduce) Tumblr (<www.tumblr. com>). Consider projecting Tumblr, showing students the blog you created, and then introducing the Tumblr directory. Choose one category from the directory, and ask students what expectations they have about blogs in that category. Open three to five blogs in that category and discuss the blogs, using the following questions as guides:

- What assumptions about the blog's author do you make because of the blog's visual design? What do you imagine the person is like? Why?

- Look at the author's recent posts. Do they give you any sense of what the author might be like? Why or why not?

Ask the same questions of each blog you opened. Then ask:

- What do you notice is similar about the blogs that identify themselves within this category? What is different?

- Do you feel this is a community of bloggers? Why or why not? How do you define *community* in order to make this judgment?

- Would you say there is a genre of Tumblr blogs within this category? What makes them a genre or, perhaps, what doesn't make them a genre? If there isn't one large genre, do you see smaller genres emerge within the category?

End class making sure students (1) have a grasp of how Tumblr works, (2) have a definition of community, and (3) have a sense of what a genre is and how it works within Tumblr. Provide students the following assignment. You can flesh it out into a much larger project, but for here we've left it short.

Assignments

Overview
After exploring one category of your choosing in Tumblr, you will create your own Tumblr blog that you think will fit the category you have chosen.

Part 1: Analyzing a Tumblr category
Based on your interests, pick a category of Tumblr blog from the Tumblr directory. Look carefully at no fewer than ten blogs in that category.

Write a two-page paper in which you list the features those blogs share, list their differences, and discuss why you think the blogs share the features they do and differ as they do.

Part 2: Designing and writing your own Tumblr blog
Create a Tumblr blog in the category you analyzed, using a template that you think works well for the category. Send me your blog address so I can compile a list of all the blogs for class.

Over the next week create at least five posts. Each post can contain any mix of text, photos, quotes, links, audio, and video—as long as your post fits with the types of posts other users create within your category.

Part 3: Tumblr Reflection

At the end of the week, compose a text or video Tumblr in which you reflect on your week of Tumbling. Address the following points:

1. In what category did you choose to blog? Why?

2. What design template did you choose? Why? How does the design fit within the category of Tumblrs you chose to enter?

3. How well do you think your posts enter the community of Tumblrs you chose? What makes them fit? What might not make them fit?

4. Finally, comment on this overall experience. Do you think you'll keep up a Tumblr after this class? Why or why not?

ACTIVITY 4: THE CULTURAL EMBEDDEDNESS OF MEDIA

When we act as though our uses of media are natural or easy, we forget how deeply media entwine with our lives and beliefs; the chapters of this book—like this activity—work to denaturalize media so we might work with them more ethically.

Objectives

- Understand how much we take for granted in using our media.
- Consider the cultural embeddedness of books.

Considerations

- Bring to class a range of media or technology objects such as coupon books, tax forms, a magazine for a specialized audience, DVDs, memory cards, or remote control devices; the activity description below will help you think of others. Bring enough objects so each group of three to four students in your class can work with one object.

In-Class Work

Part 1: An example to discuss

Hold up a dollar bill and ask students what they need to know or assume if they are to use the dollar.

Help them think about how they need to know how to count and add, subtract, and divide; how they need to understand about money being tied to a particular country, about counterfeit money, or about how objects get valued in order to be exchanged for differing amounts of money; how they assume that other people will accept this odd piece of paper in exchange for goods and services and that they need to protect their money from others; how they trust banks, credit card companies, and PayPal to hold or use their dollars; and so on.

Also ask them to list any objects or institutions that exist because of or in order to support money: we've already mentioned banks and other financial institutions, but think of wallets and pockets, cash registers, ATMs, gift cards sized for wallets, the FBI, printing presses, and so on.

You might diagram these various observations on the board, putting a sketch of the dollar in the center and drawing connections between it and the various concepts and objects listed.

Finally, ask how what they've noted might contribute to how they act, both alone and with each other, and whether any of their values are related to the dollar bill and what they've noted. How would their lives be different without ATMs or banks, or if they had to exchange objects without the mediation of money? How would their lives be different if they didn't work for money but instead worked for food?

Point out that what you have just discussed is the cultural embeddedness of money: money is not an independent object we happen to use but rather has a history and requires and circulates among institutions, shaping our actions and values.

Part 2: Small group work and short individual writing

Ask students to form groups of three to four. Give each group one of the objects you brought (or ask them to use what they have: cellphones, credit cards, laptops, pens, notebooks. . .). Ask them to analyze their objects as you analyzed the dollar bill: What do they need to know to use their object, what do they need to assume in order to use it, what other objects or institutions exist to support their use of the object, and how might their actions and values be shaped because of how the object is embedded into culture in the ways they describe?

Have them diagram the object as you did.

Then give each group a book or have them pull out a classroom text. Have them discuss and diagram the book-object exactly as they did the other object.

When they finish, ask them to write individually: What aspects of the embeddedness of any of the objects do they not like, and why? About what aspects of the objects' embeddedness do they think we should all be more alert, and why? What would they change about the embeddedness of the objects—and how might that change their lives?

ACTIVITY 5: KNOWLEDGE SHARING & SOCIAL TAGGING

This activity draws on all the chapters of part 1: through research and information shaping, students confront how their technologically supported choices shape what they can communicate with others.

Objectives

- Explore the conversations surrounding the value of *Wikipedia*.
- Explore the role of metadata in saving and sharing information.
- Consider the role of audience in sharing academic knowledge through writing.
- Consider the role of audience in choosing metadata.

Considerations

- While we've used this assignment as a four-week unit in a course, its length depends on the length of the paper you assign, the number of sources you request, and the amount of in-class work desired.
- When using Delicious, consider devoting a class period to exploring the interface and learning how other users tag information.
- Consider a day in class when students tag the course readings for future students. What tags make sense to them? Why? Ask them to articulate the reasons certain tags make sense in particular rhetorical situations.
- To explore tagging further, assign the Prologue and chapter 1 of David Weinberger's *Everything is Miscellaneous* (available for free at http://www.everythingismiscellaneous.com).

Assignments

The following suggest steps for, and descriptions of, assignments for helping students learn about knowledge sharing and social tagging.

Overview

You will write a feature article for your college newspaper on the various conversations surrounding the value and impact of *Wikipedia*. Your primary audience is faculty across campus, particularly those who feel students have no business using *Wikipedia* as a research tool. While it is not your job to convince them otherwise, it is your job to inform them of the various conversations both laypeople and scholars have on the role and value of *Wikipedia*. Along with writing the paper, you will make your research available for your audience through the use of Delicious bookmarks. Finally, you will write a justification paper that explains the reasons you chose the tagging system you did.

What is Delicious?

Delicious is a Social Bookmarking service, which means you can save all your bookmarks online, share them with other people, and see what other people are bookmarking. It also means we can show you the most popular bookmarks being saved right now across many areas of interest. In addition, our search and tagging tools help you keep track of your entire bookmark collection and find tasty new bookmarks from people like you. (www.delicious.com/help/learn)

Part 1: Research

Find twenty to thirty web resources—with a mix of academic and popular sources—that discuss the value and implications of *Wikipedia*. These sources should inform your writing and should also provide further information for your article's audience should they choose to dig deeper.

Create a Delicious account—http://www.delicious.com—where you will bookmark your articles by employing a tagging system. If you already have a Delicious account, please create a new account solely for this assignment so the readers of your article can easily find your sources by going to www.delicious.com/[yournamehere].

When you save an article at Delicious, you are required to tag it. Consider the audience for your tags as the audience for your newspaper article. What tags will make the most sense for those interested in your topic? How will you justify your choices rhetorically?

Part 2: The Article

Compose an 800-1000 word article for your college newspaper that explains the various conversations surrounding *Wikipedia*. Your primary audience are faculty on campus who dismiss *Wikipedia* as a research tool. It is not your job to convince them that *Wikipedia* should be used in all situations, but it is your job to provide them with a range of ideas on the validity and value of *Wikipedia* so that they can make a more-informed choice about its use. The article needs to reference at least five of your sources, and must point readers to your Delicious bookmarks so that they can read more should they choose to.

Part 3: The Tagging Justification Paper

Compose an approximately 1000 word paper that explains to others in class the reasons you chose the tagging system you did. First, list the tags you included in your Delicious bookmarks. Second, explain why you believe these particular tags will be effective given your perceived audience. How will these tags help them understand, make sense of, and find your bookmarked articles?

Part 4: The Tagging Reflection Paper

Write a short, informal paper in which you reflect on how you thought about tagging as you carried out this assignment. Use the following questions as a springboard to thinking about how tagging shapes your relationships with information, other people, and your own composing processes.

How did you have to shift the ways you thought about sources, this assignment, or your audience in order to create the tags you did? Do you think having to tag your sources—and make your tags available to others—shifted how you remembered and thought about your sources?

If you have not used Delicious before, do you think you will continue to use it? Why—or why not?

How has your use of tags—and how you think about what tags to use—shifted as you have worked with them?

What do you see to be the usefulness of tagging?

How does tagging ask you to think about others who use Delicious or who use other social media that requires tagging, such as Flickr or some blogging software? Do you feel as though you are collaborating with them, or is there some other relationship you feel with them?

ACTIVITY 6: THE FEEL OF COMPOSING

This activity draws on all the chapters of part 1 to ask students how their composing and communicating processes shape their felt sense of their bodies.

Objectives

- Consider how our uses of our composing technologies shape how our—and others'—bodies feel and move.

- Strengthen our abilities to observe our own bodily responses.

Considerations

- We describe this as a three-week activity, but you could shape it to extend over three days or over a full semester.

- You could drop the first observation and writing we ask for in the activity—the observation of others—to shorten this assignment.

Assignments

Overview

You will perform three different observations: first, you will observe how others hold and move their bodies as they compose and communicate; second, you will observe your own usual composing and communicating processes; third, you will observe how you feel and move when you change your own composing and communicating processes.

For each observation, you will describe what you have observed, and—after you have finished the three observations—you will write a reflection about what you have learned from thinking about how we use our bodies when we compose and communicate with others.

Part 1: Observing others—and writing about your observations

Over the next week, any time you are in a coffee shop or library, on public transit, or in a place where you can discreetly and unobtrusively watch others and take notes, observe—from a distance—how others hold or move their bodies as they use communication technologies or compose texts. For example, if you watch others at computers, are their bodies tilting forward into the computers or are they sitting back? How do people hold their phones and how do they move while they are talking? (Do you get a suggestion of their relation with the person on the other end by how they move while talking?) How do people sit or stand as they read?

As you observe, try to name styles of body use and describe the styles. That is, do you observe relaxed, tense, languid, elegant, effusive, or shy styles (obviously, many other adjectives are possible for naming how people move)? What body postures characterize the differing styles?

Try to observe at least ten to fifteen differing styles.

After you have observed for a week, write up your observations. Name the styles you saw and why you named them that, describing how people held or interacted with their technologies.

As you write, also address the following questions: How do communication technologies themselves seem to shape how people hold their bodies and move while using them? For example, how does the shape and size of someone's computer or a book suggest or encourage the postures and movements bodies can make while using it? How does the shape of a body seem to shape the movements it can make while using a communication technology? What other considerations do you think shape how people hold and move their bodies while they compose or use communication technologies?

Part 2: Observing yourself—and writing about your observations

For a week, write down how you hold or move your body any time you use a communication technology or compose a text. For example, if you are writing a paper, do you sit or walk around—or some mix of both? How does your body feel as you write? Do you hunch your shoulders and hold a pen tightly or do you type, feeling like a pianist elegantly in control of a score? How do you hold your body when you text or e-mail others or talk with them on the phone?

It is hard to observe oneself. One way is to set a timer for fifteen to twenty minutes—and then let yourself start composing or communicating so that you get lost in the work; when the timer goes off, stop and take notes about how you are sitting, standing, moving, or holding your body. You can also—after you have finished a bout of writing, typing, or texting—simply close your eyes to remember how it felt and to visualize how your body was moving. (You can also ask someone else to observe you.)

After you have observed yourself for a week, write up your observations. Name and describe your styles for composing and using communication technologies. Where do you think your styles come from? Do your styles change depending on what you are composing or communicating? How might your communication technologies themselves be affecting how you hold your body or move? Are you surprised by any of your observations about how your bodily movements entwine with your composing processes and uses of communication technologies?

Part 3: Trying new movements—and writing about your observations

From your *first* observation, pick a style (or two) that differs significantly from how you compose and communicate (as you noticed in your second observation).

Try on that style or styles several different times over the week—and try to maintain the style for more than a few minutes.

Also, try sitting or standing in a place where you usually don't when you read or write. As you change how you hold or move your body, observe how the changes feel. Take notes about what you observe about your body and how it feels.

After you have tried several different styles, write up your observations. How does it feel to hold and move your body differently? Was it easy or hard to do this? Did anything about how you composed or communicated change—or were you simply distracted? Where do you think the changes—or the distractions—come from?

Part 4: Reflection

Thinking back over all three observations, what most stood out for you? How do you think our composing processes and uses of communication technologies shape how we can use our bodies—and vice versa? How might the designs of our communication technologies enable more styles of communication—or restrict them to fewer styles? How might our bodily styles when we compose or use communication technologies affect how we hold our bodies and move in other situations, including when we are face to face with others?

PART 2

MEDIATING BODIES ∧ MEDIATED BODIES

What sorts of productive relations with texts help us sense and understand our—and others'—bodies most capaciously?

What sorts of productive relations help us open new potentials and relations?

8 CRAFTING NEW APPROACHES TO COMPOSITION

Kristin Prins

In her essay "Writing on the Bias," Linda Brodkey describes her childhood approach to ballet as a series of rules that taught her "that dance is discipline, and discipline is a faultless physical reenactment of an ideal." She notes that while codifications of practice into rules are meant to instruct, their use by those new to a practice "as often as not ground a ritual fascination with rules, the perfection of which is in turn used as a standard against which to measure one's devotion to dance, religion, or writing rather than their performance as dancers, *religieuses*, or writers" (530). The relationship to writing Brodkey implies here is one between a writer and rules, the text produced and an ideal text. This relationship is asocial, ahistorical, and immaterial. As Brodkey illustrates, however, writing is actually "seated in desires" and "subject to the contingencies of performance," just like dancing and sewing, practices that are also called skill, art, craft (547). Echoing Brodkey's dissatisfaction with writing instruction, Anne Frances Wysocki, in "Opening New Media to Writing," describes much writing pedagogy as "attempts to get abstract thought present in the most immaterial means possible," concealing "the kinds of embodied, temporal positions that we need to be able to see" (22).

In what follows, I will be arguing that by revising our understanding of writing to understand it as craft—as a particular set of actions and relationships between people and between people and things—writing's value explicitly shifts from being located in a writer's ability to reproduce ideal discourses to the roles textual production plays in shaping writers and the uses a made object such as writing has in social circulation. Craft invites us to consider things and actions, craft as noun and verb. It calls to mind a maker, the tools that maker uses, and the materials that maker shapes into an object. And as the tradition of craft guilds illustrates, craft also implies a complex of relationships between a maker's identity, her interactions with others, and the things she makes. This way of thinking about writing brings to the foreground many issues already important to Rhetoric and Composition, but I believe that considering them together as craft can help us to understand these ideas in new ways that can guide us as composing and composition continue to shift in the twenty-first century.

WHY SHIFTING HOW WE THINK ABOUT WRITING MATTERS

In "Rhetoric and Ideology in the Writing Class," James Berlin argues that "social-epistemic rhetoric" should shape our teaching of writing. This approach to rhetoric—which Berlin believes is shared by no fewer than fourteen named scholars (including Kenneth Burke, Kenneth Bruffee, Ann Berthoff, Lester Faigley, David Bartholomae, and Patricia Bizzell)—is grounded in the belief that rhetoric is "always already ideological," already has embedded in it assumptions about what exists, what is good, and what is possible (717, 719). For Berlin, writing is "a political act involving a dialectical interaction engaging the material, the social, and the individual writer, with language as the agency of mediation" (717, 730). He asserts that rhetoric "cannot escape the ideological question, and to ignore this is to fail our responsibilities as teachers and as citizens" (736). Broadly, I share Berlin's beliefs about rhetoric and feel compelled to address "the ideological question" at hand: in first-year composition (FYC) courses, what do I believe to be, what do I believe to be good, and what do I believe to be possible?

I believe that FYC courses can be opportunities for students to examine their various positions—"embodied and temporal," as Wysocki writes—and to consider how those positions influence the kinds of writing students can choose to do. Because the writing students do in FYC is constrained by what instructors ask of them, I believe assignments, classroom activities, and goals for FYC courses should be designed to solicit consideration of these positions from students. My goal for this consideration is for students to understand themselves and their writing as working in complexes of social, historical, and material conditions that all people are embedded in—and that they can work to change. I believe that through the acts of considering our positions, learning more about them through writing, and sharing our writing with readers and listening to what they have to say in response, we can reposition ourselves, shift our subjectivities. I believe that the reasons to do this are to build a more thoughtful, caring, ethical, equitable, democratic world. And I believe that doing so is both good and possible—and that engaging with writing as craft can help us to achieve such a world.

WRITING AS DESIGN

Before considering in more detail what I mean when I ask that we think about writing as craft, I would like to discuss a similar idea developed by those who would have us understand writing as design. Design opens up many of the possibilities I find compelling in craft and will discuss below, such as emphasizing the materiality of tools, technologies, and texts, as well as bringing to our attention in new ways the transformative power of writing—the action as well as the object. However, I believe there are short-comings to the notion of design that are better accounted for in craft, as I will explain later in this essay.

Perhaps the most influential argument for understanding writing as design comes from the New London Group. In "A Pedagogy of Multiliteracies," the writers propose a new literacy pedagogy for the twenty-first century—a time characterized as "culturally and linguistically diverse and increasingly globalized," shaped by "information and multimedia technologies" (9). Attempting to answer new needs they perceive in literacy pedagogy, the writers developed a now well-known metalanguage of multi-literacies that centers on design, which refers to both the process of design-ing and the structure of what's designed. The New London Group propos-es that we consider all semiotic activity to be a matter of design that involves three elements: available designs, designing, and the redesigned. This sys-tem helps to highlight the fact that meaning making is about more than rules and is instead a recursive, dynamic, active process of making in which is available designs are made into the redesigned, which becomes an avail-able design for others to use and to which they respond.

The New London Group's pedagogy of multiliteracies allows us to retain a number of values I believe are central to composition: their pedago-gy is developed from the position that "human knowledge is embedded in social, cultural, and material contexts" and that "'abstractions', 'gen-eralities', and 'overt theories'" are developed through social interaction and "must always be returned to it or to a recontextualized version of it" (30–31). This commitment reflects Brodkey's, Wysocki's, and Berlin's: that social, historical and material conditions are necessarily inseparable from writing. As Marilyn Cooper puts it, "Writing is not a matter of autonomous-ly intended action on the world, but more like monitoring, nudging, adapt-ing, adjusting—in short, responding to it" ("Being Linked" 3). The New London Group's work also stems from a belief that pedagogy "is a teaching and learning relationship that creates the potential for building learning conditions leading to full and equitable social participation," and, as they note, literacy pedagogy plays "a particularly important role in fulfilling this mission" (9). These commitments deserve to be emphasized as part of the New London Group's work—and ours.

The design paradigm also encourages us to consider multimodality, a well-established concept in composition studies. The purposeful generality of the metalanguage of multiliteracies—and its situation within media- and technology-saturated cultures—is one that is well suited to the "new key" of composition that Kathleen Blake Yancey calls for, one that "brings the notions of practice and activity and circulation and media and screen and networking to our conceptions of process" (320). While the reading and writing of print texts remains primary in composition instruction, multimo-dality not only fits with the convergence of modes that occurs in increas-ingly pervasive digital technologies, it also helps writers in composition classes see their composing of print in new ways. Jody Shipka argues in "A Multimodal Task-Based Framework for Composing" that when students are asked to choose the "production, delivery, and reception" of the work they do in her composition course, they are able to

(1) demonstrate an enhanced awareness of the affordances provided by the variety of media they employ in service of those goals; (2) successfully engineer ways of contextualizing, structuring, and realizing the production, representa-tion, distribution, delivery, and reception of their work; and (3) become better equipped to negotiate the range of communicative contexts they find them-selves encountering both in and outside of school. (283–84)

From this perspective, multimodal composition can make more appar-ent to students their options for composing and the choices they make as they write. By explicitly engaging multiple technologies in not only the pro-cesses of composing but also in the final graded product—from paper and pen to computers and various software to the boxes, bags, and web pages Shipka's students use in their projects—students can become more self-conscious designers.

Wysocki describes the design approach as being "tied to the develop-ment of useful (instead of readable) objects," which she believes "tends to foster a more concrete and bodily sense of audience, purpose, and context"; designers are "more likely to develop what fits" because they are encouraged to work "by exploring and testing possibilities" (qtd. in Cooper, "Being Linked" 19). Taking these ideas to their logical conclu-sion, Cooper argues that understanding writing "as embodied, as biologi-cal and technological as well as social and cultural, means taking a design approach to creating texts and encouraging students to do so" (19). Students often come to composition less habituated to designing multi-modal texts in a school environment than they are to writing essays printed on paper. This inexperience frees instructors and students alike to expe-rience a "gradual attunement of movement and perception that comes dominantly through practice, a lot of playing around with stuff" (20). In college writing classes, students also bring different experiences regard-ing textual production, which we might note in varieties of academic and nonacademic writing, the kinds of writing students have done in and out-side of school, and so forth. It seems more difficult, however, for instruc-tors and students alike to articulate and work in meaningful ways with these differences between kinds of textual compositions. Practicing mul-timodal composition might serve to help students experience composing practices that encourage them to revise and refine the work they do in textual production.

As I hope these examples illustrate, the design paradigm offers much that is desirable to composition. But it also seems to ignore Berlin's question of ideology: while designing creates the potential for developing equitable social conditions, it does not necessarily lead to those conditions. And amid the New London Group's emphasis on a globalized, competitive, highly technological world, the question they ask is about "educational success" (10). That success is first defined in terms of people's work lives—and only later in political and personal lives (10–17). While each of these arenas is likely important to FYC students, and while education in general and higher education in particular are commonly understood in the United States to be a vehicles toward more desirable employment, I do not believe this focus is the best way to fulfill either my or the New London Group's stated goals of building a more equitable, more democratic world. What the notion of design lacks is a clear ethical direction because it can be appropriated for too wide a variety of purposes.

WHY MOVING FROM DESIGN TO CRAFT IS IMPORTANT

There is nothing in what I've written above about using design as a way to think about writing that I find seriously objectionable, except for the lack of a clear ethical direction for design work. I do, however, find this direction in notions of craft as they have been developed through various writers. In order to transition from design to craft, I would like to turn first to Min-Zhan Lu's uses of the New London Group's design paradigm, which I see as a place to start working toward a more complete understanding of what it means to approach writing as craft. Secondly, I will review multimodal work being done outside composition that illustrates some of the directions I think we should consider for composition.

ARTICULATING THE CRAFT OF DESIGNED COMMUNICATION

Min-Zhan Lu employs the concept of design to argue for the kinds of equitable purposes the New London Group allows for but does not demand. In "An Essay on the Work of Composition: Composing English against the Order of Fast Capitalism," Lu asks us to take into account the many contexts, purposes, and audiences of writers as they use varieties of English as available designs. She argues against attitudes about English that would position any English user as needing to fulfill language rules to please "self- or socially identified Native-Speaking, White, and/or Middle Class users of English" in the fast capitalist corporatized, globalized economic order that demands English (25). In a world where success is often defined primarily in terms of this economic order, many users of English are both explicitly and implicitly compelled to use standard American or British English in order to appeal to employers and consumers in the most lucrative markets.

Instead, Lu argues that responsible use of English by writers and readers necessitates giving up the fantasy of standardized English "and the fear of a world (ordered by U.S. interests) collapsing under the weight of Other languages and englishes" (25). In order to overcome these myths, Lu believes that we—as individual writers, readers and teachers of writing in English—need to work against associations between any variety of English and "the image of someone first buying or inheriting a ready-made, self-evident, discrete object—a tool (of communication) or a key (to success)—and then learning to use that object like an expert" (25). Pointing to the relational, complex, and in-process relationships to language that every designer necessarily has, Lu proposes a method of reading (and, by extension approaching writing) that begins with two assumptions:

> (1) all users of English (self- or socially identified Native-Speaking, White, and/or Middle Class users of English and users Othered by those labels) are actively structuring the english they are acquiring, its relation to other englishes, and the relations of peoples invested in the competing englishes; (2) in every instance of discursive practice, all users of English are working with and on very specific, often complex and sometimes dissonant, discursive resources and for potentially complex and conflicting purposes. (25–26)

In Lu's formulation, writing in English isn't already a known entity, part of a totalized standard of correctness. It is, instead, produced in various ways with various materials in order to meet the needs of any given designer in her specific contexts. As teachers and readers of writing in English, we need to be actively interested in all kinds of uses of English and to teach students to be, as well—design doesn't demand that from us.

MULTIMODALITY: FROM DESIGN TO CRAFT

While design opens up many possibilities for multimodal work in composition, I haven't explicitly looked at how multimodal work might be used to build the kind of world I'm working toward. In this section, I will explore some examples of composing that digital technologies open up, examples that I think help to illustrate the distinction I am making between design and craft and that point to uses of digital technologies I believe are most useful to composition.

From law and economics, Yochai Benkler, in *The Wealth of Networks: How Social Production Transforms Markets and Freedom*, describes one way networked digital technologies can be used to express democratic values: he finds something democratic in the idea that "anyone, using widely available equipment, can take from the existing cultural universe more or less whatever they want, cut it, paste it, mix it, and make it their own—equally well expressing their adoration as their disgust, their embrace of certain images as their rejection of them" (276). Benkler believes that the "plasticity of digital objects... improves the degree to which individuals can begin to produce a new folk culture, one that already builds on the twentieth-century culture that was highly unavailable for folk retelling and re-creation" (299). Through individuals' working and reworking of basic cultural themes, Benkler sees the emergence of a new folk culture making culture "more participatory," rendering culture "more legible to all its inhabitants" (299–300). Benkler draws a direct line between the kinds of work people can do with widely available digital technologies (like computers in labs on college campuses that are furnished with software like Photoshop and iMovie and are connected to the internet) and the degree of freedom people have in commenting on, contributing to, and therefore—even in some small way—reshaping the culture they live in.

Similarly, from Media Studies, Henry Jenkins asserts in *Convergence Culture: Where Old and New Media Collide* that digital media actually find us enacting in new ways older forms of culture, in which folk culture influences mass culture while mass culture influences folk culture. He writes that while modern mass media may have subsumed nineteenth-century American folk cultural traditions, networked digital technologies once again provide opportunities for "everyday people to actively contribute to their culture" (132). Blurring divisions between producers and consumers, Jenkins sees participatory cultural production encouraged by the nature of digital artifacts and the distribution system of the internet:

> Once you have a reliable system for distribution, folk culture production begins to flourish again overnight.... Much of [what amateurs create] will be good enough to engage the interest of some modest public, to inspire someone else to create, to provide new content which, when polished through many hands, may turn into something more valuable down the line. That's the way the folk process works and grassroots convergence represents the folk process accelerated and expanded for the digital age. (136)

In short, networked digital technologies make the kinds of nonmarket production that have always existed both more visible and easier for people to do.

For example, Lisa Nakamura has explored user-made Instant Messenger (IM) buddy icons and pregnancy bulletin board avatars as evidence of embodiment in digital networked environments. In both cases, she found that many users choose graphics that have been made outside of corporate production, homemade by amateurs who have taught themselves how to make buddy icons and avatars and distribute them for free. Many users choose these graphics instead of professionally made icons—for example, the ones AOL makes available for free to IM users.

Anthropologist Mizuko Ito investigated barter and gift economies of Japanese fan culture and found that "otaku culture destabilizes certain key sociocultural categories," including distinctions between professional and amateur cultural production, as well as the commodity form of media (55). In otaku culture, participants build their own grassroots networks or "sub-economies," in part using digital technologies, "where young people gain a sense of expertise, deep knowledge, and validation from knowledgeable peers. In other words, these are expert communities, although not professional ones" (64).

The subjectivities Ito describes—similar to those in Benkler's, Jenkins's and Nakamura's work—might not be defined as "successful" by many measures in the world order Lu criticizes. Instead, their measure of success is in small networks. For participants who take up these subjectivities, the work they do making cultural objects becomes part of who they are and what they do—not as paid work that participates in a fast capitalist economy (although they might also do so), but as defining the kinds of relations they have and seek to have with others through social production, barter, and gifting. This kind of cultural production could be called design, but more specifically, I believe this production participates in the traditions of craft. While digital cultural production (making artifacts like essays, images, music, and movies) is in many ways different from traditional crafts (like weaving, pottery making, knitting, and crocheting), both are modes of craft—the hand production of cultural objects.

WRITING AS CRAFT

I propose that, as an approach to composition pedagogy, craft offers many of the advantages of design while moving us into realms where I see design lacking. Similar to the New London Group's definition of design as referring to both organization/structure and the process of making, craft invites us to consider how something is made and the act of making—it is also both noun and verb. Additionally, craft highlights subjects, objects, and relationships. It implies a maker, tools used to shape materials into an object, a user or users for that object, the time it took for the maker to learn how to use the tools and work with the materials, the time it took to make the object, relationships between the maker and thing made as well as between maker and users. And this is where I see craft as a more useful paradigm for composition than design.

In *Critical Theory of Technology*, Andrew Feenberg writes about the importance of making relations between people and technological systems less uniform. His answer to this is to recognize "the human significance of vocation, the acquisition of craft." Craft, Feenberg writes, recovers "the reciprocity of the relation of the subject to object." In a craft approach to making, "the subject is no longer isolated from objects, but is transformed by its own technical relation to them. This relation exceeds passive contemplation or external manipulation and involves the worker as a bodily subject and member of a community in the life of the objects" (qtd. in Wysocki 21). Wysocki notes that "Feenberg argues for this notion of craft—for people to take up the careful, individual, crafted making of objects—in order to work against the standardization of our industrial corporatized world" (21). Similarly, the experiences of writing, of designing, of crafting their own texts is one way that students and their teachers alike learn—and learn again—the lesson that even when using they are forms of English that might be called "standard" or "academic," they are also often not.

Furthermore, their writing cannot be produced following an industrial or corporate model. This is not to say that writers who craft aren't working in relationship with others: they emphatically are. Instead, I am emphasizing that craft must be done manually, one word, one page, one screen at a time, whether one uses a crayon and the back of an envelope or professional publication software on a sweet new computer. By engaging in social and digital production of texts, as the New London Group reminds us, writers are transformed by the experience of looking closely at available designs, considering them in the contexts in which they are writing, engaging with fellow writers and potential readers, and finding themselves reflected in what they make. As Wysocki formulates it, "When someone makes an object that is both separate from her but that shows how she can use the tools and materials and techniques of her time, then she can see a possible self—a self positioned and working within the wide material conditions of her world, even shaping that world—in that object" (21). That possible self can be developed through approaching writing as craft.

To further define craft, I find it useful to consider its popular opposition to art, one that has only developed in modern usage. As Richard Sennett writes in *The Craftsmen*, at the root of this difference is a notion of art as the original expression of individuals, while craft "names a more anonymous, collective, and continued practice" (66). The individual, original nature of artistic production began to develop during the Renaissance, culminating in the Romantic notion of art as the expression of individual genius (66, 84). Contemporary uses of the term *craft*, which can implicitly mark its difference from *art*, still share important similarities to *art*—and, of course, for all the differences in their usage, the two terms still overlap and are often used to define each other. People who practice arts and people who practice crafts both develop specific skills, often work in collaboration with teachers and colleagues, express themselves through their work, and sometimes become well known for their work. Most importantly, those practicing both arts and crafts are involved in productive activity: they are making things. Another useful distinction is between industrial and craft modes of production. As a manual art or handicraft, a craft mode of production is on a human scale. According to Josef Chytry, Marx advocated for craft production because "the concrete individual, whose individuality is manifested in the immediate activity that makes or creates the object," sees production from beginning to end (242). This end, we might say, is the created object.

Or, as objects are often used for something, it is that use that is the end of craft: the object in use, in circulation. The circulation of a crafted object might be very narrow, limited even to the maker herself. Potters make many clay pots before they make one anyone else sees or uses, and we have all written text for our eyes only. But many crafted objects are meant to circulate more widely: a knit blanket to an expectant mother, a video mash-up to an internet forum, an essay to a journal read by a professional group. We are often able to predict what will be done with objects by their users, as the new baby will likely get wrapped up in the blanket and the video will be praised, criticized, and maybe even remixed online. And then again, the blanket might be regifted or used as a wall hanging; the journal essay might become part of a collage. The "ends" of made objects, of course, aren't fully predictable. And part of the fun of making something is to see what it can be used for, how it will be interpreted and reinterpreted by those who come into contact with it.

As Lu illustrates, the New London Group's metalanguage can be used to approach composition in a way that foregrounds our responsibilities to each other; in fact, their writing attempts to emphasize this dimension. On the other hand, craft demands, in ways that design doesn't, that we take into account those responsibilities. As Andrew Ford has noted, the term *craft* "has attractive democratic overtones—anyone can acquire a craft through honest application—and suggests old world social relations" (32). In the New London Group's framing, design is almost necessarily done using digital technologies, while craft seems to suggest the opposite, bringing our attention back to pen and paper, to readers who will interact with and respond to what's written. It's important, therefore, that an understanding of writing as craft is able to take into account all kinds of technologies for production that writers and readers use—and use to construct new kinds of social relations. We should be cautious of approaching composition as craft, if craft symbolizes nostalgia: to use craft as a metaphor for composition demands that we take into account the varieties of technologies writers use, from pen and paper to computers and other digital technologies—as well as the kinds of social relations and understandings of self that those technologies help to facilitate.

CRAFT AND SUBJECTIVITY

Several thinkers have considered how craft and subjectivity are related and how making things, circulating them to other people and seeing them used, shapes a person's conception of self. The trajectory of my own thinking on this traces from Hegel to Marx to Morris. Contemporary philosophers from Levinas to Lyotard to Butler have shaped the ways I understand relationships between self and other. With these influences present, I turn now to the work of feminist economic geographers Katherine Gibson and Julie Graham, writing together as J.K. Gibson-Graham, who critique the Marxist tradition's totalizing version of economy, which draws from Hegel and runs through Morris's work.

In this tradition, capitalism is a system with no outside—all production, regardless of how it is done or by whom, is part of the capitalist economy. This system sees nonmarket relations as existing in support of or even as part of the economic relations referred to by the term *capitalism*. As they note in *The End of Capitalism (As We Knew It)*, traditional approaches to capitalist economy identify manufacturing as what drives the economy, while other sectors, such as agriculture, services, government, and households, are identified as relying on or derivative of manufacturing (Gibson-Graham 106–7). Even in the globalization narrative, capitalism is figured as "inherently spatial and naturally stronger than other forms of noncapitalist economy (traditional economies, 'Third World' economies, socialist economies, communal experiments) because of its presumed capacity to universalize the market for capitalist commodities" (125). Gibson-Graham trace this understanding of capitalism back to Marx: "Capitalist production destroys the basis of commodity production in so far as the latter involves independent individual production and the exchange of commodities between owners or the exchange of equivalents" (qtd. in Gibson-Graham 125).

Citing Judith Butler's assertion that the fiction of binary gender is used to regulate sexuality as heterosexuality, Gibson-Graham deconstruct the regulatory fiction that capitalism is, in fact, how the world works (2). Seeking to counter an all-encompassing notion of capitalism, Gibson-Graham have devoted their work not only to redefining "the economy" as nonpervasively capitalist, but also to action research projects that seek to develop noncapitalist subjectivities. Drawing on the language of gender studies, Gibson-Graham deduct that if "capitalism/man can be understood as multiple and specific; if it is not a unity but a heterogeneity, not a sameness but a difference; if it is always becoming what it is not; if it incorporates difference within its decentered being; then noncapitalism/woman is released from its singular and subordinate status" (44). How, then, do we learn to understand capitalism as "particular set[s] of activities practiced by individuals"—and to see noncapitalist activities as such? Gibson-Graham argue that we must learn to see all kinds of household and social production as different from and outside of capitalism:

> If we grant that nonmarket transactions . . . account for a substantial portion of transactions and that therefore what we have blithely called a capitalist economy in the United States is certainly not wholly or even predominantly a market economy, perhaps we can also look within and behind the market to see the differences concealed there. (261)

These transactions include the social, networked digital production illustrated above by Benkler, Jenkins, Ito, and Nakamura.

By participating in these kinds of nonmarket relationships through social production, Gibson-Graham argue in *A Postcapitalist Politics* that we can cultivate subjects—ourselves and others—who can "desire and inhabit noncapitalist economic spaces" (x). These new subjectivities highlight relational, complex, in-process conceptions of self that can be made more apparent by social and networked digital production and demanded by Gibson-Graham's noncapitalist economies. These ideas of self are central to the notion of craft I am working with and to the field of composition I believe would benefit from approaching writing as craft.

As I have tried to articulate here, engaging with others helps us to discover who we are. And those engagements can be structured by a variety of economies. As the New London Group does, but far more thoroughly, Gibson-Graham explore how we might shift subjectivities through varieties of noncapitalist social engagement with others. Lu has explained what that engagement might look like in an FYC course—understanding writing choices as choices instead of as accidents or mistakes, taking others' choices seriously, and working to understand why a writer might make the choices she did, as well as what we might need to learn about a writer's social, material, historical, political, linguistic, and other conditions in order to more fully appreciate her choices in context. Similarly, Lu demands that we take our own varieties of conditions into account as we engage with others' compositions: How are our own experiences and expectations of texts shaping our understanding of writers' choices? Through engaging with others, we are able to reflect on our own subjectivities, the realities of others' subjectivities, the worlds we share, and our roles in those worlds.

And through engaging in craft, what Sennett calls a "practical activity," "labor is not simply a means to another end. . . . The craftsman represents the special human condition of being engaged." This engagement happens when "people can feel fully and think deeply about what they are doing," seeing the immediate work they are doing in a wider context that includes both the entire production of the object and the relationship that object represents between the maker and the world (20). In the very act of learning to craft, our subjectivities shift: as Bourdieu formulates it, what is "learned by body . . . is not something that one has, like knowledge that can be brandished, but something that one is" (qtd. in Atwill 59). For this reason, craft production also carries connections to the idea of craftsmanship, in which good work is done for its own sake, apart from the kinds of efficiencies associated with industrial production and capitalism (9). Contrast this with the New London Group's ideal: "In an economy of productive diversity, in civic spaces that value pluralism, and in the flourishing of interrelated, multilayered, complementary yet increasingly divergent lifeworlds, workers, citizens, and community members are ideally creative and responsible makers of meaning" (36). This ideal is more encouraged by craft than by design.

CRAFT TECHNOLOGIES AND SOCIAL PRODUCTION

In its current cultural position in the US, craft is intimately tied up in networked digital technologies. In their essay "Notes on Weavin' Digital: T(h)inkers at the Loom," Teshome H. Gabriel and Fabian Wagmister note that there is a deep connection between weaving and digital technologies, explaining that computing vocabulary borrows from backstrap weaving (using terms like *texture, pattern, layering, links, nodes, sampling, net, web, weaver, threads*) and that early computers were extensions of mechanized looms (pars. 5–6). Connecting digital technologies and contemporary craft culture in another way, Stella Minahan and Julie Wolfram Cox argue in "Stitch'n Bitch: Cyberfeminism, a Third Place and the New Materiality" that digital communication networks have in part enabled the massive return of traditional craftwork as a popular mode of cultural production in the digital age. In addition to their crocheting, macramé, and modding, crafters' work now often includes the digital production that supports handicraft. Craft culture is sustained by the blogs, websites, online tutorials, and streaming video that crafters use to share their projects, as well as digitally crafted artifacts themselves—the music, movies, mashups, images, and stories that Benkler, Jenkins, Nakamura, and Ito write about.

The social production people engage in using these craft technologies is, according to Benkler, "a sustainable pattern of human production given the characteristics of the networked information economy" (106). Echoing Gibson-Graham, Benkler believes that the "social production of goods and services, both public and private, is ubiquitous, though unnoticed. It sometimes substitutes for, and sometimes complements, market and state production everywhere" (117). Likewise, Jenkins emphasizes that the social production in which many people participate through networked digital technologies occurs outside any formal educational setting and without formal training (255). In composition, Kathleen Blake Yancey has noticed that writers gather in online spaces like chat forums, listservs, and shared-interest websites, and that these "members of the writing public have learned—in this case, to write, to think together, to organize, and to act within these forums—largely without instruction and, more to the point here, largely without our instruction" (301). Today, these writing publics also include large-scale collaborative writing projects like *Wikipedia*, local service-barter collectives like Women Empowered~Chicago that connect through their websites, and massive collective intelligence games like the one Jane McGonigal describes in "Why I Love Bees: A Case Study in Collective Intelligence Gaming."

But because craft encourages us to consider how one learns a craft, I don't believe we can take familiarity with and full access to networked digital technologies for granted. Although many of us and our students do use digital technologies like cell phones as technological extensions of our biological selves, as Cooper sees her students doing in "Being Linked to the Matrix," writers like Susan Kirtley remind us that students come to FYC courses with widely divergent experiences with and attitudes toward digital technologies. Kirtley suggests that composition teachers include discussions about and devote class time to looking at composing on computers (223–24). Similarly, Christina Haas's studies on writers' use of different writing technologies have illustrated that how we compose is in part shaped by the kinds of writing allowed, encouraged, or made difficult by the technologies we use. For example, it's difficult to write a long blog entry in the tiny text box in Google's Blogger, especially if you are used to the full-screen text box provided by Microsoft Word. Similarly, text messages are often short and full of abbreviated and otherwise nontraditionally spelled words in part because of the small screen and, originally, lack of "qwerty" keyboards.

It is important to note, however, that despite these inconveniences, people do text, and quite a lot. In fact, as the *New York Times* reported in January 2008, "The year-end best-seller tally [for 2007] showed that cell phone novels, republished in book form, have not only infiltrated the mainstream but have come to dominate it" (Onishi). Despite the fact that it might seem easier to write a novel with pen and paper or on a desktop computer, many writers enjoy the convenience of composing on their cellphones. As Sennett argues in *The Craftsman*, craft draws our attention to tools not only because one must learn how to use them, but also because one might repurpose them, use them in unintended ways that allow crafters to do new things in new ways.

And this is where students and instructors alike might find an advantage in working with tools and technologies they are unfamiliar with, composing in ways that are new to them: they might discover unintended uses for composing tools and technologies, such as writing novels on a cell phone. While Sennett argues that this kind of invention is the work of a master craftsman, untrained crafters can make their own discoveries, if they have the time and space to play. This play is part of the work—the writing and revising and rewriting and revising that we would recognize in FYC classes.

MAKING CRAFTED OBJECTS

Craft both engages and extends many practices common to FYC. It invites us to carefully consider the social, historical, and material contexts of composers and users; the materiality of tools, technologies and texts and how we might differently engage those tools and technologies; and the social and ethical implications of the texts we produce and ask students to produce. Working within a craft paradigm, we can emphasize the importance of thoughtful, careful future building through the crafting of objects.

With all this in mind, I've included below several suggestions for course design and course practices. I recommend them with not only the ideas I've written about here but also my own experiences as a student and teacher of writing in mind. Some of them you might already be familiar with, while others could be new to you. And depending on the courses you teach and the department and institution you teach in, they may or may not be of practical use to you—but I hope they at least help you to consider ways of teaching writing as craft.

COURSE DESIGN

- Shift the language of the course from a vocabulary of "writing" to "making," which better accommodates nontextual and multimodal composing.

- Assessment should allow for more experimentation—what constitutes "failure" should be a lack of engagement with the tools and technologies of production, not a lack of technical skill.

- Ask students to self-identify their strengths and get into project or peer-review work groups that include a variety of different strengths. Encourage students to rely on and learn from each other in their work groups.

- Explain the learning outcomes for the course and invite students to help you build the schedule and project requirements that will best help them to fulfill those outcomes.

- Ask students to circulate their final projects to each other several weeks before the end of the course. Have them analyze and suggest revisions for each other's work based on questions of use: Who is this for? How can it be used? How well does it work?

- Consider with students various ways their work should circulate, to whom, and why—and then put that work into circulation for feedback.

- As a final course reflection, ask students to remix one of their classmates' projects in another form (an essay could become a video or image) and write an analysis of that remix.

COURSE PRACTICES

- Partner with other sections/courses/schools to work collaboratively on your topic via shared-author blogs or wikis. Include ample space for reflection on how individuals productively participate. (I highlight digital publications here because they are usually cheaper and easier to circulate if your institution has networked digital technologies already in place. In lieu of this, other kinds of collaborative writing are also useful.)

- Have students keep course blogs (to track their research or as a space for reflection, for example), and ask students to comment on each other's blogs regularly.

- When focusing on writing explicitly, ask students to consider various technologies of writing (crayons, pencils, pens, lined and unlined and grid paper, chalk, markers, classroom boards, typewriters, computers, text editors, layout and design software, websites, digital networks, SMS messaging, etc.). Ask students to try writing different kinds of things using different writing technologies and reflect on how different technologies shaped their work.

- When looking at making more broadly, ask students to consider why they might choose one kind of media over another for a project: What do we usually think text, image, and sound (and various combinations of them) are good at? What nondigital media should be considered? Are academic arguments (or the kind of writing your course focuses on) best made in text (digital or nondigital)? Why? (These questions can also serve to clarify what qualities are valued in certain kinds of writing and get at different ways you and your students might be thinking about the work your course asks them to do.)

- Ask students to work on one idea or project in several different media (which will likely include learning new software or production techniques and experimenting with process and form).

Encourage experimentation and "play" with different media as students work. When they are done, ask students to reflect on which media worked "best" for their projects and why, as well as what they learned by making each iteration of their projects.

- Focus discussions of students' work on the choices they've made and the effects those choices have. This is often easier for students to discuss with nontextual projects at first, so you might find it useful to frame a discussion of choices by looking at work done in multiple modes—say, a printed essay that includes figures, a blog post that includes pictures or embedded video, and a collage made in a graphics editor. Finally, ask students to consider what wasn't a choice, what they didn't have control over or didn't consider as they worked.

While this certainly isn't an exhaustive list, I hope it gives you additional ideas for how you might reframe your own and your students' approach to writing, to shift the focus from rules to performance, from writing to making—to craft.

9 BODIES OF TEXT

Aaron Raz Link

1. THESIS

In 2007, the University of Nebraska Press published the book *What Becomes You* in a series called "American Lives." The book is a collaborative memoir in two voices. One of the voices was mine. The other voice belonged to my coauthor, Hilda Raz. The topic we used to shape the book's questions about media and embodiment was sex change, and the sex change we looked at was my own. How we defined our two voices in print, and how those definitions related to the way audiences responded to the physical bodies of the authors, is the subject of this essay.

For eighteen months after the book was published, I worked with material from the book as a visiting artist and teacher. My physical presence was an important part of that material because the book is about the ways body and identity affect our points of view—as writers and readers, speakers and listeners, people being seen and people who are looking.

The first paradox of this essay is that the role of speaker/writer is usually assumed to have authority over the role of listener/reader—that the person who is talking is in charge, and the disenfranchised role is to be "talked to." Interestingly enough, in person the speaker role is occupied by someone whose body is being looked at, and the listener role is occupied by people—often a social community of people, an audience—looking at the speaker. Much ink has been spilled over the ways a person being looked at is subjected to the authority of a majority viewer's gaze, and the way the authority of that gaze protects the group doing the looking.

But when a person occupying both authority and minority roles steps onto the stage, the role of the speaker is also the role of the person being looked at, subject to scrutiny and evaluation, engaged in a performance. The speaker's success (and therefore reputation, dignity, job, survival) is defined by the eyes of others. Money may change hands. To stand vulnerably in a position of authority before a group is also to be a minority object of a majority's gaze. We can call this role "Stepin Fetchit," or "beauty queen," but we can also call it "teacher," "stage fright," or "humanity."

The space in which this paradox plays out is a theatrical space—the space of classrooms, auditoriums, stages.

The Brazilian theatrical activist Augusto Boal defined *actor* as any person taking action. I'd like to offer *teacher* as a parallel term here. For those of us whose physical presence is a teaching tool (and that may be all of us at one time or another), the idea that space and time can be neatly divided into "onstage" (or "teaching") and "offstage" (or "not teaching") is an illusion. This issue turns out to be especially important in tightly knit, physically segregated communities—college campuses, conferences, departments, ghettoes, and community centers of color, culture, gender, and sexual minority. These island communities can be what sociologist Erving Goffman called "asylums." I'd like to offer the option of seeing identity politics itself as an asylum. As Goffman pointed out, a prison can be an asylum, but so can a safe space. They are miniature universes in which people reside—not defined as good or bad places but as self-policing and self-referential ones. As such, their core questions are, "Who is in charge?" and "Do you belong here?"

When the subject is sex change (or any trans experience: transnational, transcultural, perverse, multiethnic, interracial) these questions are constantly present, without clear answers. In an asylum, nothing is more frightening than a person whose status is unknown.

My coauthor points out two basic questions to ask writers and readers of creative texts (here, nonfiction writing): "Who says?" and "Who cares?" That is, where does the authority of the text come from? And can the audience connect empathically with that authority as a human being? For instance, my co-author can be identified as "writer, poet, and editor of *Prairie Schooner*, one of the oldest literary quarterlies in the US." Or perhaps as "feminist scholar and professor of women's and gender studies." Or maybe as "my mom." Who says? Who cares? In *What Becomes You*, we asked these questions about the subject of sex change. In the spirit of the feminist observation that the personal is political, we chose the radical step of answering the first question, "We say. We've lived these issues." We chose an equally radical response to the second question, by asserting that "You do." Meanwhile, in the asylum of identity politics the audience asks the authors, "Who's we?" and "Who are you?" "Do you belong? Are you in charge?"

These questions proved difficult. I chose to answer them as clearly as possible in our book. How people then answered them about me depended a great deal on what they thought of my body.

For instance, I can say "I was female for twenty-eight years, intermediate for one year, and male for sixteen years (at the time of publication). I can say I am a man, or I am a transsexual man, or I am diagnosed in reactionary terms as an autophilic sexual fetishist, in conservative terms as a female transsexual, and in liberal terms as a female-to-male transsexual or transgendered person. Or I can say I am an historian and philosopher of science, a specialist in museum education who has worked for half a dozen of the nation's major institutions." Or perhaps "I'm a peer advocate for people facing homelessness and discrimination. Or a professional performer." Though all this information is highly specific, the majority of readers of the book and this essay still have no idea what I look like. Without knowing what I look like, it's very difficult for many people to know what to think of me.

We may add that my race is either white or nonwhite, depending on where, when, and whom you ask. We may guess from this information that my skin color is not very dark, but a friend in the same racial category (or lack thereof) is about the same shade as a Damson plum, so all bets are off. In print, of course.

In person, my apparent social identity is obvious. However, the categories to which I obviously belong have changed several times. I have been seen as unambiguously male, female, androgynous, transgendered, cisgendered, nonwhite, white, bourgeois, working class, highly educated, from a street background, lesbian, bisexual, heterosexual, and gay. At this point, you may begin to notice some difficulties with theories about prejudice and difference that depend on intrinsic, mutually exclusive identity categories.

For the past eighteen months, the dominant issue in my work with the book has been that I am obviously a middle class, highly educated, straight-appearing, white, able-bodied male. At other times in my life I equally obviously have been working class, street acculturated, queer, nonwhite, disabled, and female. As a result, I can be imagined as a stereotypical oppressor, a stereotypical oppressed person, and everything in between. In becoming transsexual I also became male. (Similarly, by finding refuge in communities of color I became identified as white, and by entering serious poverty I became identified as middle class.) Therefore, the story of my survival as a member of perhaps the most disenfranchised minority in the United States is also a story told by a person who looks, to the communities most likely to care about this particular story, like the villain. Let me explain.

2. EXPLICATION DE TEXTE (ANALYSIS OF LANGUAGE)

In common terms, *to hail* someone is to recognize them with a core gesture of welcome, a greeting—hello! In the terms of Louis Althusser, widely adopted by intellectuals studying difference, *to hail* means to deny a person's individuality, replacing it with assumption and stereotype. In everyday terms, *a gaze* is the lyrical act of looking. In the terms of critical theory and identity politics, it is an act of oppression. In common terms, *a privilege* is a benefit we strive for and may receive. In the language of identity politics, it is a form of safety or pleasure that prejudice denies to some of us; we despise the crime of having it, though having it is exactly what would end our oppression. Meanwhile, those of us who do enjoy it must give it up, though of course we cannot do so since we are granted it by others because of characteristics of our bodies or histories we usually cannot control.

We have therefore eliminated words for greeting and concepts of human difference as sources of ethical power or pleasure. We have replaced them with the idea that justice is a zero-sum game and equity is a nonrenewable resource, and that the only way to gain them is to steal them from each other. In such a language, the only ways to be just or kind are to delete our bodies or imagine we should all be the same.

Of course we cannot eliminate the human need to greet each other, see and be seen, listen and be heard. And every human struggle for justice, however theoretical, requires that we do these things. If the language available to us offers only a catalogue of sins, the question becomes not what forms of contact across differences are acceptable (none, apparently), but who are the most acceptable people to make contact?

Who's in charge? Do you belong here?

For instance, if I am welcomed (and you may consider the *I* in this sentence to refer to trans men, men of color, gay men, disabled men, male survivors of colonialism) into feminist spaces when our nontrans, white, straight, able-bodied Anglo-Saxon protestant male colleagues are not, our belonging is built on uncomfortably familiar terms: that trans, black, brown, "Oriental," gay, disabled, native men aren't real men at all. Do we want to promote the idea that a man has to be in charge to be real?

3. JOURNALISTIC ARTICLE

This story follows the first week at school—in an MFA program of a top US school with a strong progressive reputation—for someone we'll call Joe. Joe represents the promise of a university degree as the American ticket to an equal playing field. Joe is a returning student. For most of his life, he's struggled to survive.

> Every year, there was a round of layoffs—last hired, first fired. After a while it's always you. These days I can't get a job, and sometimes I wonder why, but there's no provable discrimination. If you think about it too much it makes you crazy.

Joe tries to keep a positive attitude, which he says is important for a non-Christian from the heartland with a Middle Eastern background.

> There were always swastikas in my school, white power leaflets with crosses, people screaming "faggot" and "Bomb Iran" when you walked by. I took a university history class and the teacher started by giving us pamphlets about Jesus, so I dropped out. But at the same time these people are the families of your friends. I lost my one Muslim friend when her family joined the Nation of Islam.

I understood, I mean my mother's friends all escaped genocide; my uncle was fighting when he was sixteen. In Germany then, I'd be dead. In Baghdad now, dead. In America now . . . I'm Middle Eastern. I'm not Christian. I'm gay. When somebody calls me a name, I understand—I may lose my job or my home, they may try to kill me. But somehow you have to give up on hate.

Joe says his main reason for returning to school is to get a job with health insurance. With medical problems from years of inadequate health-care, his biggest fear is that he can no longer fill his financial gaps with day labor. But his dream is to become a college teacher.

4. INTERNAL MONOLOGUE

Everybody's wearing five-hundred-dollar glasses and everybody's got five-hundred-dollar words for things they've never done. I've done things I've got no words for. What the hell am I doing here? I've been busting ass for years to get to school, for chrissake, and now my voice is too loud and my arms go around when I get an idea and everybody acts like I'm King-fucking-Kong. I was so scared they were going to think I was trash, at the Goodwill all the time looking for decent clothes, and now white kids with more money in their back pockets than I've seen in a year are call-ing me the oppressor cause I'm wearing a dress shirt. If I'm the oppressor, how come I'm the only one here buying at the Goodwill? I've got the wrong glasses. If I can get the right glasses, is it going to make things better or worse? Maybe they don't want me here. Of course they don't want me here. Well, I guess as long as I can play the Man . . . I can't sit still in a chair for three hours without moving or talking, I mean who can do that? Where the hell did they learn how to do that? Where was I?

5. EXPERIMENT

I need two volunteers from the audience. One of them can be a mirror.

One other thing. I need your body. Actually, you need your body, which in a way is the whole point. But in a zone of intellectual discourse the body is a dangerous object; it sticks out of text.

I don't mean to alarm you, but you are already sticking out of text. Move your eyes just slightly beyond the margins of this page. (If you are blind, feel for the audio player.) On the other side of my words, you will discover hands or hand-like objects of some kind. You're already part of this experiment.

One could say that as a reader, you're on display only to yourself. One could say that you wouldn't be on display even to yourself if I hadn't just mentioned that you are, and any bad feelings you may have now are my fault. One could even argue that if you don't notice you have a body, it's just the same as not having one. One would be wrong, but I'm not going to argue. We're here now; you've noticed that your particular hands are the ones holding my particular words, and it's too late to go back.

The next step on this journey asks you to imagine that the gaze looking at you now might be your own. And therefore that the gaze of the Other, looking at this text, looking at yourself, at me, at us, could also be your own.

There is nothing I can do to make you trust me but I am going to leap off the page now anyway, and I am going to trust you to bear with me, to bear me, to step away from the page and catch me. A thought experiment will not work. We need to do this for real.

Stand up now. Carry this text with you.

Somewhere near you there should either be a mirror or another person. Stand in front of whichever is closer to you right now.

Read the following paragraph out loud:

> Most of the people who became rich and famous doing blackface minstrel shows were Jews. A lot of women in this country feel victimized. White guilt doesn't do me any good. Every generation believes they can change the world and then they get old. Looking at me, how would you know where I'm from, what my family looks like, if I have a uterus, a penis, how big it is, how many children I've had? I like being seen, I don't like being stared at. Why are you looking at me?

Now go find those other people and choose a body that seems as different as possible from your own. I am going to mention the words *sex, skin color, age* and *size* and *voice* and *dress* and *hair*. In spite of all apparent differences, the country in which people have bodies is literal. Here, in this literal place, if you can reach another pair of eyes and ears, you can trust that they are close to the same level as your own. I'll give you a line break in case you need to go greet someone and ask them to come into a literal place where you can reach them.

Now, give this other person the copy of the text you've been reading so they can read the following paragraph out loud:

> Most of the people who became rich and famous doing blackface minstrel shows were Jews. A lot of women in this country feel victimized. White guilt doesn't do me any good. Every generation believes they can change the world, and then they get old. Looking at me right now, how would you know where I'm from, what my family looks like, if I have a uterus, a penis, how big it is, how many children I've had? I like being seen, I don't like being stared at. Why are you looking at me?

The differences between the two texts you have just experienced are not in the two texts. But because these differences can be clearly seen, heard, smelled, tasted, felt, they strike us directly. Such an unexpected and violent strike is known medically as an insult. Insults take our full attention. They mean, technically speaking, that we might be hurt. They cause a reaction, or perhaps even a response. But since differences in our bodies, our voices, and our clothes will not show inside of text, it is almost impossible to account for them there—or rather here, in an authoritative zone of silence and invisibility.

Here in text we are safe and bodiless, here we can have a discourse on sex and color and size and other properties of bodies. But we are talking about bodies in a zone that has excluded them, and the actual appearance of bodies in such a discourse can feel like a gauche and terrifying invasion from another country.

6. APPEAL TO AUTHORITY

When a stranger comes into our presence, then, first appearances are likely to enable us to anticipate his category and attributes, his "social identity"...We lean on these anticipations that we have, transforming them into normative expectations, into righteously presented demands.

Typically, we do not become aware that we have made these demands or aware of what they are until an active question arises as to whether or not they will be fulfilled. While the stranger is present before us, evidence can arise of his possessing an attribute that makes him different from others in the category of persons available for him to be, and of a less desirable kind....He is thus reduced in our minds from a whole and usual person to a tainted, discounted one. Such an attribute is a stigma....It constitutes a special discrepancy between virtual and actual social identity....Note, too, that not all undesirable attributes are at issue, but only those which are incongruous with our stereotype [in a particular situation] of what a given type of individual should be.

It should be seen that a language of relationships, not attributes, is really needed. (Goffman *Stigma* 2–3)

7. A LANGUAGE OF RELATIONSHIPS

Scene:

A space devoted to media and embodiment. It is separated into two unequal parts by a thin scrim covered with printed words.

Characters:

Text, the scrim, does not speak but remains on stage constantly, like a mime.

Territories are defined by the presence of the scrim. These never speak directly but silently influence the action at all times. Their names will vary by location:

The Individual and Society
The Writer and Reader(s)
Media and Its Audience (or Consumers)
Virtual Reality and Physical Reality

On Stage and In The Audience
space for actors and more space for actors
Subject and Object, in no particular order.
and
Two Voices, whose proper names are *Passive Objective* and *First-Person Singular,* but they're used to being called *Theory* and *Practice.*

At Rise:

TwoVoices come from one side of the scrim, though there is no evidence that they see each other; a second scrim, or an extension of the first, may separate them. Neither *Voice* can be seen from the other side of the scrim, where any observers will be sitting. Both *Voices* may be played by the same actor.

Passive Objective (Theory) is dressed in the latest fashion. Everything is custom tailored and tightly pressed. *First-Person Singular (Practice)* wears distressed clothing, which might be very antiquated and down-at-heel or just extremely avant-garde.

Theory, who always speaks in the objective voice, has just finished reciting a quote from Erving Goffman. *Practice* tries to peer through the scrim, then checks clothing for cat hair.

Practice:
What *Theory* is saying is that we're in a terrible bind. All of you, and us, have assumptions about what's supposed to happen here: what we are and aren't supposed to talk about and what we are and aren't supposed to say. Being the personal voice, I'm in the spotlight right now... and I'm not even supposed to be here. Unless this is creative nonfiction, or maybe something avant-garde in Media Studies or Performance Studies, something like that. (*Looks around.*) American Studies. Yeah, okay. But some of you are probably Canadians. Or, you know, something else. Colonial. Postcolonial. Whatever. Shit. Sorry. If you think of text as a kind of performance, and performance as a kind of text, we'll probably be on the same page.

Promise you'll take me seriously and I promise I won't use words like *syntagma* and *dialectic.* That's a social contract, right?

So the reason I'm here and I'm speaking in the personal voice is that we're talking about a body. What we mean when we talk about a body of *Theory* is something really different.

Theory:
Stigma is a Latin word meaning a "mark" or "brand." It derives from the Greek verb *stizein,* meaning "to tattoo." The basic Indo-European root word appears in English as the word *stick,* which is both a piece of a plant's skeleton and the verb for the act of pushing something into a living body in order to cause a response. *Merriam-Webster* defines *stigma* as:

1 a : archaic: a scar left by a hot iron: BRAND
  b : a mark of shame or discredit: STAIN
  c : an identifying mark or characteristic; specifically: a specific diagnostic sign
    of a disease
2 a : stigmata plural : bodily marks or pains resembling the wounds of the cruci-
    fied Jesus and sometimes accompanying religious ecstasy.
3 a : a small spot, scar, or opening on a plant or animal.
  b : the usually apical part of the pistil of a flower which receives the pollen
    grains and on which they germinate.

In other words, all forms of stigma—identifying stigmas, perjorative stigmas, holy stigmas, openings, points of fertility—require bodies. To discuss
the question of stigma, which is a pressing question in the issue of media
and embodiment, it is necessary to talk about bodies, examples of bodies,
and the question of what happens when media/text encounters a human
body. This is the place where theory meets practice.

Practice:

So the real question is, how do we talk about the way my body and voice
affect your idea of who I am, what I'm trying to say, and what might happen
if people listen? How do we talk about the same issue for each of you, when
different bodies create different experiences for the people living in them,
so different people are going to come to different conclusions? Because
thanks to *Text*, we can't really see or hear each other. Okay, pretend I'm
doing that old *Twilight Zone* thing, you know, staring out at you and pounding on the inside of the screen. (*Pause. Distant scream. Sound of pounding.*)

Okay, that was cornball. But those old stereotypes exist for reasons...
which is kind of my point. All of us on both sides of this paper are in a space
with a one-way mirror, and both sides of the mirror face out. We're having
a conversation, but we can both only hear half of it, and they're different
halves. As a performer hanging out in the world of cultural studies, the ele-
phant in the room is that you're talking a lot about embodiment, I mean,
everything you're talking about depends on embodiment...but your medium is text. You know, no seeing, no singing, no dancing.

Theory:

Whenever lack of conformity makes a person's physical, embodied presence in a particular space dangerous or unimaginable, text and other
forms of nonembodiment provide an alternative for avoiding or managing
stigma. They enable individuals and groups to be heard in circumstances where they might be stigmatized into silence (and therefore isolation)
in an embodied setting. Networking, theorizing, and sharing of resources
become possible. These collective actions are usually required in order to
change the expectations that lead to a particular stigma in the first place.

The geometric rise in popularity of the internet (primarially a text-based form until quite recently), as well as internet resistance to top-down controls, gives one measure of how much more freedom from stigma people can have in text than in person. As bodies become common on the internet (in the form of video, audio, and pictures), the culturally perceived level of danger from the medium increases, as do government, legal, and corporate attempts to control it.

The first influential voices in cultural change in the West are usually writers. For instance, the text-based work of women like George Elliot, Emma Goldman, Audre Lourde, and Betty Friedan could change social discourses that were closed to the bodies of the writers themselves. When people cannot avoid stigmatization in person, they can create equal representation through text.

Since stigma is the result of a visible difference between the person/author/subject expected and the person/author/subject revealed, avoiding embodiment—never revealing or discussing any particular body or its physical differences—promises freedom from stigma. The degree of equality in these situations is the degree to which embodiment can be avoided.

Practice:
Which explains a lot about academic culture. (*aside, to audience*) What *Theory* really means is, if you pay attention to the folks behind the curtain, they're gonna try to get you suppressed.

Theory:
(*Aside, to audience*) Preoccupation with bodies is characteristic of working-class and masculinist cultures.

Practice:
Good point. Might explain why fewer and fewer men and working-class folks are graduating from college. You know, the first generation to really talk about a problem isn't usually writers, that's the second generation. The first generation is usually a mix of street fighters and clowns. But writers have an easier time in academic culture, as you just pointed out. I mean, it's pretty hard to get into a conference if you're naked except for a bunch of bananas, or dressed up as a cock. Except as the entertainment. I mean, unless you're dead. That's kind of a problem, if you get what I mean.

Theory:
And you would prefer we paid live African Americans to appear at conferences as animals?

Practice:
Or professors, maybe. Look, I didn't say this was gonna be easy. It's a significant argument for *hijab*. People who completely cover their bodies don't

have to deal with stigma about their physical appearance, at least as long as everybody's doing it. I really wonder why American academics don't require the veil for everyone, especially in identity studies.

Theory pauses.

Practice:

What you're going to say next really depends on whether you think I'm a woman. Or wearing a veil. (*Taps Text*) Too bad you can't tell.

Theory:

Intellectual discourse, especially in academia, must be transparent. Ethics requires a system where it's possible to confirm whether the author of an idea is in fact the author, and whether s/he is who and what s/he claims to be.

Practice:

As opposed to, say, the internet, where men are men, women are men, and twelve-year-old girls are the FBI. Or at least so they say. Whoever "they" are. Maybe it's that guy whose book was on *Oprah*, you know, the expert on drug addiction.

Theory:

Professional standards exist for good reasons.

Practice:

Yeah, to teach people how to speak *Theory*. Otherwise you might have people masquerading as experts on drug addiction who've never been addicted to drugs. Analyses of masculinity by people who've never been men. Or of femininity by people who've never been women. Things like that.

Theory coughs politely.

Practice:

Which brings me to my point. The only professional standard I'm claiming is the standard of practice. In practice, we have bodies. Not theoretical bodies (*taps scrim*). Not (*taps scrim again*) virtual bodies. Physical bodies. And theoretical language doesn't always admit we have bodies and that they make a difference. Which makes it hard to talk about, which brings us back to stigma.

Theory:

(*Long pause*) In theater, communication is understood as a feedback loop in which reality is controlled as much by the way it is perceived and understood by the audience as by the way it exists in the intent and action of the actor. In a personal communication, theater scholar Joan Schirle referred to this idea as *the observer effect*. The ways audience members respond to an actor reveals what they have observed, and the audience's collective conscious and unconscious communication of its interpretation constantly guides the actor's understanding of what is happening. As each performer adjusts to communicate more successfully with each audience, the message's reception guides its creation. As a result, live performance is a collaborative consensus between

(individual and society)

(producer and consumer)

(subject and object of the gaze)

(performer and audience)

in which we decide what is actually happening.

Practice:

Damn, you are good for something. (*pause*) I . . . I mean, I know you're . . . y'know, I can do it . . . I mean I have to . . . I don't have any choice, I mean I do, but I don't, but I . . . I just can't talk about it.

Theory:

The standard of intellectual professionalism is still the depersonalized passive or objective voice. It is the voice of collective experience. It's the only medium available. I want to . . . (*pause*) What we have here is a failure to communicate.

Practice:

You could say that. Actually, you could mean a whole lot of different things depending on exactly how you said that, you know, like your tone of voice. And what you look like. Which I can't tell. I'd have to trust you. I've got no reason to trust you. I've just finished saying it's no good deciding somebody's good or bad from their name on the title page. I mean, even looking at somebody's face...I don't know who you really are. Will you respect me in the morning? (*pause*) Because in practice, when our bodies are different and we're not really seeing each other, telling a story is all I can do.

8. RESOLUTION

Any conclusions drawn from an essay like this one go beyond the scope of the text, and therefore beyond my ability as an author to create. Resolutions that matter will have to be embodied, which means it's time to put down this text and do something together about it.

10 WHOSE BODY?
Looking Critically at New Interface Designs

Ben McCorkle

The personal computer has given us two things: bad metaphors and bad posture.

—Tom Willard

Think of it as the thin chrome line, the literal contact zone between the human body and the personal computer. Industry insiders refer to it as HCI—the human-computer interface—and it represents the convergence of the two data sets identified by Tom Willard in the epigraph above, exemplified by anyone suffering from mouse-induced carpal tunnel syndrome or confused by the concept of dragging a compact disc icon into a trashcan in order to eject it. It is along this thin line of demarcation that I propose we focus our critical attentions because soon that line will become blurred and indistinguishable, or will even disappear altogether.

Beyond the questions of aesthetics or ease of use, our gazes should be concerned with the ways in which designers of digital interfaces—and by this, I mean to suggest a broad categorization including the interface design of various operating systems, software applications, and even hardware itself—assume unquestioned subject positions for the user. We can begin this critique by revisiting the conversation arguing that the current interface paradigm anticipates an impossibly idealized universal user through the repetition of common design tropes and metaphors, as well as physical functionality. In the spirit of such scholars as Christina Haas, Steven Johnson, and Christine Neuwirth, I contend that these common design features actually privilege a certain subject position at the exclusion of others, and that the construct of the universal user serves as a mechanism to devalue those bodies outside that position.

From this foundational critique, we can look ahead to examine sites that offer us glimpses into the likely future of interface design, among them advances in touchscreen hardware, voice/handwriting recognition software, ubiquitous computing and internet appliances, and virtual reality—all of which suggest an increased attention to embodiment in the interface design paradigm. Again, the critical question of whose body (or bodies) is being assumed in the development of these new interfaces is crucial, especially as it applies to implications of gender, class, race, and the able body. While some artifacts from the future, as it were, are designed in an attempt to conceal their interfacial properties from the user, creating the illusion of direct, in-the-world manipulation of content, we can also glimpse hopeful sites of resistance, notably in a counterbalanced set of artifacts designed to remind us explicitly that we are interacting with the machine. Without such a critical counterbalance, the predominant logic of the new interface will likely be reified via a variety of mechanisms: the language used to frame the user experience (in advertising and technical documents, for instance), the sanctioned uses to which new technology is put (touch-sensitive table displays intended for corporate settings), and the deeply embedded assumptions about how the body ought to behave in the face of new technologies. Collectively, these formal and discursive factors will result in a thin chrome line that only certain types of bodies are allowed to cross, bodies that have historically known the privileges associated with the technological vanguard. Ultimately, then, this chapter serves as a call to extend the conversation of access initiated most forcefully by Gail Hawisher and Cynthia Selfe. I argue for a more expansive notion of access so that it applies not only to the material availability of hardware and software, but also to the symbolic economy of interface design. It is in part this barring of access that potentially limits certain bodies' capacity for learning and communicating within digital media environments.

For teachers and scholars of composition in particular, the stakes in this encroaching shift are high. For one, we have an opportunity to be ahead of the technological curve, helping to act upon it rather than react to it, unlike other moments of technological transition across our history. With that opportunity comes an obligation to insist on maintaining an ethical character to the ongoing conversation affecting how we develop these new technologies, how we recognize the variety of eloquent and useful new forms that will undoubtedly emerge, and how we teach people to communicate effectively using them (in the realms of both academic and civic discourse). As a field, we risk being caught flatfooted if we think the next technological paradigm will simply mark a return to orality; instead, we will be entering a stage of digitally augmented communication, one that will involve a complex combination of alphabetic, aural, video, graphical, haptic, gestural, and oral elements. Consequently, we need not only to develop new pedagogies for teaching how to compose using these new technologies, we must also teach students to develop a robust awareness of the tools we will use. This is necessary so they not only acquire the skills necessary to use them, but also so they recognize how such tools operate as manifestations of broader sociocultural forces, and even muster the courage to challenge any potentially harmful conventions before they ossify.

DEFINING EMBODIMENT

Our body is not primarily in space; it is of it.
—Maurice Merleau-Ponty (1945)

Before we can contemplate the historical changes in the digital interface, a digression is in order. We would be well served to revisit the definition of *embodiment,* a concept that has suffered from "feature creep" over the years, but one that is useful to our purposes if used in a very precise way. Specifically, looking to Maurice Merleau-Ponty's original phenomenological schema of embodiment gives us a useful vocabulary to describe the kind of paradigm shift we are approaching in digital technology: from a metaphorical state to a more seamless virtual state of embodiment, or rather from a state in which we are acutely aware of our bodies as we interact with digital technologies to one in which we are likely to forget them.

In his 1945 book *Phenomenology of Perception,* Maurice Merleau-Ponty first gave us a philosophical model for explaining how a subject is constituted as an in-the-world being. These bodily aspects of subjectivity, which stand a priori to any second-level conceptualization, make up the ontological condition Merleau-Ponty termed "embodiment." Embodiment is at base the experience of one's body as a unified potentiality or capacity for acting in the world through time and space. In this model, Merleau-Ponty distinguishes between the more authentic phenomenal body (the body I inhabit, as it exists as an active force in-the-world, reacting without conceptualization to the phenomenological data it collects) and the static abstraction he refers to as the "objective body" (that physiological mass of quivering flesh to which each of us can point and say "my body"). As Merleau-Ponty famously proclaimed in *Phenomenology,* "Our body is not primarily in space; it is of it," emphasizing the spatiotemporal habit of being over the empirical thing-ness of the material human body.

By way of illustration, I can sit at my desk writing, and as long as things go as expected for me, my experience of my body is subjective, phenomenal, embodied. In Merleau-Ponty's parlance, the desk, chair, pen, paper, and any other objects I interact with in the course of my act of writing constitute "equipment" for me, so long as that interaction does not present any novel impediments. The second I turn the sheet of paper over and get a paper cut, however, I am temporarily removed from the embodied state, and my experience of my own body is objective. Here, Merleau-Ponty would say a "breakdown" has occurred. Thus, embodiment involves a state of comfort, which allows us to forget our bodies as objects. In the colloquial sense, embodiment is the state of being in the moment.

As HCI designs move from virtual to actual embodiment, the user becomes less aware of her body as object—less aware of how her subjectivity is constructed—both the means of mediation and the awareness of the integumental body become subject to erasure. Consequently, the phenomenal experience becomes the more privileged design goal. Although those in the business of designing human-computer interfaces may not have conceptualized the shift in quite these terms, the shift is still a powerful one. For instance, in Jay Bolter and Diane Gromala's 2003 book *Windows and Mirrors: Interaction Design, Digital Art, and the Myth of Transparency*, the authors claim that in spite of the important digital arts perspective offered by the designer camp—to view the interface as designed object—the prevailing trends in HCI lean towards the structuralist camp, who want the interface to function as a transparent window through which the user can glimpse content without disruption. The more entrenched this paradigm becomes in the future, the more likely it will be that users will assume the embodied interface represents the way they "ought" to interact with digital technologies, to the point that the interface becomes naturalized. It is also at this point that users' inabilities to interact properly or effectively with these technologies will result in the kinds of breakdowns for which they will blame themselves ("I'm just no good with computers!"), potentially damping access to powerful new means of communication in the process.

A BRIEF HISTORY OF HCI

Of course, in the earliest days of computing, interaction with the machine was quite literally a direct physical activity, often requiring the direct manipulation of mechanical components. Depending on how one draws the history of the computer—beginning with the Babylonian abacus (ca. 2400 BCE), Charles Babbage's nineteenth-century analytic engine and prototypical difference engine, or the more recent iterations of supercomputers such as UNIVAC, ENIAC, and similar room-sized machines developed during and just after the Second World War—the human operator's relationship to the machine was an embodied, phenomenal one because of the direct feedback afforded by the mechanical apparatuses of these early technologies. In a sense, it is not until the age of the digital computer that we first see traces of what we can identify as the modern interface language, where virtual layers of metacontrol exist between human and machine. Therefore, in the interest of focus and brevity, we can construct our historical overview from a more recent staring point: the shift from the alphabetic interface of the command line to what is presently our far more pervasive interface language, the visually oriented desktop.

The shift in interface paradigms from the command line interface (CLI) to the graphical user interface (GUI) standard can be traced back to 1968, when Doug Englebart invented and publicly demonstrated the computer mouse, which would eventually become the predominant device for navigating the GUI. The programming and design team at Xerox's Palo Alto Research Center had developed the first functional GUI in the late '70s, around the same time the personal computer was first introduced to a mass market. This innovation remained dormant for nearly a decade, as the CLI remained the dominant mode of screen interaction for all platforms until Apple "borrowed" (unscrupulously stole, some say) the GUI model from Xerox in the early '80s, incorporating the familiar desktop environment into their groundbreaking Macintosh desktop computer. Until the release of OS X in 1999, all versions of the Mac operating system basically had the same look and feel, as the code was built upon the same basic conceptual platform.

The initial difference in interface standards caused much verbal warfare among the technogeek culture—depending upon where the allegiances lay, they either saw the GUI as childish and the CLI as sophisticated and "pure" or the GUI as user friendly and the CLI as cryptic and unnecessarily clumsy. This attitude definitively changed in the early '90s with the introduction of the PC platform's answer to the Mac GUI—Microsoft's Windows 3.11, the breakout version of an operating system the company had been developing since 1985. At this point in our history, when both major computing platforms had adopted the GUI as the primary interface of their respective operating systems, the paradigm shift had occurred in earnest. Today, the familiar GUI icons, as well as the ingrained series of keyboard and mouse interactions, is a standard that can be seen in most second-level software applications; additionally, the same iconographic logic pervades much of the World Wide Web.

Accompanying this shift, as we might expect, were efforts to research the educational and efficiency benefits—or drawbacks—of the GUI. Early attempts to research the effects of human-computer interface design on the learning capacities of users have been characterized as naïve in methodology. Two such studies, which suffered a barrage of criticism after their publications, were Dan Barker's 1991 report "Gender Differences between Graphical User Interfaces and Command-Line Interfaces in Computer Instruction" and M.P. Halio's 1990 article for *Academic Computing* entitled "Student Writing: Can the Machine Maim the Message?" Barker concluded that neither gender nor a shift in interface design was an influential factors in computer instruction outcomes, but was attacked for using too small of a data set for too short a duration. Alternately, Halio argued that students using Macintosh computers (which came with a toy-like GUI) wrote at a significantly lower reading level and pursued less serious topics than students on IBMs; this conclusion upset readers because of the study's methodological inadequacies as well as what was alleged to be unacknowledged subjective bias. Studies like these began a more robust line of scholarly inquiry in the field of education; scholars in Rhetoric and Composition and Technology Studies also began examining the ideological assumptions behind interface designs, drawing critical attention to the equipment itself and, in so doing, raising important questions concerning which identity groups have easier or more difficult paths to access based upon those designs.

By this point, it isn't new thinking for us to consider technology as having a gender bias—moreover, technology is often the product of other privileged positions as well: class, race, ability, language, logocentrism. These lessons have been taught to us by the likes of Cynthia and Richard Selfe in their 1994 article "Politics of the Interface," Billie Wahlstrom's "Communication and Technology: Defining a Feminist Presence in Research and Practice," and Johndan Johnson-Eilola's 2001 article "Little Machines: Understanding Users, Understanding Interfaces." Built into computer interface designs are a series of semiotic messages that support hierarchical regimes along the axes of identity—think of the servile white-gloved hand that serves as a cursor, the white, professional figures depicted in clip art, or for that matter, the identity implications behind the entire desktop environment. These images send powerful associative signals to nonwhite, lower-class, or otherwise marginalized users that to enter the world of the interface is to enter a world constituted around the values of white, male, corporate professionalism. The Pew Research Center's Internet and American Life Project supports this claim, as data from a number of surveys indicate disparities in rates of connectivity and usage habits between historically privileged and historically underrepresented identity groups. The very symbols so familiar to certain social or cultural groups become so much cognitive noise—breakdowns in the equipment that lead to a self-conscious objectification of the self—for those who do not inhabit bodies of privilege.

THE NEW INTERFACE

Although the desktop-themed GUI might seem commonplace and ubiquitous for computer users today, it is important that we keep in mind that it has been with us only a relatively short time and that we will likely become witnesses to its demise in the coming years. In fact, we can already see evidence of a shift away from the iconographic, metaphorical GUI standard. This shift challenges Steven Johnson's claims that the function of metaphor is crucial in order for an interface to make sense to the user. In his book *Interface Culture*, Johnson says the real cognitive energy of the desktop metaphor is that it approximates, but doesn't duplicate, an actual desktop. Someone like interface design expert Donald Norman, however, sees a much more powerful alternative in the "invisible computer" concept, where the interface is completely absorbed by the task defined to a given appliance, such as weather/traffic displays on car windshields, or exercise clothing that monitors your health vitals while you're jogging. As the state of technology changes, so does the state of art and design. Faster processors, more storage capacity, and the miniaturization of components are leading to experimentation with the language and landscape of the interface, the net effect of which is to create or amplify the sense of embodiment. Increasingly, Johnson's vision of the interface is being replaced by Norman's; it is precisely because of this move towards invisibility that we should become more critically vigilant observers of this shift.

What will characterize the look and feel of future technologies? What symbolic or actual equipment will we be called on to manipulate, and how can we identify whose body will be best suited for the task? What precisely should we watch for in order to dispel the beguiling effects of the new interface? Basically, the machines are becoming smaller, more tactile and ergonomic, easier to synchronize data with one another, willing to listen to us and to look us over ever so closely (as in the retinal and finger security scanners that are becoming more accessible to the general computer-buying public). Touch-sensitive screens and handwriting and voice-recognition software, long thought to be impractical, are being continually upgraded—these types of interfaces allow us to have more direct contact with our machines rather than having a white-gloved avatar stand in our place on the computer screen. The illusion of direct haptic control, very much like the interface Tom Cruise's character manipulates in Spielberg's almost-believable sci-fi film *Minority Report*, is one manifestation of this shift. The real-life promise of such enticements is already being fulfilled. Market-ready instantiations of the touch-sensitive interface are already here and wooing us, as in the case of New York University's Jeff Han and his research with multitouch graphical screens (http://www.cs.nyu.edu/~jhan/ftirtouch/), or Microsoft's similar product called "Surface," a coffee-table display targeted to business professionals, around which users gather to manipulate digitized objects such as videos, slideshow presentations, and spreadsheets with their very own hands. Currently, the most popular consumer example of this haptic interface shift is perhaps Apple's iPhone, which has a virtual "lock" the user slides her finger across in order to activate, after which she is able to scroll through lists of contacts, play songs, and navigate and resize web content simply by touching the display.

The pathway to the embodied interface doesn't just reconfigure the experience of bodily contact with the machinery; in some cases, the goal is to minimize or eliminate that contact altogether, creating an almost telepathic conduit between user and device to create an augmented mode of being that doesn't feel augmented. To offer an example, MIT's Laboratory for Computer Science, in an initiative begun by the late and long-time director Michael Dertouzos, is currently pursuing the Semantic Web project with the WWW Consortium, an attempt to imbue web content with connotative meaning so that it behaves in a more humancentric fashion. Of course, the problems inherent in this project involve constructing models for how "the human mind" functions and acknowledging linguistic fluidity, but that is a critique well beyond the scope of this present work.

In concert with technological developments seeking to create the invisible, mentally augmented interface, we can also see that our cultural discourse is already beginning to embrace the notion. In addition to Dertouzos's pursuit of creating an interfaceless computer that thinks with the user, I find many similar claims of the mind-to-machine linkage in popular discourse. For instance, the software company PacificVoice has a slogan urging the consumer to "speak your mind. Digitally." A 2001 article for *WIRED* magazine by *Dateline* correspondent and disability pundit John Hockenberry voices a similar philosophy: "The brain-body-machine interface doesn't seem to need the body as much as we believe it does. We hybrids are part of a universal redrafting of the human design specification." Despite the problematic potential inherent in such statements, in which technology stands as a monolithic "cure" for all disability and thus potentially erases the need to speak of a culture of disability, the impulse to create invisible, natural interfaces persists. Futurist and assistive technology inventor Ray Kurzweil predicts that the second half of the twenty-first century will see the realization of artificial intelligence, but it will take the form of a merging of human and machine intelligence—what he famously calls the "singularity." Predicting that capitalism will drive this push, he sees the ultimate end of this exponential technological progression as one where "there will be no clear distinction between human intelligence and machine intelligence"—and this will be facilitated by nanotechnology (153–4). While I am personally skeptical of this kind of direct, teleological trajectory, I do think there's a concerted move in the industry as a whole to make the human-machine contact zone seamless—to hide the technological in the biological, to downplay the body's role in manipulating it, to foster the illusion of a direct connection of technology to mind. Taken as a whole, such efforts constitute a bleeding edge of interface design, one that conflates technology and body in an attempt to erase the lines of demarcation separating them, resulting in an embodied, phenomenal experience of the equipment at hand (at least for those able to afford it).

These examples of the new interface paradigm do not occur only at the bleeding edge, however. We can already see evidence of this shift emerging in more popular areas of consumer technology as well: a trickle-down effect, if you will, that targets younger users in an effort to naturalize the shift even further. The Wii, Nintendo's latest videogame console featuring motion-sensitive controllers, is significantly popular to the point that the company enjoyed significant back orders when it first launched. This popular platform is the latest and most refined iteration in a history of videogame-related input devices designed to engage more of the body than just thumbs and forefingers: recall the Data Glove, the Light Gun, or the more recent floor pad used in the game *Dance Dance Revolution!* Additionally, toystore shelves are lined with Spy Gear devices reminiscent of high-end virtual reality prototypes that allow children to pretend to see or hear better, and in some cases communicate remotely with their fellow agents.

As a final example, I return to Microsoft founder Bill Gates in order to demonstrate the trajectory charted by one of the leading forces within the computing industry. In one of his corporate communiqués, a vision statement drafted in 2001 entitled "A Software Driven Future," he offers several key insights to his employees that we are beginning to see in development today, particularly in the Surface tabletop and the Windows Media Center PC. In it, Gates stresses how the next stage of development will progress, at least in terms of Microsoft's involvement. Gates's vision emphasizes three main areas of innovation:

- The concept of ubiquity. "The screens that people carry around with them (phone or PDA) should also function as the world's nicest universal remote control. It will provide UI [user interface] for controlling every electrical gizmo in the user's world (all appliances, home, car, etc)."

- The potential of multimedia for both hardware and software development. "Inside the home, users want access to information—time, weather, stocks, calendar, news, traffic, notifications—either visually or in audio. They want access to media—music, photos, and video."

- Utilizing already familiar, naturalized technologies. "All of the communications scenarios should work against the TV screen.... All of the screens in the home should be able to display TV video." (Scheer 118)

Even as Bill Gates transitions out of Microsoft and hands over the reigns to his Chief Software Architect Ray Ozzie, the corporation's R&D trajectory largely remains on the course established by its founder: to create hardware and software experiences that blur the otherwise hard-set lines separating the desktop computer, the World Wide Web, digital peripherals, and the human user (Levy 178). To my mind, at least, it appears that Gates's goal here, and indeed the goal of this entire new interface paradigm, is to render the interaction between human and computer phenomenal—that is, of the order of nonconceptualized equipment. In short, it appears that the ultimate look and feel of this new technology is seamlessness: not only will it permeate our environment, but it will incorporate all media at its disposal without complaint, and it will take advantage of our already naturalized relations with established technologies in order to do this. Suffice it to say, though, that the allure of such efforts is that they pledge to bridge the gap between mind/body and machine; the job of the technological critic, therefore, must be to agitate that quietude by acknowledging that the gap will still exist to varying degrees, and that human programmers and designers will build their bridges based upon standardized assumptions and generalizations about the body, an impossible task in Merleau-Ponty's eyes given that the mode of human being can only ever be a uniquely singular experience.

THE TECHNO-AESTHETIC INTERRUPTION

> *The cyborg is a creature in a post-gender world; it has no truck with bisexuality, pre-oedipal symbiosis, unalienated labour, or other seductions to organic wholeness through a final appropriation of all the powers of the parts into a higher unity.*
>
> —Donna Haraway ("A Cyborg Manifesto")

While the aforementioned hardware and software make up the most prevalent logic of the newly emerging interface paradigm, wherein embodied, in-the-world behavior is seamlessly conflated with virtualized outputs (what Bolter and Gromala term a "window" interface), there also exists a counter-paradigm in which the technological apparatus is made noticably or even disruptively present for the user, constituting what Bolter and Gromala call the "mirror" interface, and fomenting, albeit in a playful manner, Merleau-Ponty's phenomenological breakdown. While I was on a teaching fellowship at the Georgia Institute of Technology in 2003, I had the opportunity to observe several experimental applications and interfaces that employed just such an interface logic, a logic that seeks to engage the user by making him or her hyperaware of the design qua design.

Georgia Tech's Graphics, Visualization, and Usability Center (GVU) utilizes traditional virtual reality technology (goggles, gloves, etc.) as well as more accessible technologies such as Macromedia's Director design software to experiment in areas ranging from interpersonal communication, adaptive technology for the disabled, habitation practices (i.e., smart homes), learning strategies, and gaming. One example of the center's research is *Alice's Adventures in New Media*, an attempt to create an immersive, augmented reality version of the Mad Hatter's tea party scene from Lewis Carroll's novel by placing the user in the role of Alice in order to help shape the plot. Additionally, the Topological Media Lab, directed by Sha Xin Wei (currently affiliated with Concordia University in Montreal), supports the development of projects using fabric-based, wearable computers and gesture-based projection systems. Erick Conrad's *Aether* is one such project, creating a haptic reading experience for the user by projecting words onto a liquid surface that respond to touch—the words move and rearrange themselves when the user dips his or her hand into the pool. Diane Gromala's *Biomorphic Typography*, a project out of Georgia Tech's Biomedia Lab, displays an animated font that responds to a user's biofeedback data; shape, color, and size change according to corresponding changes in the user's physical and emotional state. These examples, and others like them, are interdisciplinary projects that draw inspiration from academic fields far beyond computer science and engineering, including psychology, cognitive science, cultural studies, fine/performing arts, kinesthetics, physiology, and sociology, among others.

It is worth looking at examples of these experimental applications because they offer us potential strategies for critical resistance, means by which we can recognize the implicit political dynamics of the comparatively seamless interface designs emerging from commercial counterparts. In these sometimes-joyful/sometimes-disorienting interface experiences, I can't help but be reminded of Donna Haraway's iconic figure of the cyborg, itself an ironic embodiment of technology and biology fused together, a figure who exists to deconstruct the line separating the cultural from the natural and thus highlight the constructedness of the entire system. Like the cyborg, these interfaces don't simply celebrate the technological, they complicate it. They allow us to "see the window" in order to create the potential for strategic political maneuvering within the technocultural space. As Haraway's epigraph above states, the cyborg is (among other things) "post-gender," a fluid, multiplicitous mode of being capable of maneuvering around cultural gender constructs as well as so-called "natural" biological categories. This doesn't mean it is necessarily beyond or past the trappings of gender, but rather that it sees gender for what it is: a politicized space for strategic performance, a space for either adhering to, transgressing, or even transcending the conventions depending upon the circumstances of the moment. Ontologically speaking, Haraway's cyborg is an exaggerated metaphor for the human condition, imbuing Merleau-Ponty's notion of embodiment with a self-aware, strategic instability that takes advantage of the ever-shifting material reality of being in-the-world. The cyborg reminds us that we are always already enmeshed with the equipment of the social world: its politics, its ideology, and its technology.

Conceptually, this alternative series of technological applications, software, hardware, and so forth challenges the emerging paradigm of the new interface, making present the seamlessness of the embodied interface by aestheticizing the interaction between person and machine, making the user acutely aware of the technological space he or she inhabits at that moment. Beyond the technical, beyond the aesthetic, these alternative interfaces are politically subversive, enacting Nedra Reynolds's feminist politics of interruption. According to Reynolds, the practice of interruption allows the marginalized subject to reclaim a sense of agency through discursive practices, in effect minimizing the effects of ideological interpolation emanating from positions of power (59). Awareness of the state of embodiment—an interruption of the phenomenal state aspired to by dominant interface design—is a vital means by which users can recognize their own roles as technological agents when producing or consuming new media texts. Such interruptions are invaluable for technoartists and designers to create in the first instance; they are also invaluable for new-media theorists and critics to acknowledge and critically study in the second instance. Collectively, such interruptions provide us a clearer glimpse into Selfe and Selfe's "contact zone," the politicized space where human and machine meet, and demand that we question the constructedness of that space.

We shape and we are shaped by one another through our technologies of communication. As Michel Foucault's conception of biopower makes clear, newly emerging technological paradigms operate according to two complementary forces: an "anatamo-politics of the human body" and "a biopolitics of the population" (139). Together, these forces work to discipline a population in order to impose hierarchies of order and regulatory systems of control. While technological standardization is not necessarily in itself insidious, it does create conditions by which control is exercised over people: by sanctioning purposes of use (valuing business and commercial interests, devaluing artistic, civic, or informal ones), reinforcing literacy thresholds (rendering learning or physical disabilities impediments to proper learning), and validating certain styles of delivery over others (devaluing gender or cultural differences marking how people speak or move). By making the familiar strange, by interrupting the stealthy march over the line to the embodied interface, we can potentially open up spaces for greater access, allowing those groups who have historically been technologically marginalized a means by which to spot, cross, and even shape that line themselves.

CONCLUSION

As the virtual boundary between human and machine becomes intractably blurred, it becomes increasingly important to give voice to a number of questions and concerns that orbit this approaching shift in interface design paradigms, questions and concerns to which—borrowing from the language of Cynthia Selfe—it would do us good to pay attention. One overriding concern potentially threatens the critical work that has already been done in the area of Technology and Media Studies: specifically, that it will be deemed impertinent or inapplicable to these new design standards, and that the assumptions identified by this work will be allowed to continue without scrutiny. In order to stave off this analytical obsolescence, we ought to extend the conversation of *access*—that crucial buzzword that seems to offer us a way of bridging the digital divide between the technological haves and have-nots—so that it applies broadly to the realm of interface design. The technological challenges driving assistive/adaptive technology give us a good starting place to begin the critical work of assessing the design decisions underlying the material conditions of newer technologies, but can we also identify bodies altogether left out or unconsidered in these new interface designs, claims of individualized customization to the contrary? As we know from Merleau-Ponty, a necessary component of the embodied state lies in its hidden nature; when comfortable, when properly functioning in-the-world, the body hides itself from itself. My concern is that the push towards an embodied interface will facilitate real-world practices of silencing and marginalization, in effect essentializing difference. In other words, will the mistakes that were previously blamed on bad interface design, because the technology will go into hiding, by default fall into the lap of the user? In such a state, we risk forgetting to ask whose body is assumed or privileged by this new paradigm, and thus the need for more critical scrutiny on this point becomes increasingly important as we enter this shift.

We should remain cautious about a reflexive return to the prevailing cultural myths about technology, the kind that Christina Haas outlines in her book *Writing Technology*. When the machinery itself becomes hidden, when we forget our integumental bodies, conditions are prime for a reiteration of technology as a transparent, neutral tool that merely facilitates the transfer of information with no inherently politicized bias built into it. On the other end of that spectrum lies the myth that technology has a liberatory, all-powerful essence. As an aside, we can already see these myths taking shape in the aforementioned comments of Bill Gates, Steve Jobs, and John Hockenberry. As critics, it is our responsibility to identify such instances of myth substantiation and analyze how these discourses contribute to certain reality effects within our culture.

In addition to concerns about the philosophical or cultural impact of the embodied interface, we should pay attention to the material impact as well. A pervasive quandary exists in the conflict between the unique phenomenological condition of embodiment and a marketplace whose logic is predicated on normalizing mass production. This conflict presents one mechanism of exclusion and should be studied, but more overt and familiar mechanisms will remain in play, such as cost and availability of technology. What role will market forces play in the development and dissemination of this new technology? At the very least, financial standing will likely, then as now, limit some groups' abilities to benefit from interacting with these new interfaces, maintaining or perhaps even further expanding the digital divide.

Lastly, where can we identify sites for resistance? Certainly, we should continue the pursuit Cynthia and Richard Selfe call for when they suggest that we become "technology critics as well as technology users"—this applies to our scholarly work as well as the work we encourage our students to do in the classroom. But in addition to becoming critical readers of the new interface, we should think of ways of participating, for example, in the design process of software as end-user tech consultants making up part of a professional collective. And insofar as it's in our power as writers of grants, influencers of policy, and purchasers of technology, we should strive to see that technology is designed and distributed equitably. Even as creators of digital media texts, we should strive to create the kind of work that interrupts the ideological lull brought on by new interfaces and foments a productive breakdown, dragging otherwise hidden ideologies into the critical light. As academics, education professionals, and even artists, we should try to position ourselves at the reception and production ends of the technological assembly line, one small way of ensuring that our push towards participatory democracy in the digital world can be realized—for everybody, and every body, involved.

11 QUEERNESS, MULTIMODALITY, AND THE POSSIBILITIES OF RE/ORIENTATION

Jonathan Alexander and Jacqueline Rhodes

There are times in life when the question of knowing if one can think differently than one thinks, and perceive differently than one sees, is absolutely necessary if one is to go on looking and reflecting at all. . . . But, then, what is philosophy today—philosophical activity, I mean—if it is not the critical work that thought brings to bear on itself? In what does it consist, if not in the endeavor to know how and to what extent it might be possible to think differently, instead of legitimating what is already known?
—Foucault, *The Uses of Pleasure*

Ultimately, throughout, and before we even begin, we log on, we ask: How might I represent my own queerness? How might I figure queerness multimodally? More specifically, how might multimodality embody the queer in dynamic and productive dimensions? What is a multimodal queerness? What are its possibilities, and what are its limitations? We can read, see, hear, perhaps even touch the queer—and have it touch us through multiple senses, potentially even interactively. But what does such touch mean, particularly for those who may not be queer?

The internet and the emergence of a variety of collateral multimedia composing and publishing tools have given us a nearly unprecedented capacity to represent ourselves, our interests, our communities, and our investments—personal, political, and otherwise. With such a capacity has come the possibility that our views, beliefs, and ideas may themselves be challenged by others, putting out there their own multimediated visions. Such is certainly true for the multimediated representation of queerness, which has been represented in richly multimodal ways—to foster community and awareness, particularly among those struggling with their sexual orientation, to mobilize queer activists as they reach out for political change, and (indeed) to foster hatred and intolerance through sites such as *God Hates Fags*. Such sites aside, we believe that exploring queerness through multimodality—that is, taking advantage of increasingly rich ways of figuring and composing—may help us develop productive insights into the experiences of the queer, the possibilities of multimodal composing, and the possibilities (and limits) of figuring the queer.

In this chapter, we want to forward a theoretical approach to the multimodal composition of queerness that situates such figuring as a challenging possibility for queering sexuality, for queering our understanding of the queer and the heteronormative, and for queering our interaction with multimedia and multimodal texts. To undertake this queering, we want to construct a set of queer genealogies—from Jean Cocteau to *Craigslist*, from *Gay.com* to lesbian cut-ups—that sees in the multimodal composition of queerness possibilities for reorienting our understanding of sexuality and how it moves in the world, and for how it orients us along certain paths, particular trajectories on which we may, or may not, wish to travel. Most audaciously, perhaps, we want to suggest that multimodal composing offers us rich resources for representing a complex queerness—and that such resources have a history, however unexplored, that may be illuminating, even inspiring. With this view in mind, we attempt to perform in this chapter our own encounters—as sexed and sexual beings—with a variety of texts. Combining scholarly discussion, theoretical explorations, and autoethnography, this essay fleshes out our understanding of how sexually engaged interactions with new media problematize sex/sexuality/gender as it creates a space for producing new sexual positionings.

MULTIMEDIATED QUEERNESS: SOME THEORETICAL AND HISTORICAL CONTEXTS

To offer a framework for our exploration of queer multimodality, we set two narratives against one another:

1. the narrative of scholarly exploration of queerness online and through multimediated texts
2. an homage extolling the unacknowledged work of Jean Cocteau as both queer artist and multimedia artist

These two narratives, not contradictory but rather in tension, offer us a way to conceive of the possibilities of queer multimodality as a function of both a recovered and an emerging history of queer multimedia.

1

THE NARRATIVE OF SCHOLARLY EXPLORATION OF QUEERNESS ONLINE AND THROUGH MULTIMEDIATED TEXTS

With both its capacity to disseminate a variety of complex new media texts and its proliferation of sex, erotica, porn, and fetish sites detailing a seemingly infinite diversity of sexual pleasures and possibilities, the internet has arguably done more to "queer" sex than any other medium. For some queers, internet sex offers not only a way to safely approach desires and pleasures deemed illicit by larger cultures, but it also serves pedagogically to introduce people to the range, possibilities, and even techniques of queer sexual pleasures. Of course, porn and erotic sites are often banned by ISPs in a variety of locales, with some entire nations (such as Iran and China) forbidding access to internet pornography. Still we should not underestimate its potential value for queer people. As Irmi Karl points out, "It is important to recognize that online media themselves are not consumed in isolation. Rather, they constitute part of a broader set of everyday techno-practices and information and communication technologies" (46). With this in mind, we can think of queer multimedia and even online erotica as ushering queer sexualities and sexual practices out of isolation. Bridging virtual and real worlds, the internet helps some queers connect with their desires and with one another in the pursuit of pleasure.

Indeed, the Web offers us one of the richest realms in which we find a varied and diverse sampling of queer multimodal representation, so we must necessarily begin our exploration of queer multimodality by understanding online queer representation and how it has been theorized and understood, particularly as a form of multimodal composition.

Much scholarship about queers online has figured the problem of queerness as one of representation. How and to what effect do queers represent themselves online? What kinds of representational practices are used by queers (and by nonqueers) to figure queerness? What kinds of work—socially, culturally, personally, and politically—do such representations do? What are their possibilities—and limitations? Summarizing some of the very small body of research on queer practices and representations online, Kate O'Riordan and David J. Phillips write in their introduction to *Queer Online: Media, Technology, and Sexuality* that two previous collections, the anthology "*Mobile Cultures[: New Media in Queer Asia]* and [Alexander's] *Queer Webs* [for the *International Journal of Sexuality and Gender Studies*], highlight the ongoing importance of place, space, embodiment, and everyday life in the construction and production of queer techno-practices" (4). For many queers, particularly those in rural or isolated areas, the internet has been an important, even vital venue for connecting with others

2

AN HOMAGE EXTOLLING THE UNACKNOWLEDGED WORK OF JEAN COCTEAU AS BOTH QUEER ARTIST AND MULTIMEDIA ARTIST

As we have experimented with different figurings of queerness, we have searched for models and theoretical orientations to guide the trajectory of my own online, multimodal queer becoming. Curiously, Jean Cocteau has provided for us a rich tradition of queer multimodality that has informed some of our work in multimodal composition, and we have chosen to work with Cocteau primarily because he has been among the most important artists of the last one hundred years to approach queerness, even if glancingly, through his many multimodal projects. Unabashedly, we acknowledge that this project is in some part homage to Cocteau. But it is also a critical homage, in that the analyses query Cocteau's multimodal figuring of the queer.

Cocteau was among the most influential mid-twentieth-century French artists. A poet, novelist, playwright, artist, and filmmaker, Cocteau also wrote scenarios for some of the most famous ballets of the twentieth century (*Parade*, music by Erik Satie) and libretti for works by famous composers (*Oedipus Rex*, music by Stravinsky). Cocteau worked throughout his life in multiple media, exploring and experimenting ceaselessly, seeing everything he did as "composing," or making art. This embrace of what we would today call multimodal composing is perhaps best seen in his films, some of which are considered among the most important in early French film, such as *La Belle et la Bête*, *Orphée*, and *La Sang d'un Poete*. While predating contemporary work in the "new media," his multimedia experiments and innovations have much to teach us, we believe, about composing multimedia. His views can seem quixotic, as revealed in the collection of Cocteau's wide and varied writing on film, *The Art of Cinema* (translated and edited by Robin Buss), but I find his approach, even if seemingly naïve at points, refreshing in its optimism about the possibilities of media and suggestive in its potential connection to his queerness.

Cocteau argues, for instance, that "[a] film is not the telling of a dream, but a dream in which we all participate together through a kind of hypnosis, and the slightest breakdown in the mechanics of the dream wakens the dreamer, who loses interest in a sleep that is no longer his own. / By dream, I mean a succession of real events that follow on from one another with the magnificent absurdity of dreams, since the spectators would not have linked them together in the same way or have imagined them for themselves, but experience them in their seats as they might experience, in their beds, strange adventures for which they are not responsible" (*The Art of Cinema* 40). While members of the relatively contemporaneous Frankfurt school worried that the new medium, film, might be merely distracting if not stultifying to imagination, thus limiting the ability of individuals and collectives to think (and imagine) critically, Cocteau saw film as actually creating a vibrant space in which the imagination can "remix" reality, and in which "the film-maker can make 'real' the unreal figments of the imagination" (9). Such realization of the unreal is and for establishing a sense of identity and community, particularly in a queer diaspora where notions of community, even identity, must often be constructed through information steadily gleaned, sometimes at great personal and political cost, from places outside one's home of origin. Writing about the impact of the internet on Asian queer identities, the editors of *Mobile Cultures* maintain that "in spite of and alongside the commercialization of sex from Net-order brides to online Asian gay and lesbian pornography, new media have become a crucial site for constituting new Asian sexual identities and communities" (13).

In addition to acknowledging its benefits for community building, some early scholars (myself included) also saw in cyberspace the potential to create fluid and challenging representations of queerness—representations that, like cyberspace itself, figured sexuality as complex, changing, dynamic. Cyberspace as a domain of identity play seemed to complement, if not parallel, similar dimensions of queer theory that gestured toward the fluidity and performative play of sexualities and identities. O'Riordan summarizes such a position by suggesting that "the cybersubject, assumed as a fluid performative freed from embodied constraints. . . intersects with the ideal queer subject as trans, bisexual" (26). One could, for instance, adopt a variety of online identities to "play" at different subject positions, experimenting, experiencing, even if virtually, what the "other" is like, perhaps even engaging in virtual sexual practices that challenge one's own sense of sexual orientation as fixed, immutable, and essential.

While both access to information about queerness and the possibility of sexual play certainly constitute important dimensions of many people's experience of the internet, some scholars point out limitations, even dangers, in thinking about what happens when queers go online. Echoing the work of cyberscholars (such as Lisa Nakamura) writing about race and online identity, queer cyberscholars like O'Riordan argue that "although the ideal cybersubject as fluid and the ideal queer subject as fluid converge in fictions [about cyberspace] and critiques such as [Sherry] Turkle's, there is more evidence to suggest that online queer communities are stratified into fixed identity hierarchies, and anxiety about bodily identity is a strong determinant in online queer formations" (26). O'Riordan, citing the work of Joshua Gamson, connects the substantial commercial dimensions of the internet to the formation and reification of marketable categories of identity: "The successful formation of online queer communities has also fragmented into prescriptive identity menus, which serve commercial marketing purposes as much as they are expressive" (27). *Gay.com. Planetout. AfterEllen. AfterElton. 365Gay.* We note the generally commercial nature of such sites, and that, after all, commerce concerns itself (largely) with the circulation of commodities.

part not only of Cocteau's filmic project but of his approach to art in general. Indeed, calling all of his artistic endeavors "poetry," thus creating an aesthetic space in which he could mix media freely (some would say with at times reckless abandon), Cocteau sought experiences of art works that were highly emotionally evocative; he writes, "Since Arthur Rimbaud, poets have ceased to operate merely by charm. They operate by charms, using the word in its most dangerous sense. Instead of seducing, the poet terrifies: this explains the battle that is being waged against him. At the moment of waking, he unleashes the forces that govern our dreams and that people quickly try to forget" (39).

For Cocteau, these terrifying "charms" are not just evocative but also critically productive. He asserts that a "craving to understand (when the world that people inhabit and acts of God are apparently incoherent, contradictory and incomprehensible), this craving to understand, I say, shuts them off from all the great and exquisite impressions that art deploys in the solitudes where men no longer try to understand, but to feel" (*The Art of Cinema* 42). By accessing and calling forth feelings that short-circuit understanding, through this evocation of poetry, Cocteau hopes that the people he speaks to will experience a world more capaciously full of possibility, more full of the mixing and matching of dreams, and a bit less stymied by convention. He oddly parallels Walter Benjamin in this regard, even if his formulation is less directly political. Benjamin maintains in his essay "The Work of Art in the Age of Mechanical Reproduction" that "for the first time in world history, mechanical reproduction emancipates the work of art from its parasitical dependence on ritual"— with "ritual" being, for Benjamin, the old formulas of artistic patronage or the commodity prestige accruing around works of art only accessible in museums.

Art loses its "aura" of inaccessibility and becomes usable by the masses. Cocteau's formulation manages to maintain a ritual aspect—the ritual of dreams—while holding on to both Benjamin's desire that art have meaning and usefulness for people and his belief that mass art has political uses. For we cannot help but see in Cocteau's poetical dreamscapes less a lulling to sleep and much more of a desire to trouble received categories of thought. In the hallucinations that bring many different perspectives together, old modes of thinking are questioned and challenged. They are, in a word, queered. And, given Cocteau's own queerness, we are tempted to read his aesthetic approach, however loosely conceived, as at least in part a desire to make a space for that (such as the homosexual) that had previously been excluded from consideration, even from thinking—such as a love that "dare not speak its name."

More to the point of this project, we are fascinated by how Cocteau's view of art as well as his queerness may have informed his interest in multimodality. In two works, the short multigenre book *The White Paper* and the film *La Belle et la Bête*, Cocteau addresses issues of "queerness" and offers us rich multimodal figurations of nonnormative attraction, intimacy, and love. Cocteau's work thus raises for us some critical questions of how queerness may be represented or figured multimodally. Perhaps another way to put this is to sift queerness, Cocteau, and multimodality

Such commercialization and "prescriptive identity menus" have potentially global implications as queer activism goes online, with activists using the internet to disseminate information and organize for political action. While the information sharing and organizing possibilities of the internet seem unparalleled in human history, some scholars wonder what is being disseminated. Writing for the *Mobile Cultures* collection, Sandip Roy asks,

Will countries with fledgling GLBT movements risk losing the process of building a movement that is about them and their needs and end up assimilating into Western models because they are more accessible? . . . Is there a danger that the internet will not only pull together people across oceans but at the same time offer them ready packaged visions of the GLBT movement that does not account for cultural differences? Or will cultural difference cease to matter in a well-homogenized "gay world." (181)

Ultimately, O'Riordan concludes that "the productive coupling of these two discourses, of the terms cyber and queer, may be as much a stumbling block as a facilitator in helping to investigate and theorize this nexus" (13).

Other scholars have critiqued more directly the move to collapse queer theory and cyberspace into a mutually affirming realm of identity play. Nina Wakeford writes that

the impression is that cyberspace is the postmodern space par excellence . . . . Perhaps the closeness of fit is a bit too convincing? What is lost if cyberqueer research becomes merely a celebration of parody and performance, or the simplistic application of an author's reading of *Gender Trouble or The Epistemology of the Closet?*" (412)

The editors of *Mobile Cultures* echo Wakeford's questions when they point out, accurately, that "beyond a small but growing number of fieldwork-based studies, most writing on sexuality and new media has been theoretical and/

through a question: How might multimodality complicate narratives of queerness and provide richer ways of representing, figuring, thinking the queer? How might multimodality offer richer ways of being queer?

The White Paper is a brief genre-defying text that Cocteau presents as (1) authored by someone else but (2) with his own illustrations. The text frankly explores the difficulty of living as a homosexual in mid-century Europe, but, unlike other pulp fictions of the period, Cocteau identifies a homophobic society as the source of the difficulty of living and loving queerly, as opposed to anything intrinsic in queerness itself. The book recounts several "scenes," like case studies, in which the narrator attempts to come to terms with his queer desires as a young man, and several scenes of great pathos describe failed intimate encounters and unrequited longings. Throughout, though, as Rictor Norton points out, "The point of [such passages] is not to analyze homosexuality or to provide a sensational personal account of how a young man may become homosexual due to his father's latent homosexuality, but to expose the subtle workings of homophobia in the lives of people" ("Cocteau's White Paper").

In this regard, The *White Paper*'s multigenre approach sets it apart from other contemporaneous accounts of homosexuality. The dominant mode of narrating the queer in the early part of the twentieth century borrowed from sexological case studies that traced the etiology of homosexuality as a wrong turning, a sickness in the development of healthy (hetero)sexual functioning. Cocteau sets the "case study" approach, however, alongside a variety of other kinds of texts—the confession, a manifesto, a love story, and even erotic drawings—to complicate our understanding of the queer, picking up on cultural products—the case study, the confession, erotic art—to figure the queer multimodally. As such, the text functions, to borrow from Foucault, as a "reverse discourse," countering the pathologizing narratives of homosexuality circulating prominently at the time of Cocteau's writing.

Certainly, we could read the disavowal of authorship not only as a rhetorical move toward "objectivity" but also as a response to homophobia; the author has too much to risk in being too openly queer. At the same time, Cocteau's rather graphic illustrations move the text from a rather pathos-driven account of the psychological terrors of homophobia to an invitation to gaze on the eroticized male body. The reader is thus invited to become implicated—and perhaps just by lingering over the pictures becomes implicated—in the homoerotic. The two dimensions of the text—the narrative and the illustrated—work multimodally to create a tension between erotic interest and homophobic denial. Just as the text describes the intense social difficulty of homoerotic loving, the images invite you to experience the homoerotic.

But what is the experience of the homoerotic, and who can experience it? The text itself problematizes such questions. Early on, as the narrator realizes that he desires some of his male classmates, he notes,

> My sentiments were vague. I could not manage to specify them. They caused me either extreme discomfort or extreme delight. The only thing I was sure of was

or speculative, sometimes flirting with more sensational possibilities such as virtual transvestism and cyber-rape" (10). For Wakeford and others, what is "lost" in blithely celebrating the free play of the cyber and the queer is a critical understanding of what kinds of work—personally, socially, political-ly—sexual and sexual identity play might actually accomplish. What happens in the move or gesture toward sexual play, identity fluidity, and what is brought back into the "real world" after logging out of such play? Such questions remain tantalizingly open.

Certainly, the dissemination of recognizable identities has been important for queers to connect online and form community and even engage in political activism. Just as important have been the possibilities opened up for people to explore different sexual positions and subjectivities online before trying them out "in real life." At the very least the latter possibility has potentially enabled an extension of the erotic palette and imaginations of those with access and time to engage in virtual sexual play.

But I wonder what other kinds of queer work could be done (and perhaps is already being done) by the multimediated representations of queer-ness? Within the queer we find not only a move toward community or a desire for play, but also a gesture of critique—a critique of the normalizing categorizations of people into gay and straight. It is a critique, in short, of the heteronormative, of the proliferation of sexual subjectivities coupled with regimes of power that reproduce certain kinds of families, certain kind of acceptable intimacies, certain kinds of authorized lives. How might the multimediated queer perform the critical gesture of questioning, even challenging, the heteronormative?

that they were in no way comparable to those my comrades experienced. (*The White Paper* 19)

Already, the narrator feels marked off as different, as other. By the end of the short book, he is quoting Rimbaud's famous phrase—"Love is to be reinvented"—and thinking that such should be adopted as his (among others') rather queer "motto" (87). Difference and the call for reinvention—these are recognitions that the narrator's affectional and libidinal interests are not the same as those of others, and that they are potentially unknown—perhaps unknowable—to those who do not share them.

Interestingly, the very "genre" of the text raises questions of knowability. Is *The White Paper* a novel? An autobiography? A confession? A case study? A white paper? A political tract? An illustrated erotic primer? Or all of the above? The mixing of genres itself gestures simultaneously toward the reinvention of genre (paralleling the reinvention of love) and the confusion of clear knowability. It is as though Cocteau wants to carve out a multimodally rich space in which to think the queer, to enact a textual encounter that highlights the failure to grasp the queer. After all, if the sexological and psychological case studies of the turn of the century had attempted to codify and categorize a wide variety of sexual "perversions," homosexuality prominent among them, then Cocteau's *The White Paper* offers a very different experience of the queer. In mixing genres and potentially disturbing categories, we are offered not only a rich portrait of what the queer might be but a just as clear sense that the queer is perhaps not as easily knowable (as "evil," as "sinful," as "sick") as we thought. In the richness of the figuring of queerness lies a complication that itself is both part of the content of the book and the multimodal experience of the text.

While *The White Paper* is one of Cocteau's few works directly addressing homosexuality, we find traces of his queerness in others of his works, such as *La Belle et la Bête*, Cocteau's most famous and beloved film. Based on the well-known fairy tale, and the inspiration in large part for the commercially successful Disney film, *Beauty and the Beast*, Cocteau's film is a rich ménage of crisp narrative, special effects, penetrating psychological characterization, and delicious romance. We can read *La Belle et la Bête* in a number of ways, and in a number of sexual ways. A little bit of Freudian imagination might figure the Beast as the id who needs the social taming of the Beauty to restore ego balance. Along these lines, the rampant materialism of the boyfriend and other family members itself is disciplined as potentially destructive id energy. Pushing further, the story seems to valorize a particularly Freudian solution to unwieldy desire. The beast must be loved by the beauty, having left her father (to whom she seemed overly attached) to usher both of them into mature intimacy and sexuality. And indeed, they both "ascend" from the natural world at the end of the film, overcoming their potentially baser desires and connections.

Such readings are not necessarily wrong, but we believe such a glossing of the filmic text misses a key dimension of the film. Specifically, Belle, the Beauty, must come to love the Beast, even as she does not know him. Indeed, she cannot know

Surveying this past work and these critiques suggests that we should explore and develop the potentially fruitful ground between critiquing the emergence of marketable and fixed identity categories, on one hand, and lauding the internet as a space of unrestrained sexual play, on the other hand. In between identity and freeplay, we believe, lies the potential for understanding the representation of queerness on the internet as a complex endeavor with many different ramifications for identity, community, and even politics. Put another way, what we would like to do is begin to situate our own work between the critique of identity categories and the celebration of freeplay. In multimodal, even multimedia representations of queerness we see the possibility not just for fixing identities nor for ushering in untrammeled identity fluidity, but for understanding how the figuring of queerness may work identity and its construction in very specific ways—both personally and politically.

him. But the Bête can only be freed if she comes to love him without knowing who—or what—he really is. As such, the film offers its viewers what I would call a queer fantasy. At a brute level, the beast is a queer figure in the sense that he is not only not normal, but most decidedly abnormal, monstrous, frightening, and ultimately unknowable. His scenes are all set in rooms augmented with special effects designed continually to prompt us to question what we are seeing. Is that a hand holding that candelabra? We are never fully sure of what we are seeing in this powerful dreamscape. Further, despite the seeming heterosexuality of its love story (Belle is a woman and the Beast seems male), *La Belle et la Bête* shows us how someone must come to love a completely alien being—What being is this? What kind of beast is it?—in order to make a space for ascendent liberation. Put another way, the film seems to argue that liberation is only possible when we accept that which is unknowable; we do not have to know—to categorize everything in its place—in order to love. Rather, for Cocteau, love must often precede knowledge. In fact, love must exist in the absence of knowledge for it to be liberatory.

We call such a queer fantasy—even over and beyond a homosexual fantasy—because it so beautifully resists categories of knowability and suggests that our richest, most liberating experiences exist when we refuse the impulse to know and open ourselves to acceptance of the not known, maybe even of the ultimately unknowable. In both *The White Paper* and *La Belle et la Bête*, Cocteau offers us rich multimodal representations that continually invite us to question what we know about love, and about how we categorize it and attempt to "tame" it, like an unwieldy beast that must be put in its proper place. We cannot help but think of such questioning as the work of the queer, which invites us not only to consider tolerating that which is "not like us," "not like the normal," but to understand critically the moves and gestures to categorize and make knowable things as complex as intimacy, desire, affection, and love.

■

With these different histories in mind, these different narrations of queerness and multimodal multimedia, we ask:

- What kinds of representational acts figured multimodally and through multimedia contribute substantively and materially to understanding queerness in rich, varied, capacious, and (perhaps most importantly) challenging ways?

- What kinds of representations break the spell of static, flat (and flattening) tropes of identity, reprocessing digital cardboard copies of one-dimensional queer subjects?

- At the same time, what kinds of representations challenge identity while refusing fluidity (itself an ultimately untenable position—is fluidity a subject position?) either online or off?

- Finally, what are politically interventive queer acts online? And how might such acts reorient our understanding of the queer and of its efficacy as a challenge to heteronormative dominance and its orientation of our thinking about intimacy, affiliation, and identity?

Perhaps our ultimate questions about queerness and representation might be, In what is the queer invested? And in what might the cyberqueer invest its figural acts?

FROM REPRESENTATION TO ORIENTATION: QUEERNESS, AFFECT, AND IDEOLOGY

What we see in Cocteau's work is a sense, simultaneously, of queerness's unknowability and of the invitation to connect, however possible, with the unknowable queer. In both *The White Paper* and *La Belle et la Bête*, Cocteau's multimodality gestures toward a queerness that cannot quite be captured and must remain ungraspable in its queerness while also putting into motion multiple texts, genres, and sense experiences that nonetheless invite connectivity with that unknowable queerness—even as we must acknowledge that those moves to connect may be unsettling, discomfiting, uncomfortable. Indeed, what might be most critically productive about Cocteau's queer representations is that they do not represent queerness as much as they reorient our thinking about love. The reorientations, as Cocteau admits, evoke powerful feelings, calling forth "the forces that govern our dreams and that people quickly try to forget." Cocteau invites us not just to see the queer, but to simultaneously identify with it (as some identify with the story of *La Belle et la Bête*) and to be troubled by it (as some find the various narrative moves and line drawings of *The White Paper* unsettling). Such works are as much about challenging affect as they are about representing the queer.

Along these lines, the work of cultural critic Sara Ahmed and her compelling explorations of affect and ideology can illuminate what we believe to be Cocteau's aesthetic (and perhaps even political) practice—as well as what our own multimodal queer aesthetic might be. In *The Cultural Politics of Emotion*, Ahmed works the trope of orientation specifically in terms of sexual orientation; she argues that "compulsory heterosexuality—defined as the accumulative effect of the repetition of the narrative of heterosexuality as an ideal coupling—shapes what it is possible for bodies to do, even if it does not contain what it is possible to be. Bodies take the shape of norms that are repeated over time and with force" (145). Through that repetition, "Compulsory heterosexuality shapes bodies by the assumption that a body 'must' orient itself towards some objects and not others" (145). Of course, at times one experiences disorientation, usually in the face of the queer—either the queer as embodied externally in someone whose life and loves are decidedly not like one's own, or internally in stray thoughts that challenge one's assumed heterosexual orientation. For Ahmed, such moments indicate the close intertwining of affect and ideology, of how we are conditioned to move in the world. In *Queer Phenomenology: Orientations, Objects, Others*, Ahmed asserts that

> moments of disorientation are vital. They are bodily experiences that throw the world up, or throw the body from its ground. Disorientation as a bodily feeling can be unsettling, and it can shatter one's sense of confidence in the ground or one's belief that the ground on which we reside can support the actions that make a life feel livable. Such a feeling of shattering, or of being shattered, might persist and become a crisis. Or the feeling itself might pass as the ground returns or as we return to the ground. The body might be reoriented if the hand that reaches out finds something to steady an action. (157)

Ahmed then asks a pivotal question: "What do such moments of disorientation tell us? What do they do, and what can we do with them?" (158). For Ahmed, the answer in part lies in paying attention to queer orientations: "Queer orientations are those that put within reach bodies that have been made unreachable by the lines of conventional genealogy. Queer orientations might be those that don't line up, which by seeing the world 'slantwise' allow other objects to come into view" (107). Playing with the trope of orientation allows Ahmed to assert that periodic disorientation, usually brought on by the emergence of the queer or that which is not oriented along normative lines, can make us critically aware of how we are all socially, culturally, and even politically oriented to want, to desire, certain things and not others. Disorientation, in other words, reveals the normative and the normalizing in action—the powerful forces that make some lives seem so natural, others seem unthinkable. After all, disorientation is a common response among many when faced with that which lies outside of, or "slant-wise" to, the heteronormative.

Or as Ahmed puts it, to "feel uncomfortable is precisely to be affected by that which persists in the shaping of bodies and lives [e.g., heteronormativity]" (155).* Feeling such discomfort potentially creates a space for critical reflection on the various trajectories, the orientations, that point us in certain directions, valorizing some lives, disparaging others.

We can see such disorienting powerfully at work in Cocteau's multimodal compositions. The varied genres of *The White Paper* disturb our sense of how we know the queer, of what the queer is, while the special effects and fantasy narrative of *La Belle et la Bête* invite us into a world in which we must suspend our usual understanding of how the course of true love should proceed. Certainly, Cocteau understood the value of disorientation. The line drawings in *The White Paper* startle us; the Beast's visage in *La Belle et la Bête* unsettles us. In either case, the disorientation should lead to reflection: Why am I uncomfortable—and need I be? Indeed, both texts invite us to reorient ourselves, to reconsider the larger cultural forces and mandates that orient us along certain paths, calling our lives to tell certain stories. We have the opportunity of reorientation, even as our original "sexual orientation" may be left intact.

Indeed, such discomfort may constitute the pedagogical gesture of Cocteau's multimodality, of his figuring of queerness multimodally. In the introduction to Cocteau's collection of autobiographical sketches, *The Difficulty of Being*, composer and Cocteau acquaintance Ned Rorem remembers his first "textual" encounter with Cocteau. Asking for a meeting with the filmmaker, Rorem receives a cryptic note: "You yourself must find a way to meet me—miracles work better than appointments" (vii). With such a coy gesture, Cocteau offers us his understanding of love, perhaps of the queer: *I will not simply reveal myself to you—and perhaps I cannot; but you must nonetheless search for me.* Cocteau offers us then a sense of the queer as the unknown with whom connection must nonetheless be made. The beauty and the beast, that incommensurable pair, must love one another.

QUEER MULTIMODALITY

What we would like to do now is explore what a queer multimodality might look like—a queer multimodality less invested in identity and community building, or in the free play of sexual fluidity; instead, we will explore the gestures of queer critique that draw our attention to and challenge normative identity, and that probe the intermingling of sexuality and power in the West. Put another way, we will argue that queer representation involves not just figuring an orientation; queer representation means the experience—and the potentially critical re-experience—of being "oriented." Multimedia offer us some powerful (though not exclusive) strategies to invite people to experience an orientation (and perhaps even a bit of productive disorientation) vis-à-vis the sexual. Such work, necessarily personal and emerging from "the private," draws on our own sense of queerness. Indeed, this chapter serves as much as our own personal exploration of queer multimodality as it does a theoretical probing of queerness and multimedia. Thinking of Ahmed, we inquire after "real-life" meetings with the queer, with the potential disorientation of queerness. We ask, how might a queer multimodality offer a productive disorientation? And a disorientation productive of what, exactly?

JONATHAN—"PHONESEX : A DIGITAL COLLAGE" AND "DIS|ORIENTATION : A STRAIGHT CLOSET"

I conceived of these pieces specifically as explorations of queerness and multimodality. In one way, my goal was to make manifest, inasmuch as that is possible, the queer multimodally. I was interested in working toward a better sense, perhaps a more personal sense, of how multimodal composing might approach, represent, perhaps even extend a sense of the queer. Of course, there is no one experience of the queer. And there cannot be—and should not be—one way to figure the multiple experiences of the queer. At the same time, this is a queerness with a political edge as well. Monique Wittig claims in *The Straight Mind* that "discourses of heterosexuality oppress us in the sense that they prevent us from speaking unless we speak in their terms" (25). My work is an attempt to speak in other terms. And in that sense, it is a manifesto for the necessity of exploring multimodality in the effort to speak in other terms.

The following two pieces, "phonesex : a digital collage" and "dis|orientation : a straight closet," originally appeared online in *Harlot*, where they can still be viewed and explored. I designed them to explore how we interact with digital media, particularly a web-based interface, to (re)experience differing senses of embodiment and the complex relationships among bodies, embodiment, and identity. I'm drawn in particular to investigating the circulation of identities and digitized bodies—and to understanding how both get picked up in the webbed world, are remixed, and then are redistributed both to normalize identity trajectories and disturb such normative trajectories.

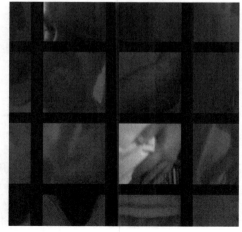

"phonesex" invites touch that viscerally implicates the interactor in what s/he is touching. At the same time, the piece frustrates users' expectations because "clicking" on the images and "scrolling down" the page take you nowhere. Instead, I intend the piece to provoke reflection on the act of "touching" images and responding to the presence of potential "links." What motivates our desire to digitally touch, to pursue linkages—particularly when the shadowed images tease and taunt—and potentially disturb? If you continue to touch, to scroll down, what—after a point—are you really looking for? And what does that say about our desires, and the role of desire in interacting with digital technologies that represent and mediate bodies?

"dis|orientation" probes how we construct online identity and represent bodily desire by linking our haptic expectations as we touch—and push—the fantasy images of advertising to realities of the sexual underground. As with "phonesex," the lingering mouse touch reveals sexualized images from the advertising world, specifically the overly sexualized images of Abercrombie & Fitch poster boys. But pushing the images takes us to postings inspired

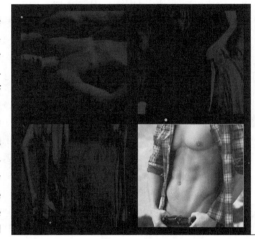

JACKIE: LESBIAN SPECTACLE

I'll start simply: *I put this picture and the one on 208 on my door and the reactions to them fascinated me.* The reactions: laughter; jokes about how Pilates was really working for me; a number of comments about how hot I was. However, a number of people—good friends, even—were disturbed: "I can't even *look* at that—it's too creepy!" The queer reading is, perhaps, obvious; in both pictures, there is a slipperiness of gender and representation, a layering of possibility and dissonance, gaps and excesses of meaning; as each reader approaches the text, she or he has different (and contradictory) interpretations of *that* body and what technology has done with it. In that mesh of possibility is a great deal of discomfort, a discomfiture courted by queer readings; for like other texts, these pictures explode the possibility of a sexuality—revealing "definitional center" for *either* the material body reading *or* the representation read. Indeed, as Eve Sedgwick writes, "A lot of the most exciting recent work around 'queer' spins the term outward along dimensions that can't be subsumed under gender and sexuality at all: the ways that race, ethnicity, post-colonial nationality criss-cross with these and other identity-constituting, identity-fracturing discourses, for example" (8–9).

So given the ease of such a queer reading, why do I propose *lesbian* sexuality as a *techné* of self? The choice is quite deliberate. In *Tendencies*, Sedgwick claims that the terms *gay* and *lesbian* still (in 1993) present themselves (however delusively) as objective, empirical categories governed by empirical rules of evidence (however contested). *Queer* seems to hinge much more radically and explicitly on a person's undertaking particular, performative acts of experimental self-perception and filiation. A hypothesis worth making explicit: that there are important senses in which *queer* can signify only *when attached to the first person*. One possible corollary: that what it takes—all it takes—to make the description "queer" a true one is the impulsion to use it in the first person. (9)

by *Craigslist* advertisements from men who are self-identified as straight but who are seeking man-to-man bodily contact. In this piece, I invite meditation on the nature of the "closet" vis-à-vis multiple identificatory practices and positions. The closet, in this case, is simultaneously the repository of A&F clothing, the perennial favorite of frat-boys and straight college kids; the homoeroticized advertising used to appeal to such kids; the pervasiveness of homoerotic behavior masked under the label "straight;" and the continued larger cultural failure to honor the homoerotic while still using it to sell merchandise. Dominant culture constructs the homoerotic as the secret, tempting desire that must still be hidden behind the façade of the "straight." I find it curious how the digital world provides access to linking different pieces of our fractured sexual landscape.

That linkage exists for me in two dimensions. First, it is an attempt to resist, in Wittig's words, "the oppressive character that the straight mind" often foists on us in "its tendency to immediately universalize its reproduction of concepts into general laws which claim to hold true for all societies, all epochs, all individuals" (27). In linking homoerotic advertising with the vast underground of acknowledged, even repudiated homoerotic activity, I want to disrupt the reproduction of a certain kind of straightness that rests necessarily on the constant reproduction of the repudiation of the homoerotic. At the same time, the piece invites your disruption through reading such reproduction in its ceaseless replication of the same, again and again, picture after picture, ad after ad.

The piece is designed to engender a bit of discomfort, and in this way I follow the theoretical lead of Sarah Ahmed, who argues that "to feel uncomfortable is precisely to be affected by that which persists in the shaping of bodies and lives [e.g., heteronormativity]. Discomfort is hence not about assimilation or resistance, but about inhabiting norms differently" (155). Such discomfort can be as simple as encountering the erotic where one didn't expect to encounter it. My colleague, Karen, a social psychologist, wrote to me the following after seeing "phonesex" for the first time: "Kewl J. I'll have to find a moment to take a closer look at them, though I must say there's a boundary there of not wanting to engage with you too sexually that seemed to pop up upon first glance." This sudden, discomfiting engagement with the sexual may inaugurate a critical engagement, and "dis|orientation" is designed to play with that engagement by asking us to think about where the erotic is allowed, and where it is perhaps allowed but simultaneously disavowed. Indeed, what persists in the representation of straightness in our culture is the reproduction of the homodenied identity, that which, even as it may partake in the homoerotic, must deny the labeling of such, must repudiate homosexual affiliation. "disorientation" invites some discomfort by making explicit the repudiated, thus prompting you, I hope, to "inhabit norms differently," to see the contours of repudiation in the maintenance and reproduction of certain kinds of identities.

As queer theory has played out in academia (for that is its only home), it has rather ironically taken on the objectivist stance that Sedgwick saw as a gay and lesbian fault. In its domesticated state, it no longer derives its critical weight—if ever it did—from first-person iteration. Rather, "queer," with its explosion of categories, signifies a particular approach to text that is necessarily discrete from the writer's body; it affords us radically disembodied bodies and desexualized sexualities to analyze. It is, perhaps, more accurately positioned as a techné or even an *episteme* of analysis—but not of self. As such—given the relative worth(s) of analysis and self in the academy—it has become "safe," or at least *legitimate*, institutionally.

In 1994, Judith Butler wrote presciently that "normalizing the queer would be, after all, its sad finish" ("Against" 21). I do not believe the queer has quite met its "sad finish"; in fact, it takes only a quick look though the CFP-L archives or MLA/CCCC programs to see that *queer* is doing at least as well as *feminist* in terms of critical legitimacy. The term still has the power to disturb, to evoke reaction, and indeed to describe a particular sense of discursive work. In using the term *lesbian*, however, I follow Terry Castle deliberately: "Indeed, I still maintain, if in ordinary speech I say, 'I am a lesbian,' the meaning is instantly (even dangerously) clear: I am a woman whose primary emotional and erotic allegiance is to my own sex" (15). It is this sense of first-person signification (to which Sedgwick alludes) that must inform any embodied feminist praxis, particularly if we keep in mind bell hooks' admonition to value the "radical possibility" that is part of living on the margin (149).

To perform lesbian first person is indeed a radical, disruptive, even *abnormalized* invocation of body, gender, desire, fear, and sensation. It is a *spectacular* act, in which we might make use of our converging alienations, our mesh of desire and want, in order to position ourselves to be—if only for a particular rhetorical moment. Even more, because of the constant exchange/deferral of need, lesbian first person increases and sustains itself through its desire, serving as the engine of its own perpetual visibility. It is, simply, one act in a generative *techné* of self.

Techné has no precise equivalent in English; it has been variously translated as "art" or "craft," "technical knowledge," or "skill." In this paper, I use *techné* as a sort of praxis middle ground, more than the "clever, bold strokes" of *phronesis* (Lyotard) or the knowledge-making systematicity of *episteme*. Rather, I pose the *techné* of lesbian sexuality as a sort of generative lived knowledge; it is a view of *techné* that points less to the prescriptive how-to sense of the term and more to the ethical, civic dimension. This *techné* has two broad parameters: (1) the acknowledgment/embrace of the idea of "spectacle," the alienating distance between bodily self and representation; and (2) the importance of lived experience to the formation of an ethical stance. The life of the body is not to be ignored.

Lesbian first person, act 1: I put the picture on my door. It raised these questions: What body? What gender? What desire? What fear? In its displacement of a "real" or even *unitary* body, it made my own fleshly, material self *present*; in its displacement of "real" or even *unitary* gender and the concomitant expectations of desire, it created an always-already exchange of image, desire, representation; in short, through technology, *I made a spectacle of myself.*

In my particular case, the absent was made present; it rather jarringly reminded viewers that "the supplement is always the supplement of a supplement. One wishes to go back *from the supplement to the source*: one must recognize that there is *a supplement at the source*" (Derrida 304). The chain of deferred meanings crafted into the Photoshop-mediated simultaneous text of [lesbian face] and [male body] lays bare the multiple disjunctures of the "seen self." In so doing—as readers tumble frantically into this rollercoaster of multiple deferrals—it makes visible the strange brew of fear, guilt, and desire with which we approach the **lesbian body**.

Any *techné* of lesbian sexuality will do well to embrace the spectacular as a force that makes fleshly bodies temporarily readable through its sustained jumbling of representation and desire. I won't rehearse decades of psychoanalytic and/or French feminist and/or poststructuralist thought here, but instead offer one proposition upon which we might agree: the body—the fleshly thing that carries us around, this ugly bag of mostly water, as Gollum would have it—is never really our own, never in existence apart from representation and desire. Perhaps we can express this relationship thusly: our self at its most simply speakable or readable is comprised of ratios between the nodes of body, representation, and desire, much like the classic rhetorical triangle of speaker, audience, and subject. And again: any *techné* of lesbian sexuality, any performance of this spectacular, must honor lived experience. As bell hooks and others have noted, experience provides a particular insight—not because of essential traits, but because of unique experience that "cannot be acquired through books or even distanced observation and study of a particular reality" (90). The "passion of experience" (90) animates this *techné*, makes it more than a relic of 1970s cultural feminism. However, it is important to remember that embodiment and experience, too, work within the ratios mentioned before. For, ironically, the spectacular lesbian is a necessarily visual *techné*: it is in the reroutings of expectation within the disjuncture between seen(s) that the yawning maw of spectacle horrifies (*Zero at the bone. You can't believe your eyes!*). In this way, the fixed seen and the fluid reading jam together in a move that invokes a radical feminist textuality, as I have argued before.

We have a world of pleasure to win, and nothing to lose but boredom. (Vaneigem 10)

After seven years of office-hour art on my door, my department knows of my Photoshop habit. Everyone also knows that I am a lesbian. I'm one of the LGBT faculty advisors on campus. I piloted one of the university's first courses in LGBT studies. My lover comes with me to department functions, and when we were married during the San Francisco wed-in of 2004, the event was announced in the department newsletter. The vast majority of my department showed up for a party celebrating us, and, in fact, the president of the university congratulated us. In short, everybody knows. Or so everybody thought. But these two specific pictures enfleshed my sexuality in a spectacular way, reminding viewers that even though they faced me directly, I am still there, "gender fucking and fucking gender," as Stephen Whittle would say.

How does one make sense and feeling of a radically expansive world of images, given the DIY incursion into public authoring? How do we make ourselves understood and felt? As more of us engage our classes in constructing new media texts, writing blogs, or just participating in listserv or Blackboard discussions, we are discovering the heady intersections of text and identity that we knew were there but had not been able to (quite) (always) make visible. These networked technologies make it easier to do such things; at the same time, I resist the idea that the technologies are all that have made it possible. In any number of my classes—graduate and undergraduate—because of inspiration, exploration, and sometimes natural disaster (flooding in the computer classroom), I use representational technologies that are nonnetworked/low end (colored markers, collage) and nonnetworked/high end (Photoshop). At other times, the network is very much our aesthetic friend; the point is facilitating access to the means of representation and distribution. To explain: in "Box Logic," Geoffrey Sirc writes about new media approaches to text and memory, writing that his primary goal is "to show my students how their compositional future is assured if they can take an art stance to the everyday, suffusing the materiality of daily life with an aesthetic" (117). Like Sirc, I want my students (and my fellow teachers) to take an "art stance to the everyday," and like Sirc, who embeds his discussion of new media within an exploration of Walter Benjamin's *Arcades Project,* I want to encourage a critical understanding of that stance. It is for this reason that I offer a "lesbian twist" on situationist aesthetics and the critique of the capitalist exchange of representation.

Lesbian first person, act 2: I am a spectacular lesbian. My visual enactment of, shall I say, "giving head" jolted the colonized lesbian body from its moorings. Its "gender confession" disrupted, ever so slightly, the ideology of heterosexism and opened a gap from which to question (if never resolve) that ideology. And it is through technology—not just the sexy stuff of cyberspace, but low-network technologies like Photoshop manipulation—that we can make readable the sustained desire of lesbian spectacle, the trembling need for knowledge we can never have, the terror of the unbidden Other, or, more succinctly, as my lover puts it, "the 'ick' factor." Can we enact, can we enflesh, a rhetoric of sexuality that embraces spectacle? Can we struggle at that point of fear? It's incumbent upon us in feminist studies, I believe, to revisit the dismissal of *lesbian* as a useful critical term; further, we should court those moments of spectacle to look bravely at flesh and desire, and to wonder, even in our horror, even if it makes us flinch—What price have we paid for hiding our bodies?

Both pieces are also experiments in "touch," in that you have to digitally, as it were, finger with your mouse the images, some of which are fairly eroticized, in order to experience the pieces. In this way, I am hoping to queer the machine, to invite active eroticization of the computer as communication technology—or, perhaps, to sense the erotic potential in the computer, in the network. Amazingly, but truthfully, we encounter new technologies and inevitably ask of them, "How can I use you to fuck better?" My question of the technology perhaps has more to do with asking questions about how we can know sexuality better, in all of its erotic, intimate, and disciplinary modalities and movements, but it also imbricates questions about how we experience the new communications technologies and new media— erotically. Again, Ahmed is useful here in helping theorize how we might understand digital touch in terms of the erotic, even as her discussion is not specifically about technology and new media. She writes that our understanding of touch generally "shows how bodies reach other bodies, and how this "reaching" is already felt on the surface of the skin. And yet. . .not all bodies are within reach. Touch also involves an economy: a differentiation between those who can and cannot be reached. Touch then opens bodies to some bodies and not others. Queer orientations are those that put within reach bodies that have been made unreachable by the lines of conventional genealogy. Queer orientations might be those that don't line up, which by seeing the world 'slantwise' allow other objects to come into view" (107). My goal in developing these media texts has been to open up a space, a touching space for a "queer orientation" that shows how certain "conventional genealogies" separate out permissible and impermissible touching—the permissible clasp of male touch in camaraderie versus the impermissible sexual contact that must be kept hidden and secret. Curiously, *Craigslist*, an internet-enabled communications platform, facilitates the illicit touching, putting "within reach bodies" otherwise "made unreachable" by the "straight mind." So, "dis|orientation" points to what "doesn't line [link?] up" so that we might see straightness, and even queerness, a bit "slantwise," or differently.

QUEER MULTIMODAL (IM)POSSIBILITY

That moment of instantiation—of the flesh made real—seems ripe for rhetorical and embodied action, one that encourages an attention to the moments of uncertainty between desire and hope, bodily self and representation, lived experience and ethical stance. It also encourages a sense of material connection to text, and a certain sacrifice of the aesthetic to the material, as writers, artists, and designers offer their work as a physical interruption of alienated representation. Finally, it encourages us to put our bodies on the line, to "risk" spectacle. Linder writes, of situationist cultural studies, that "yes, we can act in the world, and let me speak of bodies, pleasures, and paradises lost to suggest that it happens all the time. The real trick, it seems, is not in reaching Paradise, but staying there" (370).

Just as new media texts and practices prompt us to reconsider what "literacy" means, so too do they enable us to reconsider what sexuality and sexual identity (always already discursive) mean. In this chapter, we have attempted to understand the multiple layerings of sex, text, and technology as sites from which to perform queer identities. Specifically, we explored the radical, disruptive invocation of body, gender, desire, fear, and sensation that is the (new-)mediated queer self. We make use of our converging alienations, our mesh of desire and want, in order to position ourselves to be—if only for a particular, rhetorical moment—and, more to the point of this particular work, to be sexual. Through the constant exchange/deferral of need, this self-positioning increases and sustains itself through its desire, serving as the engine of its own perpetual visibility. It is thus a generative, multimodal *techné* of self, with both somatic and representational consequence.

Our view of *techné*—a sort of generative lived knowledge—points less to the prescriptive how-to sense of the term and more to its ethical, civic dimension. Our view demands that we embrace the incommensurability of bodily self and representation at the same time as we acknowledge the importance of lived experience to the formation of an ethical stance. It's important to clarify, however, that our sense of sexuality and ethics does not cover "appropriate" sexual behavior or sexual manners, but instead draws from a close examination of the discourses surrounding the sexual self. What behaviors, what subjectivities, what possibilities, and what impossibilities are created through the intersections of sex and text? It is with this view in mind that we attempt to perform in this book our own encounters—as sexed and sexual beings—with a variety of texts.

We contend that what is most attractive about queerness—theoretically, personally, and politically—is its potential illegibility, its inability to be reductively represented, its disruptive potential—in a word, its impossibility. At many different moments, queerness appears (or emerges or erupts) to trouble normalcy, legitimacy, signification. It's what doesn't fit. It's what skews, bends, or queers the realities we construct around ourselves, and that have been constructed for us to induce a heteronormative sense of stability and progress through the replication of particular kinds of people in particular kinds of families.

Queerness disrupts such stability, such progress. And as a movement of disruption, it is often difficult to track, to catch, to identify. Gays and lesbians are often positioned in relation to the normative, often as those seeking a place at the table—and many gays and lesbians are seeking that place. But in our lives as a gay man and as a lesbian, we have encountered numerous instances in which our queerness most certainly does not fit in, where it marks us as separate, as possessing and possessed by a subjectivity that is often incommensurably Other.

Those are often our most delicious moments. And the most critically insightful and revealing, for that moment of instantiation—of the flesh made real—seems ripe for rhetorical and embodied action, one that encourages an attention to the moments of uncertainty between desire and hope, bodily self and representation, lived experience and ethical stance.

NOTE

* Ahmed, to be sure, offers some interesting caveats: "I want to think about how a queer politics might involve disorientation, without legislating disorientation as a politics. . . . The point is not whether we experience disorientation (for we will, and we do), but how such experiences can impact on the orientation of bodies and spaces, which is after all about how the things are 'directed' and how they are shaped by the lines they follow" (158). Also, "In calling for a politics that involves disorientation, which registers that disorientation shatters our involvement in a world, it is important not to make disorientation an obligation or a responsibility for those who identify as queer" (177). We note such caveats, and concur.

12 IT'S MY REVOLUTION
Learning to See the Mixedblood

Kristin L. Arola

*It takes a long time to make an outfit, you know. You can go through life
and keep adding on to that outfit. Because there are different circumstances
that surround different items that you add to your outfit. When you're
dancing, these things that are in the regalia, they bring out a shine. You
actually shine out there, and you feel good about yourself. Everybody can
do that. It's not just for Anishinabe people. It's for everyone.*
— Ron Davis, Ojibwa Grass Dancer

Erase our bodies and we merely dance to music we cannot hear.
— Kristie Fleckenstein, "Writing Bodies"

Moments after dancing in my one and only powwow, I encountered something my mother, an Ojibwa Jingle Dancer (among other things), explains
as commonplace.

Having just finished a pink shawl dance—a dance organized to raise
breast cancer awareness in native communities—I stepped outside to get
some air and reflect on my experience dancing in a space I felt was reserved
for "real" Indians, not mixedbloods like me. As I tried to overcome an over-
whelming sense that the "real Indians" were staring at me and gossiping
about how I didn't belong, a woman and her two children approached
me. The woman stared quizzically at my pink shawl, slowly extended her
hand and said, "It's so beautiful, what does your costume mean?" In this
moment, my emotions were terribly mixed. At first, I was surprised to have
someone speak to me—a light-skinned, blue-eyed, more-Finnish-than-Ojib-
wa-girl—as though I actually knew something about being Indian. Surprise
was slowly overtaken by my feelings of being an imposter: "Who am I to say
anything about what my shawl means? I only know what my mother taught
me!" (which, in retrospect, is a lot). Then it hit me: "Wait, did she just say
'costume'?"

In this moment of confusion, an internal debate waged in my brain
between offering a detailed explanation of my pink shawl and making a
hasty proclamation that my regalia is not a costume but is an embodied
signifier of my past and present experiences as a mixedblood Indian. I set
aside my own dilemmas and settled on a brief explanation of my mother's

clan and the four colors, yet in that moment I acknowledged firsthand what my mother has always professed to me: regalia, that is the dance outfit one wears during a powwow, is not costume but instead is identity.

In this paper, I use the concept of regalia as a lens for looking at the MySpace profiles of three mixedblood Native Americans. While MySpace profiles and powwow regalia may seem odd bedfellows (and in spite of Facebook's takeover of MySpace as the most popular social-networking site), I assert that the materiality inferred in concepts of regalia are important for understanding online representations of self, representations encouraged by the various social-networking platforms with which we engage. Regalia is not something one simply dons atop the self for the sake of play or trivial performance; instead, regalia is an intimate expression of self. Regalia is not bracketed off from "real" life but instead is part of an ongoing process. Seeing online identities not as bracketed costume but instead as material expression encourages an examination of online identities as part of the complex ecology of meaning and not merely as an isolated snapshot of performance. More specifically, to look at mixedbloods' online expressions through regalia is to examine the material complexities of identifying as mixedblood both on and offline.

THE POSSIBILITY AND VISIBILITY OF THE MIXEDBLOOD

To be an American Indian is complicated in today's American culture. On the one hand, there are real legal requirements for how much blood is required for the federal government to recognize someone as Indian (generally $^1/_4$, although individual tribal rules vary). On the other hand, to be recognized as Indian by a non-Indian generally requires physical attributes or adornment rendered recognizable by outsiders. Additionally, being recognized by other Indians as Indian also varies, and often depends on who you know, where you grew up, and whether or not you take part in the culture of the given tribe. While there was a time in our country's history when it was in many Indians' best interest to self-identify as *not Indian*, today's new-age mysticism attached to being Indian has many folks clamoring to find that $^1/_{64}$ of Cherokee blood. Being seen as an Indian is messy, slippery, tricky, and political; being seen as a mixedblood Indian—that is, one whose parents are not both fullbloods—is often an even messier, if not impossible, endeavor. Many others before me have discussed these complications in detail (Clifton; P. Deloria; V. Deloria; Garroutte; Mihesuah) and my point here is not to rehash these discussions but instead to examine how self-representations in online spaces—specifically when viewed through the lens of regalia, which I'll discuss shortly—work to illuminate the complex materiality of being and representing the self as a mixedblood Indian. Briefly, though, I want to describe what's at stake when considering how and if mixedblood Indians identi-fy as Indian at all.

In "Blood and Scholarship," Malea Powell describes how "Un-seeing Indians gave (and still give) Euro-Americans a critical distance from mate-riality and responsibility, a displacement that is culturally valued and marked as 'objectivity'" (3). This "un-seeing" of Indians exists in part by the denial or brushing over of America's bloody past and also through the belief that "real" Indians only exist in the stereotypes of what an Indian should look like, act like, and believe in. This act of unseeing comes with a host of problems for full-blooded Indians, including an unseeing by those in power of the political, economic, and social issues relevant to today's Native American. If Western culture unsees the Indian, is there any pos-sibility for seeing the mixedblood—an identity that thoroughly disrupts neatly and hegemonically constructed racial divides? Is the only way to see mixedbloods to see them as Indian, an already problematic site of visibility? Does seeing the mixedblood work to further erase the Indian?

When considering the case of the mixedblood's visibility, Resa Crane Bizarro describes how mixedbloods "are consistently excluded from being Indians in our country today by a variety of forces" (71). These forces include real legal forces concerning what it takes to be an Indian—for example, blood quantum and enrollment cards to mark who still counts as Indian—as well as our own *mythos* of what an Indian should be. While there might be a real political or personal impetus for mixedbloods to be included as Indian, as Bizarro contends, the fact remains that mixedbloods don't fall into a neatly decided racial category. For mixedbloods to be seen as Indian, an act I'm not entirely sure is always the best option, a host of requirements are necessary.

As Eva Maria Garroutte points out in *Real Indians*, "Indians are general-ly required—both by law and by popular opinion—to establish rather high blood quanta in order for their claims to racial identity to be accepted as meaningful, the individual's opinion notwithstanding" (47). The problem for mixedbloods when identifying as Indian isn't only an issue of recogni-tion by non-Indians, it is also an issue of recognition by Indians themselves. Garroutte describes how, along with quantum, physical appearance plays a large part in who is recognized as Indian not only by outsiders but also by Indians themselves: "Many Indian people, both individually and collective-ly, continue to embrace the assumption that close biological connections to other Indian people—and the distinctive physical appearance that may accompany those connections—imply a stronger claim on identity than do more distant ones" (52).

This claim on identity, along with its ties to quantum and appear-ance, is also tied to stereotypes of the Indian. While Indians themselves don't always buy into these stereotypes, non-Indians, when looking to see Indians, often fall into this visual trap—a trap that fetishizes what it means to be American Indian. This fethishization is manifested in popular visual representations of the Indian (think your typical mascot, or your cigar store Indian), thus providing a visual standard by which to measure the "real Indian." Native artist and scholar Erica Lord describes how common stereotypical visual representations—the noble savage, the wise medicine man, the Indian maiden—have not only remained the same for the past two hundred years, but also serve to distance, or in Powell's words "unsee," the contemporary Indian. These images, Lord describes, function as "an attempt (even if it is unconscious) to keep the Native in the past, easily recognizable, simple, and, essentially, separate and different from 'us'" (1). This separation and fetishizing of the Indian serves to deny "the identities of contemporary Natives who do not fulfill the traditional stereotypes" (4). Additionally, while many contemporary Natives are mixedblood, visual representations of mixedbloods are not common, or at least not commonly recognized, in the popular landscape. Lord describes this absence:

> A visual representation of a mixed-blood individual could mean several things: that the threatening idea of miscegenation exists, that the culture is diluting and dying through the 'breeding out' of the Native, or simply, these mixed blood images do not exist because they are not as visually interesting—they do not create a story to believe in. (4)

If visual representations of mixedbloods don't create a story to believe in, what do they create? Garroutte notes that "for centuries, mixed bloods have bridged the chasms between cultures—bridged it with their bodies, bridged it with their spirits, bridged it with their consciousnesses, bridged it often whether they were willing or unwilling" (57). Mixedbloods occupy that chasm in between, representing to both Indian and non-Indian cultures the shifting and permeable boundaries of race and identification. As Ojibwa Grassdancer Ron Davis said in the opening quote, "It takes a long time to make an outfit, you know. You can go through life and keep adding on to that outfit. Because there are different circumstances that surround different items that you add to your outfit." Mixedblood's outfits are constantly made and remade, sometimes in ways in which Indians and non-Indians acknowledge them as Indian, and other times in ways in which the category of Indian begins to slip and fall away. Again, Garroutte's words seem relevant: "Though one's actual blood quantum obviously cannot change, the definition of identity that depends upon it can and does. Biological Indianness, just as much as legal Indianness, can wink in and out of existence, sometimes with remarkable rapidity" (53).

I feel there is value in learning how to see not only the Indian—be she traditional or modern, powwow or hiphop, rez or urban, dark or light skinned—but also the mixedblood. To unsee the mixedblood, or to only see her in terms of Indian or non-Indian, is to view *Indian* itself as a static category trapped in stereotypes and outsider expectations. This narrow way of seeing, particularly if it only sees Indian as one thing, facilitates a world-view in which Indian culture is so fixed and tied to traditional ways that it risks being seen as dying. Additionally, to see the mixedblood would mean grappling with slippery categories of race and acknowledging the various reasons someone may want to be seen as Indian or non-Indian. I do believe there is something to be said for those, such as Vine Deloria, who ques-tion and challenge mixedbloods' desire to be Indian, and I am not asking you to see mixedbloods necessarily as Indian, but instead as what they are: mixed. As a mixedblood myself, I ask others to see me as mixed, as a blend-ing of cultures, as one whose sweatlodge is the Finnish sauna. I propose that a starting place for reseeing the mixedblood in contemporary terms is to look online—to the spaces where users are asserting their identities in ways that illustrate not only the existence and persistence of the mixed-blood, but whose visual, aural, and textual choices illustrate the complexi-ties of this category and the embodied nature of the online self.

SEEING THE MIXEDBLOOD THROUGH REGALIA

In order to resee (or perhaps fully see for the first time) the mixedblood in online spaces, I caution against theorizing online identities as bracketed performances separated from the material realities of the body.

In the article "Beyond Anonymity, or Future Directions for internet Identity Research," Helen Kennedy argues that online selves are inextri-cably linked with offline selves, and for this reason "it is necessary to go beyond internet identities, to look at offline contexts of online selves, in order to comprehend virtual life fully" (861). Kennedy encourages us not to "lose sight of identity as embodied experience" or "as identity-as-prac-tice" (873). She argues against Sherry Turkle's sometimes lauded and sometimes contested assertion in *Life on the Screen* that anonymity online can equal power—at least in the sense that it can free one from raced, classed, and gendered bodies that may otherwise be discriminated against. In her own study of the homepages of minority working-class women in the UK, Kennedy discovered that "students showed no sign of wanting to hide their gender and ethnicity and so 'benefit' from the possibility of anonym-ity that cyberspace offered them" (867). In this way, identity online is, for many users, a continuum of their offline selves and a place where they can represent various pieces and connections that make them who they are. As Kennedy describes, "Online lives are lived and produced in the context of life offline" and I would argue that the reverse can be true as well. Online and offline life functions in a feedback loop where materiality matters.

The theoretical belief that users online can easily create and embody any online identity is particularly problematic when it comes to issues of race. This belief that users will strive for anonymity when beneficial, or that they even can achieve some level of anonymity, imagines online identity as costume where any and all identifying marks are made available to individuals who can unproblematically try on different masks as their mood, need, or desire suits them. For example, were one able to merely don an identity costume online, then the mixedblood could play white/black/Asian/Hispanic, or Indian instead of being materially enmeshed with a body that is, in daily life, read in particular ways. Thinking of online representations as costume implies a separation of offline life from online life. This division erodes the possibility of seeing how one is not separate from the other, and how both are material spaces.

To bracket materiality is to deny the complex ecology that goes into identity. Kristie Fleckenstein, when speaking about the concept of embodied literacy, says,

> Meaning is always about an identity that has no existence outside that system. . . . Identity for any single aspect of meaning is embedded within the dynamic of the jointly crafted context. We cannot excise one element and attempt to define it outside its immersion within a system of relationships. Nor can we point to a single site within the system and say that identity starts or stops here. It is dispersed throughout the entire system. (*Embodied Literacies* 166–67)

This dispersal of relationships transcends the off/online barrier and acknowledges that meaning, identity, and in this case race, are all dependent on an ecology of relationships. So as to acknowledge the social and cultural meaning of production—whether it be the production of the self online, or the production of an idea through writing—we cannot view identity online as a separate, immaterial costume. Instead, I propose that identity in online space can be seen as regalia.

To understand online identity as regalia is to understand it as an embodied visible act that evolves and changes, and that represents one's history, one's community, and one's self within that particular moment. Regalia, in the sense I'm using it, refers to the outfits worn by powwow dancers. In a powwow, the regalia functions as an expression of dancers' lives and represents a range of the dancer's experiences: families, hobbies, dreams, and religious beliefs. Most dancers make clear that regalia should never be referred to as costume, as "the term costume denotes artificiality and wear that is donned for an event that is not part of one's ongoing life" ("The Regalia"). Just as thinking of online representations as costume negates the

ecology of meaning tied up in any representation, calling a powwow dancer's regalia a "costume" denies how regalia is "part of one's ongoing life."

Regalia firmly positions one within a shifting continuum of embodied
identities. The act of identification continues to change, just as some powwow dancers change their regalia from year to year, powwow to powwow. I
know one woman who, on the first day of a two-day powwow, wears a jingle dress. After a day of jingle dancing, she changes and performs in a traditional dress on day two. She makes this change in regalia in part because
her feet hurt after a day of jingle dancing, and in part because she feels
the need to engage in both dances. Change in regalia also happens based
on gifts a dancer has received, things a dancer has learned, dreams a dancer has had, and any meaningful encounter the dancer feels is important to
represent. For example, throughout the years, dancers may add ribbons,
feathers, beadwork, or other appliqués to their regalia. While the representation may change, it remains a material act enmeshed with the everyday.

Similarly, for powwow dancers there is no contradiction in blending historic elements with modern (or, perhaps, seemingly "untraditional") elements. For example, at a recent powwow I saw a young girl with beaded unicorns on the skirt of her regalia and a number of young men using bright
neon colored ribbons: neither unicorns nor neon green have any cultural
significance for the Ojibwa people of the Upper Great Lakes. Additionally,
a colleague recently told of an amusing discovery: she found her uncle's
regalia from the mid-1980s donned with elaborate beadwork representing
the popular Atari game *Space Invaders.*

Before moving on, I want to make clear that I am not trying to negate
the spiritual element of powwow regalia, nor am I trying to equate that spiritual element with any element found on a MySpace profile. Caveats aside,
I believe that thinking through online identities through the lens of regalia as it is understood in powwow culture opens up possibilities for reseeing identity and can provide a framework outside the familiar with which to
investigate identity not as merely a costume worn in online spaces in order
to shun bodily binds such as race, class, and gender, but instead as a continuum of the offline self which mixes and remixes components of the past
and present in order to arrive at an unfixed identity. Regalia acknowledges the shifting self, and can help us see the mixedblood outside the traditional lenses afforded.

MYSPACE MIXEDBLOODS

In order to explore how regalia can help us see online representations, I
explore the MySpace profiles of three mixedblood American Indians. These
profiles were chosen based on my personal knowledge of these three individuals; that is, I knew they were mixedblood and was curious to see how

they negotiated race in the template-driven parameters of a MySpace template. Each profile, as seen through the lens of regalia, opens up possible ways of questioning and reseeing the mixedblood through the permeable boundary of offline and online lives. Additionally, these profiles indicate how "mixedblood" isn't an available category for some users, both within the confines of MySpace as well as within their daily lives. Some of my analysis might seem arguably problematic in that I'm looking for identifiable traits that users enact to represent themselves as Indian, as mixed, or as Other. This looking for what is or is not Indian easily can slip into stereotyping, but I hope this analysis illuminates how the category of "mixed" is difficult to see and represent within the confines of a social-networking template.

For those who skipped over MySpace for the world of Facebook, let me offer a brief reminder of how the space itself worked (and still does, to varying degrees). Much like Facebook, users can sign up for free, and in doing so create a profile. This profile is represented through a webpage that can include the user's photos, interests, blog, general stats (height, weight, race, birthplace, etc.), and comments from and links to other friends within MySpace. Figure 1 shows a screenshot of Adam's MySpace profile. Adam is a mixedblood of Ojibwa and European descent. While MySpace includes an option for indicating one's ethnicity (and note that MySpace uses the term *ethnicity* and not *race*), users can only select from the following categories: Asian, Black/African decent, East Indian, Latino/Hispanic, Middle Eastern, Native American, Pacific Islander, or White/Caucasian. There is no option for checking more than one race, and Adam's profile indicates no ethnicity. Along with not self-identifying as white or Native, Adam doesn't include any identifiably Indian traits on his MySpace page—that is, no powwow pictures, medicine wheels, AIM logos, comments about his race, or anything else one might look for when trying visually seek out the image of an Indian. When asked why this absence in his profile, he said, "I have great hesitancy about self-identifying as either native or mixed race when I don't have an opportunity to explain in full what that means to me." Similarly, Adam rarely identifies as native or as mixed in his daily life except in academic circles where he engages directly with native philosophy—a space in which he has the room to define and describe his own positioning. For Adam, online space, similar to most of his offline space, does not allow enough room for the explanation he feels is required to identify as mixedblood.

In looking at mixedblood profiles, Adam represents one end of the spectrum—no visible acknowledgment of his mixedbloodedness. For all intents and purposes, looking at his pictures we might simply assume he's a white man, given his light skin and that "white" is often a cultural default race for anyone not qualifying themselves as, or appearing as, "other." If we look through the lens of regalia, considering how his representation

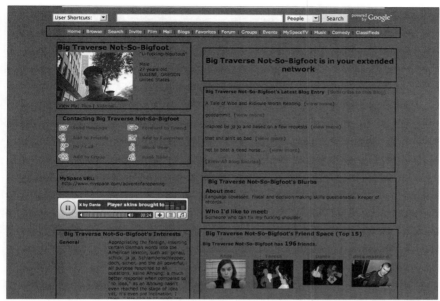

Figure 1

reflects his life experiences, we can see a pastiche of music, friends, and stories—yet none of these in any way explicitly refers to being mixed. Just as regalia represents one's history, one's community, and one's self within that moment, Adam's profile represents his material discomfort with identifying as mixed.

On the other end of the spectrum lies Jamie (fig 2), an artist and traveler of Ojibwa and European decent. When I first encountered Jamie's profile, there was no listed ethnicity, yet his profile at the time included a powwow song from the Bear Creek Singers, numerous photos of native art, multiple references to powwows, and an image of him playing with the Redstone Ojibwa drummers. At the time, when asked about the absence of a labeled ethnicity, Jamie said, "I dunno really why I didn't check the ethnicity box, I guess I did in the beginning but y'know we all change our songs, and our images." Days later I noticed Jamie had checked the box, and now quantifiably identifies as Native American on his space. Additionally, a photograph of Jamie in his powwow regalia now serves as his profile picture.

Jamie's profile, as seen through regalia, clearly represents his connections to a native community, acknowledgements of his history, and indicators of his self within the moment. Through his images, words, and musical choices he makes numerous references to powwow culture—thus visibly positioning himself within a native community. This community is also represented through the acknowledgement of his history, in that he includes an old photo of his native relatives (fig 3) looking very colonized.

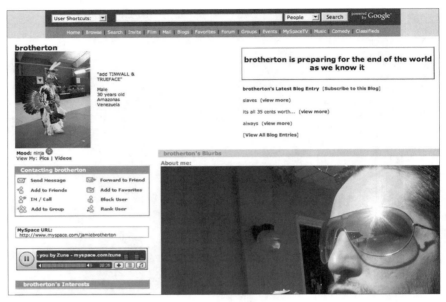

Figure 2

By including pictures of himself and his girlfriend, images of his paintings, powwow references, and poetry he has written we also get a glimpse of Jamie as he is positioned within the moment. Given the available ethnicities within MySpace, and given that Western culture doesn't have a way of acknowledging or seeing the mixedblood, Jamie might be read within this context as native—particularly because of his self-identification as such.

As opposed to Adam, Jamie has more "authentic" markers of what some of us might recognize as being Indian, and in this way we might even see Jamie as Indian, and perhaps not necessarily as mixedblood. When asked if he felt any of his design choices represented who he was as a mixedblood, Jamie explained that "there is a struggle to define what is and what isn't Indian, . . . being caught in the illusion of separation is detrimental to the progression and growth of our human family, of which none are excluded." And perhaps this is exactly what I'm doing here—looking for qualifiers of what is and isn't Indian—yet I do so in the spirit of finding the mixedblood so that the mixedblood can become part of our racial landscape, not an either/or but just as is. Interestingly, though, while Jamie cautions me on doing this sort of analysis, he himself acknowledges at one point a small sense of what he feels it is not to be mixed but to be Indian.

Most of Jamie's blog postings on MySpace include his poetry, yet in one particular entry Jamie speaks about the first time he met his father when they were both locked up in county jail. He describes their initial encounter and then goes on to describe the final day they were locked up together:

Figure 3

The last day we talked a lot. He told me stories of his own wild youth, the trouble he caused, the hearts he broke. Bands and music that he had played, he was a local guitar legend. His scrapes in the cities. The hard life of booze, basically. He told me to stay away from the stuff. I have mostly. A strange thing happened on that last day while we were in that cell, strange to me anyway. Just like anything I suppose, as strange as meeting your father, who you never knew, at seventeen, in jail. The strange thing was that while we were in there on the TV comes this movie called *Lakota Woman*, it was about the American Indian Movement, and the siege at Wounded Knee in the seventies. We stood there watching that movie. Father and son. Two orphans of their tribe, arms resting on cold, gray, jail cell bars. Fuck, how much more Indian could you get than that?

While eschewing a separation of what is and isn't Indian, he does have a sense, if even a sort of sarcastic sense, of what is Indian to him, or at least what others might acknowledge as Indian, for better or worse. While Adam felt it was too complicated to identify as Indian or mixed, Jamie seems to feel a connection to his sense of Indian and represents it through images of his past and present and tales of his life—some of which conjure up what Indian, but not necessarily mixedblood, means to him.

Unlike Adam, who feels he cannot identify as mixedblood or Indian, or Jamie, who feels comfortable identifying not as mixed but as Indian, Erica's profile (fig 4) represents the only profile of a mixedblood I have come across that offers some possibilities for identifying not as Indian, or as other-than (be it black, white, Hispanic, or Asian), but as mixed. Erica, a self-proclaimed Finndian—mixed Finnish, Athabaskan, and Inupiaq—is an

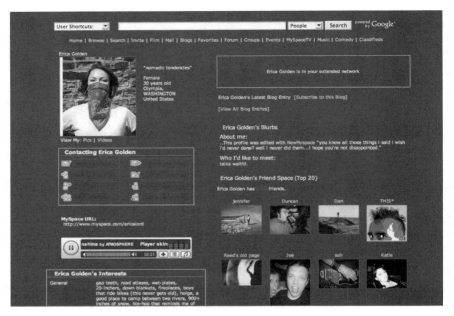

Figure 4

artist whose work questions issues of her own identity, which she describes as "a shifting self whose qualities seem to surface and diminish, depending on her context or present environment" (Erica Lord). Within the online space of MySpace, Erica lists her ethnicity as Native American, but upon closer inspection one sees that her identity is not this simple. Erica makes a nod to her mixedblood heritage by listing the hometowns of her Indian and Finnish families: Nenana, Alaska, and Chassell, Michigan. Additionally, she often makes references to being "Finndian," and includes some of her artwork that directly confronts issues of being mixedblood, for example a self-portrait (fig 5) in which she has self-tanned the phrase "I tan to look more Native" onto her back.

This self-portrait isn't existing merely online for Erica or as some part of a separable online identity, nor is it used as a mask to hide from her white or her Indian blood; instead this photo addresses mixedbloodedness and visual expectations of the Indian straight on, while also representing a continuum of her off- and online self, and of her questioning, resisting, complicit, and contradictory body. This profile is her regalia, not a costume but an embodied visible act that evolves and changes, and that represents her history, her community, and her self within this moment.

When asked if she used her MySpace profile to identify as mixedblood, Erica said, "Well, I think, I can't remember which box I checked for ethnicity. But as for the pictures and all, I think I try to be ambiguous. In a

Figure 5

lot of my representations, I think I try to be a little mysterious, or ambiguous, to allow for those slippages, with maybe small clues as to my background." Perhaps these clues are more visible to me than they would be to others, in part because I have spoken with Erica about her background and her choices. Yet, unlike Adam, who "seems" white, and unlike Jamie, who "seems" Indian, Erica's profile provides contradictions and slippages that indicate an identity that is unfixed, continuing, and appropriately mixed.

I don't mean to suggest that Adam or Jamie is being inauthentic when identifying as white and Indian respectively. They both, for various reasons, feel the need to do so in both their online and their offline life. Within the continuum of Indian identity (which itself is by no means fixed), both of these options are entirely reasonable personal choices. Yet I believe it is important to find the middle ground, a space where the mixedblood can identify as such without pressures to conform to one identity or the other. Erica's profile illuminates this possibility, one where mixedblood identity embraces slippages and acknowledges the messiness of being situated in the middle.

SEEING THE MIXEDBLOOD

Understanding the online mixedblood identity as regalia—that is, as in constant conversation with offline identities, as an act that evolves and changes, an act that represents one's history, one's community, and one's self within that moment in a continuum of embodied identities—provides visibility to mixedbloods. Were online personas merely costumes, Adam, Jamie, and Erica wouldn't have their choices so enmeshed with their own

it's my revolution.

Figure 6

material ecologies. For example, Adam is fairly light skinned and doesn't identify as mixed or Indian in most offline settings—the same holds true for his online self. Jamie doesn't get too hung up on what is or isn't Indian, and in his offline life participates actively with a native community and identifies as such—the same goes for his online profile. Erica provides an interesting twist in that when she is at her mother's home, where most people and relatives are white, she very much stands out as Indian. Yet, when Erica is at her father's home, where most people and relatives are Indian, she again stands out, but this time as white. For Erica, identifying as mixed illuminates these contradictions, and so she does so—both off- and online. Seeing online identity as regalia offers a means of generating and exploring a rhetoric of mixedblood identity—an identity, as one of Erica's pictures and captions suggests, might just be a revolution (fig 6).

In an arguably post-MySpace era, we continue to represent ourselves online through various social-networking platforms. The more we engage in these spaces, the more we may see our online and offline lives as woven together more tightly than we once did. Yet, if we want our online spaces to encourage mindful representations, be it mixedblood or otherwise, it is worth paying close attention to how we understand identity and representation to function in a highly templated online world. Regalia might just help us resee ourselves and each other.

13 VISIBLE GUERRILLAS

Karen Springsteen

Figure 1. Copyright © 1989 Guerrilla Girls, Courtesy www.guerrillagirls.com

DO WOMEN HAVE TO BE NAKED?

The representation above, created by the feminist art activist group the Guerrilla Girls, is a disruption of much more than the multitude of lounging, creamy-skinned women who line the walls of museums, silently offering come-hither looks. Not only does this image place a gorilla head on what should be Ingres's beautiful grand odalisque, and not only was it displayed as posters on New York City busses, its use of words allows the concubine to speak, enacting a sarcastic challenge to the representation of women in the city's Metropolitan Museum. It is disruptive precisely because those abilities of women to speak, question, challenge and act were rarely accounted for in the tradition of painting from which the nude comes.

I need not rehearse the history of women conceived as sexual property, as beautiful, passive objects to be gazed upon or used in the service of men. Critics T. J. Clark and John Berger (both men) agree:

> A nude, to repeat, is a picture for men to look at, in which Woman is constructed as an object of somebody else's desire (Clark 131).

> ...

> In the art-form of the European nude the painters and spectator-owners were usually men and the persons treated as objects, usually women. This unequal

relationship is so deeply embedded in our culture that it still structures the consciousness of women (Berger 63).

I need only point to some pages from glossy "women's" magazines like *Allure* and *Cosmopolitan,* or start to parse the rhetoric of 2008 female presidential and vice-presidential candidacies in the United States, to signal that this history is still in process, still structuring some aspects of a collective conscience. The subject-object dichotomy, in which women can be painted but not painters, carries such historic and psychic weight because it has long been aligned with and reinforced by other binary oppositions. In what follows, I offer a brief sketch of these (mis)alignments, as well as some key feminist responses to them. I offer this sketch in order to provide a context for the arguments I set forth in this chapter—namely, that visual modes of representation are integral (not just incidental) to the rhetorical work of the Guerrilla Girls and that an understanding of this function of visual modes is dependent upon a more primary understanding of how the subject-object dichotomy took on its gendered valence.

In her classic study, *The Man of Reason: "Male" and "Female" in Western Philosophy,* Genevieve Lloyd traces, from Plato to de Beauvoir, the philosophical development of the association of masculinist ideals with ideals of human reason. Lloyd quotes Philo writing in the first century CE, as he echoes both Plato and the Pythagorean table of opposites formulated six centuries earlier. Philo wrote:

> The male is more complete, more dominant than the female, closer akin to causal activity, for the female is incomplete and in subjection and belongs to the category of the passive rather than the active. So too with the two ingredients which constitute our life-principle, the rational and the irrational; the rational which belongs to the mind and reason is of the masculine gender, the irrational, the province of sense, is of the feminine. Mind belongs to a genus wholly superior to sense as man is to woman. (qtd. in Lloyd 27)

Lloyd does not suggest that Philo was self-consciously aware of the long-term social implications of this kind of description. Yet, we see in Philo's description an articulation of several oppositions that stack up and then flatten or compress into a dense dichotomy still with us today. This dichotomy includes not only the subject-object opposition but also the male-female opposition in which reason, the mind, and causal activity are gendered male while the irrational, passive domain of sense (and, by extension, the body) is gendered female. The former is dominant; the latter "in subjection." It is no coincidence, then, that female nudes served for centuries as subject matter for male painters. Their bodies were exactly that: matter, material, object, the stuff of men. And the dichotomy thickened further when the display of nudes on canvas was accompanied by a simultaneous rejection of the bodies of living, breathing women as inappropriate for active engagement in the public sphere, resulting in yet another layer of opposition: public versus private.

It is important to note, at this point, that much of the build-up of this dichotomy was and is ideological rather than purely descriptive: the dichotomy reflects the world-view of interested parties who tell versions of history for benefit or convention, versions to which feminist theorists and activists can and do respond. For example, in "Rethinking the Public Sphere: A Contribution to the Critique of Actually Existing Democracy," Nancy Fraser writes that the notion of the public sphere, idealized in the work of Jürgen Habermas, "rested on, indeed was importantly constituted by, a number of significant exclusions"—exclusions rooted in processes of class formation, in masculinist gender constructs, and in the precepts of racism (73). Fraser draws upon revisionist historiography to demonstrate the existence of multiple public spheres, multiple public arenas, and multiple "competing counterpublics," including "nationalist publics, popular peasant publics, elite women's publics, black publics, and working-class publics" (75). She points out that the version of the public sphere that rejected the work of these bodies was, in fact, a bourgeois, masculinist, white-supremacist conception.

The Guerrilla Girls themselves also bring levity to what I have described as the dense dichotomy through their use of gorilla masks and fake names. When asked who they are, the Guerrilla Girls offer the following response:

> We're a bunch of anonymous females who take the names of dead women artists as pseudonyms and appear in public wearing gorilla masks. We have produced posters, stickers, books, printed projects, and actions that expose sexism and racism in politics, the art world, film and the culture at large. We use humor to convey information, provoke discussion, and show that feminists can be funny. We wear gorilla masks to focus on the issues rather than our personalities. Dubbing ourselves the conscience of culture, we declare ourselves feminist counterparts to the mostly male tradition of anonymous do-gooders like Robin Hood, Batman, and the Lone Ranger. (Guerrilla Girls)

Maintaining anonymity, the Guerrilla Girls can't be pinned down. Their gorilla masks not only play on the alignment of women with the irrational animal body but also resist the kind of objectification that often accompanies public visibility, especially for women. Hiding individual identities, they resist what Susan Miller has called, "the political silence of the individualistic *I am*" (500, emphasis added). Moreover, the Guerrilla Girls take the names of dead women artists to increase conscious awareness of women in art who have been active producers, engaged in "causal activity," as Philo puts it—women who have been the painters rather than the painted. By keeping their names before us—Alma Thomas, Eva Hesse, Lee Krasner, Paula Modersohn-Becker, Emily Carr, Alice Neel, Chiyo Uno, Romaine Brooks, Rosalba Carriera—the Guerrilla Girls do not allow these women to be forgotten or overlooked. Prying open subject positions from which to move, the Guerrilla Girls say: "We could be anyone. We are everywhere." They refuse to stand within the kind of formation Lloyd describes in her conclusion:

> Our ideas and ideals of maleness and femaleness have been formed within structures of dominance and of superiority and inferiority, norms and difference, positive and negative, the essential and the complementary. And the male-female distinction itself has operated not as a straightforwardly descriptive principle of classification, but as an expression of values. We have seen that the equation of maleness with superiority goes back at least as far as the Pythagoreans . . . . Within the context of this association of maleness with preferred traits, it is not just incidental to the feminine that female traits have been constructed as inferior—the "feminine" itself has been partly constituted by its occurrence in this structure. (103–4)

Do women have to be naked? Well, yes—if we are to continue to be constituted within the structures and values Lloyd critiques. And, of course, no—we can revise that inheritance. Such revision is the source of my interest in the Guerrilla Girls.

My point of departure is as follows: if, as it seems, women have been devalued as irrational creatures who are tied to our bodies and "therefore" problematically located vis-à-vis an ideological public sphere, how might we create new embodied identities that are neither self-annihilating (transcending the body) or locked into a dominant masculinist logic that offers options like sexy and dumb, unable to speak, or dowdy and intellectual, the female figure gaining public credibility for what she lacks in femininity? How might we create a break with old, constricting options and compose ourselves anew, in ways that allow for revised patterns of recognition? In response to such questions, the Guerrilla Girls' revision of the odalisque functions in at least two ways. (1) The Guerrilla Girls are themselves "painters" who call into question the bourgeois, white supremacist, masculinist spectator-owner position by placing the art outside museums and into the city's public transit system. After all, who rides the bus? And (2) the odalisque becomes a subject who speaks with desires of her own. I read that question—Do women have to be naked to get into the Met?—as coming straight from the mouth of the woman wearing the mask.

In this chapter, I identify a key strategy (appropriative reproach) by which the Guerrilla Girls carry out such revision. I argue for the vital rhetorical function of this strategy in the Guerrilla Girls' effort to confront gendered dichotomies and construct new identities for women in art and in the larger world. I demonstrate why such an effort not only benefits from but necessitates the use of visual representation, a claim that has implications for compositionists who are considering the role of visual media in writing courses (George; Hess; Hocks; Selfe, *Multimodal Composition*; Shipka; Wysocki et al.; Yancey). To begin, I turn to a historical example that resonates with the contemporary work of the Guerrilla Girls.

OLYMPIA

Appearing in 1865 at the Paris Salon, Édouard Manet's *Olympia* was stark and scandalous. Viewers and critics did not know what to make of her. The following are characterizations of *Olympia* that appeared in French newspapers at the time.

> A sort of female gorilla, a grotesque in India rubber outlined in black, apes on a bed in a state of complete nudity, the horizontal attitude of Titian's *Venus*: the right arm rests on the body in the same fashion, except for the hand, which is flexed in a sort of shameless contraction. (Amedee Cantaloube, *Le Grande Journal*, qtd. in T.J. Clark 94)

> ...

> The august *jeune fille* is a courtesan, with dirty hands and wrinkled feet; she is lying down, wearing one Turkish slipper and with a red cockade in her hair; her body has the livid tint of a cadaver displayed in the morgue; her outlines are drawn in charcoal and her greenish, bloodshot eyes appear to be provoking the public, protected all the while by a hideous Negress. No, never has anything so...strange been hung on the walls of an art exhibition. (Ego, *Le Monde Illustre*, qtd. in T.J. Clark 96)

Who was this figure with the corpse-like color and dispassionate stare? How dare she flex her hand so immodestly? From whom do those flowers come and why is she painted with such thick and disgraceful lines? She is accompanied by a black woman, who is clothed and actively working. To what extent is the offense compounded by the presence of this woman? What is her role? And the cat?

Unlike the idealized nudes of the neoclassical style, the realist Olympia did not blend away softly as the passive, consumable object, despite her class status as a prostitute (*une fille publique*, or "public woman.") Olympia violated the traditional form of the nude, a violation that brought her identity, body, and purpose in the painting to be of issue. Her lack of passion was provocative; although nude, she had to be recognized as something

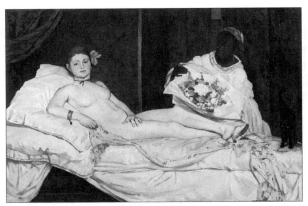

Figure 2. Manet, Edouard. Olympia. 1863.
Musèe d'Orsay, Paris.

else. Manet wrote his friend Baudelaire, "I really would like you here, my dear Baudelaire; they are raining insults on me, I've never been led such a dance" (qtd. in T.J. Clark 82).

Yet it was possible for Manet's Olympia to be successful in another regard. The painting startled the viewer into recognizing his own position of sight because Olympia recognized it, with her gaze, in no way modestly turned to the side, returned to the viewer. Because Olympia issued a different mode of address to the viewer, that viewer was kept from relaxing into the conventional position he had heretofore not considered to be a position at all. He was now at least temporarily aware of the relationship of looking between himself and the alien canvas. In a chapter entitled "Olympia's Choice," which emphasizes the agency of the woman Manet depicted as I am doing here, T.J. Clark concludes, "In order that the painted surface appear as it does in Olympia, the self-evidence of seeing—seeing the world, seeing Woman—had to be dismantled and a circuit of signs put in its place" (139). In other words, the shock of Olympia registered when the conditions that had seemed natural and obvious, the truths men took to be self-evident about women on canvas and in the world, were forced into a breakdown, such that instead of the impenetrable density of the subject-object/male-female/reason-sense/active-passive/public-private dichotomy, there was now a "circuit of signs"—that is, a dynamic system of representation, laden with values and recognized as such. I argue that the work of the Guerrilla Girls seizes on the value of visibility in this system.

The Guerrilla Girls could writing scathing editorials to the *New York Times* all day long about the ill representation of women in the Metropolitan Museum, and their words would likely stay at the level of commentary. By appropriating visual modes to issue reproach, the Guerrilla Girls avail themselves of the operant forms in an inherited structure and exploit their self-awareness of their position in history. This is the move that necessitates visual representation and generates revision right before the public eye.

In this way, the work of the Guerrilla Girls can be read by composition-ists as an indication that visual media is worthy of attention not because a picture is worth a thousand words, a cliché that reinforces what T.J. Clark terms the self-evidence of seeing; not because there is some built-in "affor-dance" of visual representation that is distinct from writing, as Gunther Kress has sometimes suggested (78); not because visuals are simply hip or cool; and not, as Diana George makes clear, because students are some-how positioned as unsophisticated consumers of visual media who need to be inoculated against its harmful effects (32). Rather, the work of the Guerrilla Girls can be read as a call for compositionists to consider the role of visual media in writing because both forms of representation—visual and verbal—are coimplicated as producers and products of an inherited circuit of signs that carves out spaces for people to live and breathe.

To the extent that compositionists want students to be able to inter-vene in such a circuit, in what Min Zhan Lu calls "the living process of language" ("Composition's Word" 193), important pedagogical questions remain. How do we teach people to have some consciousness of historical and philosophical contexts like the ones Lloyd and Fraser describe, while also teaching them to employ active literate practices by which they may speak back to that history and philosophy? In other words, how do we teach subjects to both articulate and intercede in the context of symbolic rela-tions that affect their very lives? We are not faced here with an either/or choice. Just as we do not have to choose between visual and verbal compo-sition, we do not have to choose between analysis and design, thinking and doing, consumption and production, or reading and writing. The work of the Guerrilla Girls demonstrates just how tightly interwoven are modes of representation, social positions, rhetorical strategies, and historical-philo-sophical formations of gender, race, class, and bodily potential.

Susan Miller has suggested that compositionists have lost an awareness of this interweaving and erred on the side of unrelenting reflective anal-ysis. In "Technologies of Self?-Formation," she claims that "by teaching texts rather than their making, by teaching awareness rather than rhet-oric, and by teaching the power of meanings rather than the making of statements, we inadvertently reproduce a politics that is aware but passive" (499). Miller suggests we take a dose of "vulgar composition" (499). She believes writing courses "should focus on what powerful writers know and do" and direct students "toward practice in manipulating genres . . . toward Guerrilla stylistics . . . toward strength to withstand forces that prevent their critiques from wide acknowledgement" (499).

In the next section, I respond to Miller's suggestions for writing classes by positing the Guerrilla Girls as examples of powerful writers. I highlight a key productive strategy—appropriative reproach—that enables them to confront, dismantle, revise, reject, and resist sexism and racism in the art world, politics, film, and the culture at large. And I remind readers that looking at the Guerrilla Girls' work in a writing classroom does not restrict the people in our classes to the role of passive analysts, observing a powerful rhetorical practice from the outside—lest we forget that, in fact, the Guerrilla Girls could be anyone; they are everywhere.

APPROPRIATIVE REPROACH

I define appropriative reproach as taking possession of a commonly accepted or normalized form and altering it such that it is implicated in a design that disgraces, discredits, shames, or blames an offender, an offender who is often instrumental in the creation and maintenance of the appropriated object. In the opening image of this chapter, the Guerrilla Girls claim the form of the traditional nude and disrupt its typical appearance by adding the mask, changing the location of its display, and injecting words that question the credibility of a museum in which a large number of women ("nudes") are kept naked on the walls. Likewise, in Figure 3 the Guerrilla Girls take hold of the George W. Bush administration's rainbow colored terror alert chart by adding "for women" to the title.

Repetition of "President" as the first word in each level of warning identifies the offender who is to be disgraced, shamed, or blamed. True to form, each of the five warning levels issues an increasingly severe reproach; the lowest level simply mocks the president's cowboy antics, whereas the most severe level invokes the murder of innocent people.

In Figure 4, the *New York Times Magazine* masthead indicates the object being appropriated.

The group of men, who are piled together and posed in a studio, face the viewer directly. Arnold Glimcher, the man responsible for this scene, is seated front and center with his art world all-stars backing him up. The text directly below Glimcher on the magazine cover explains to viewers the substance and importance of the photo. Below this, in a signature typeface, the Guerrilla Girls issue their reproach: hormone imbalance, melanin deficiency. The Guerrilla Girls diagnose what is wrong with this picture and take both Glimcher and the *New York Times* to task for glorifying an exclusively white, male artistic ensemble.

Appropriative reproach, however, is not just a strategy for counterstatement or backlash. Figure 4 has less to do with Arnold Glimcher or the *New York Times* than with exposing the sexism and racism that are plastered across the cover of a national magazine. Similarly, Figure 3 is not just an

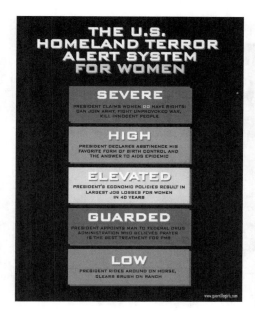

Figure 3. Copyright © 2003 Guerrilla Girls, Courtesy www.Guerrillagirls.com

Figure 4. Copyright © 1993 Guerrilla Girls, Courtesy www.Guerrillagirls.com

anti-Bush poster. As the title suggests, it is a poster for women. It is a feminist articulation of the global terror of war, disease, poverty, and a leadership out of touch. Indeed, Figure 1 may take issue with the Met, but it is the gendered subject-object dichotomy—the deeper problem reflected on the surface of that image—which holds the locus of the critique. Whether the Guerrilla Girls use a magazine cover, a government terror alert chart, a traditional nude, or—as we will see shortly in Figure 6—a movie poster that displays women in bikinis, these images are the status quo and are symptomatic of a world in which particular groups of people are rendered speechless, invisible, marginal, objectified, expendable. The Guerrilla Girls' effort to change this rendering is quite literally an effort to change how we see. Their work changes not only the image, but also the ways in which we think about the world that produces that image. In this sense, then, appropriative reproach is a strategy for revision in the most global sense.

MAKING FUN

The Guerrilla Girls show how forms of visual representation that have helped hold up dichotomous structures and annihilate subject positions can, in fact, be penetrated. The Guerrilla Girls make fun of such forms. And while not all of the Guerrilla Girls' representations do so by drawing

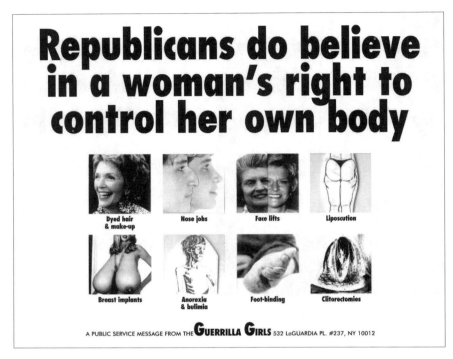

Figure 5. Copyright © 1995 Guerrilla Girls, Courtesy www.Guerrillagirls.com

upon the strategy I have labeled appropriative reproach, as evidenced by Figure 5, the full body of their work does contain a sarcasm, parody, irony, and humor that cannot be denied.

Figure 5 is representative of much of the Guerrilla Girls' work. Making bold written statements, the Guerrilla Girls most often directly and candidly address the public, using simple declarative sentences or rhetorical questions, set in thick, black no-nonsense type. Their visual work is matter-of-fact in tone and straightforward in style, relying like enthymeme on audiences' abilities to induce "correct" conclusions from declarations and questions as they are paired with statistics, lists, photographs, and statements of fact. Calling themselves the "conscience of the art world" and the "conscience of culture," the Guerrilla Girls serve the public with an ethos that combines whistle-blowing, objective revelation of evidence, and adjudication. Substantively, their representations can be read as public service messages. Stylistically, they make visible facts and predicaments that had been hidden, unknown, or avoided. In Figure 5, what is the connection between face-lifts and clitorectomies? Both are painful bodily mutilations; yet, placing visual representations of these practices in the context of a message about women's self-determination and political control yields some degree of ironic pleasure for sympathetic

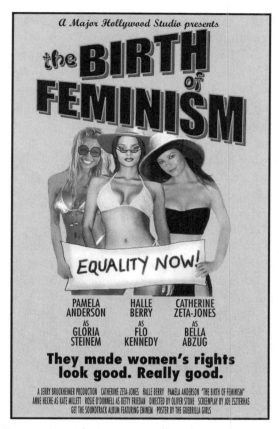

Figure 6. Copyright © 2001 Guerrilla Girls, Courtesy www.
Guerrillagirls.com

audiences—perhaps a smirk, if not an outright laugh. This pleasure is important as it marks a departure from earlier feminist approaches to the subject-object dichotomy. For example, in "Visual Pleasure and Narrative Cinema," Laura Mulvey also sees women enclaved in the "to-be-looked-at" position and ultimately suggests the destruction of pleasure as a radical antipatriarchal weapon that would work at the site of the scopophilic male spectator. She writes that "the ultimate challenge [is] how to fight . . . while still caught within the language of the patriarchy. There is no way we can produce an alternative out of the blue, but we can begin to make a break by examining the patriarchy with the tools it provides" (35). If pleasure was one such tool, Mulvey's suggestion resulted in a brand of progressive but anesthetic film. Absent pleasure, what reason do people have to go to the movies?

The Guerrilla Girls, on the other hand, provide pleasure. In Figure 6, for example, they work on material provided by "a major Hollywood studio."

They appropriate the common form of a movie poster and push the to-be-looked-at position to the point of farce. The pleasure they create is both embodied and derived from public visibility of injustices and hypocrisy rendered so ludicrous they are laughable. Indeed, there is some visceral satisfaction in the exercise of power we see in this poster. It is a remaking of matter that is clearly tied to the body, has implications for the body, and registers in the body when the viewer laughs. Perhaps this is why Miller refers to the kind of writing instruction she privileges as "vulgar composition" (499). Perhaps Miller would like for students, like the Guerrilla Girls, to be able to look at the world and, commanding a sarcasm that betrays deep analytic ability, create this statement: They made women's rights look good. Really good.

The jest the Guerrilla Girls take part in by creating representations like the ones I have showcased in this chapter does not displace the very real pain that was likely a motivating factor in their creation. In the context of bodies driven to commit literal and symbolic acts of violence upon each other and upon themselves, the pleasure the Guerrilla Girls provide is political. It generates strength to withstand war; it offers strategies to create peace. For these reasons, among others I have outlined here, the sort of visual/verbal work carried out by the Guerrilla Girls offers a rich site for analysis and production in composition classrooms.

14 AFFORDING NEW MEDIA
Individuation, Imagination, and the Hope of Change

Kristie Fleckenstein

On a dark stage, postindustrial music characterized by screeching electronic feedback loops and assorted noises fractures the silence. The skree of a computer connecting via modem to the internet complements the dissonant pulse of sounds. Then, an LED display, situated above the stage but still a part of the set, breaks the darkness, locating the play and the audience virtually. It flashes: *"Welcome to Trangress O Yes.Com . . . that's www.TOY. com! Real*Live* Bodies* Make* Art *4 * U!"* In the midst of the cacophonous sounds and disorienting visuals, two actors emerge from the wings, responding to the off-stage instructions of an invisible manager to change into their costumes for the night's activities.

So begins artist-activist Coco Fusco's searing one-act drama *The Incredible Disappearing Woman (IDW)*, a traveling social protest that Fusco has performed at four different international venues. Combining feminist performance art, activism, and twenty-first century multimedia, *IDW* takes advantage of the possibilities of new media technologies for social change and weds those possibilities to embodied actions. As an example of social action, this dramatic protest demonstrates new modes of citizenship and civic participation that integrate material and virtual technologies in ways that hold implications for the composition classroom, especially for teachers who envision writing as a tool for social action. My goal in this chapter is to explore those implications, focusing specifically on the interface of identity, symbol systems, and new media, which I define as any technology or combination of digital technologies that enables easy manipulation, replication, and distribution of representations of reality. As my title suggests, I ask how we might teach with new media so that we emancipate identity without repressing social action or denying the need for social action.

Drawing on Fusco's performance art project, I claim that new media can serve liberatory goals—both individual and collective—and can be taught in ways that serve those goals when aligned with what legal ethicist Drucilla Cornell calls the minimum qualifications of individuation: bodily integrity, access to symbol systems, and protection of the imaginary domain. I use Fusco's multimedia *IDW* to illustrate the activist possibilities of melding media sensitive to this triad of qualifications. I conclude by abstracting from this union of theory and activist-artistic performance a set of heuristics to generate classroom strategies for using use new media to foster individuation, invite participation in social change, and nurture collective action.

THE ACTIVIST POTENTIAL OF NEW MEDIA

Circulating throughout Fusco's *IDW* are three intertwined elements integral to social action—identity, symbol systems, and technology—and these three elements are equally significant to writing instruction, especially when the focus of that instruction is social action. Teaching writing as a means of social change inevitably requires dealing with identity: its constitution, its options, and its possibilities. For, if there is no agent of action—individual or collective—how, then, can there by any action? In addition, identity is also bound up in symbol systems; constructing identity involves access to and mastery of a particular array of organized symbols shared with a community. Psychologically and rhetorically, identity is created from the raw materials of those systems. This relationship between identity and symbol systems is rendered even more complex when we factor in the additional complication of technologies of production and dissemination. The means by which any identity is fashioned—the instruments through which symbol systems are physically manifested and distributed—influences the nature of the identity and the nature of the social action. For instance, the choice to create an identity via words through quill and foolscap or via images through Photoshop affects the material representations of the self. In addition, the means by which an identity is delivered to the audience—while standing in the agora, performing on stage, or contributing to a MySpace page—also influences the identity an author can create and the social action an author can advocate. Any mode of fabrication opens up or curtails options for identity and social action, highlighting that some identities are more readily available through particular media and less available through others. In a neat sleight of hand, media, then, are potentially both emancipatory and repressive, enabling some options while disabling others.

Fusco highlights the contradictory potential posed by new media technologies for identity and social action. For instance, she claims that, in spite of the performative element intrinsic to digital technologies, new media—through the ease of manipulation, replication, and distribution—tend to disengage bodies from minds, expelling bodies from the virtual imaginary (188).[1] It is not the enfleshed body that is represented via new

---

1. German writer-critic Tilman Baumgärtel notes that the dematerialization of bodies is a characteristic of all electronic media; however, the process is particularly acute with the rise of digital media, affecting art and activist art.

media; it is a coded construct that has no anchor or referent in the materi-al world and therefore no stakes in that world.[2] This expulsion of the body from the virtual imaginary has both aesthetic and political consequences. Disembodiment hides (and detaches) not only the enfleshed user, but also the material act and impoverished situation of the people who assemble the components of digital technologies (184–200). As material artifacts, technologies are literally produced in low-wage, outsourced factories by members of an underclass that, because of their socioeconomic position-ing, will likely never have access to these new media and thus never have access to the options for identity and social action enabled by these new media. The illusion of digital transcendence—that all identities are avail-able for all people with sufficient technological resources and savvy—over-writes the fact that new media carry with them the inequities of their own production even as they promise new modes of identity formation and pro-test.[3] Therefore, Fusco contends, any ethical use of new media must reveal an awareness of its own limits, the conditions of its own making, at the same time it celebrates its intrinsic possibilities. Otherwise, it diminishes hope for substantive individual and social change.

The incorporation of new media into a composition classroom focused on writing as social action, then, requires that we teach with technologies in ways that increase our students' options for identity making and social justice by increasing their engagement with (rather than disengagement from) material realities. Such a requirement is even more pressing with the increasing digital expertise of Generation M: students who arrive in writ-ing classrooms with digital proficiency and digital habits, including disen-gagement, already in place. Legal ethicist Drucilla Cornell provides a the-oretical construct—the three minimum qualifications for individuation—that can serve as a blueprint, a heuristic, for generating a socially active new media writing pedagogy.

THE MINIMUM QUALIFICATIONS OF INDIVIDUATION

Identity and social change are integral to Cornell's agenda as a legal ethi-cist and her efforts to evolve a means by which legal decisions concerning controversial issues such as pornography, abortion, and sexual harassment can be resolved in ways that support individuation. The primary purpose of any law is to provide a safe space for people to develop their personhood, their individual identities, Cornell asserts. Cornell defines personhood as

---

2. Jeff Rice makes this point implicitly in *The Rhetoric of Cool* by his elision of corporeality in digital writing. In making his case about "cool" as a metaphor for new media writing, Rice identifies five characteristics—appropriation, juxtaposition, commutation, nonlin-earity, and imagery—none of which is linked to users' material realities and investments.

3. David M. Sheridan, Jim Ridolfo, and Anthony J. Michel make exactly this point in their nuanced account of access (807–13).

an active rather than a static or stable entity. Identity is always an unfinished project, "a possibility, an aspiration which . . . can never be fulfilled once and for all" (*Imaginary* 5). People have an array of "personae"—imposed and assumed versions of identity—that are experienced wholly or partially, voluntarily or involuntarily. Personhood results from the "endless process of working through personae"; identity is what "shines through" the personae, and that shining through is what must be protected (4). "For a person to shine through, she must first be able to imagine herself as whole even if she knows that she can never truly succeed in becoming whole or in conceptually differentiating between the 'mask' and the 'self'" (5).

To protect this process of individuation, however, something other than the current legal gold standard is required. At present, Cornell explains, the means by which questions involving sexually charged cases are resolved depends on a hard-won, but flawed, precept: the assertion that women are equal to men. The criterion of equality fails to support the necessary process of individuation because it elides the very real material differences between men and women. In addition, the equality criterion is problematic because it fails to provide a space for sexual identities that are not heterosexually based. Thus, judging a law's adequacy on the basis of its equality reduces the scope of a citizen's efforts to develop identities differentiated from both male and heterosexual norms.[4]

In place of this flawed criterion, Cornell proposes a triad of the minimum qualifications for individuation—bodily integrity, access to symbol systems, and protection of the imaginary domain—as a means to assess the degree to which a law is just or unjust. The key question to ask in regard to any law—in its creation, application, and revision—is, How well does a law preserve the minimum conditions for individuation? This triad can also be fruitfully used to shape and answer key questions in composition studies: How might we shape a new media writing assignment to foster social action, and how well does that assignment preserve the minimum conditions for individuation? Just as each element of Cornell's triad of bodily integrity, access to symbol systems, and protecting the imaginary domain is essential for legal decisions, so can it also be productive for generating new media pedagogy for a writing classroom focused on identity building and social change.

---

4. Although focused predominantly on women's issues in the public sphere, Cornell's arguments are equally applicable and equally powerful when applied to people marginalized by race, ethnicity, class, or disability. Because the white, middle-class, heterosexual male identity continues to be taken as the norm—that is, it sets the bar against which all other identities must be measured to ensure equality—the criterion of equality jeopardizes the individuation project of anyone who cannot comfortably assume that persona. Thus, while Cornell provides examples and builds arguments based on her concern with individuation for women, her precepts can be easily and fruitfully applied to the individuation project of all people, particularly those who do not align for whatever reason with the legal norm.

The first criterion of bodily integrity functions on both a material and imaginary plane. Bodily integrity refers to an individual's right to protect his or her body and to make decisions concerning that body. It encompasses the right of an individual to travel freely without fear of physical or psychological assault; it protects the right of every person to pursue sexual satisfaction and make reproductive decisions without interference from the state. Thus, arguments concerning a woman's access to abortion would no longer focus on issues of individual privacy, which is the current foundation for Roe v. Wade, but on the element of bodily integrity. For instance, a woman's ability to pursue abortion as a legal option should be based on her right to determine the limits, purposes, and boundaries of her own body. Such a right is crucial to her individuation, her development of an identity that ensures happiness.

The criterion of bodily integrity also includes the imaginary as well as the corporeal body: one's ability to conceive of different ways of being in a body, different ways of realizing what Cornell calls a *sexuate* identity, from homosexuality and bisexuality to transgendering. The legal implications of the imaginary body are just as far reaching as the legal impact of the corporeal body. To illustrate, the criterion of imaginary bodily integrity justifies the existence of zoning laws designed to prevent a business (or a website) from exhibiting sexually explicit literature, photos, or paraphernalia in window displays (or home pages). Such laws would protect passersby (or internet surfers) from the assault of images that insult their imaginary bodies (*Imaginary* 103). However, these zoning laws would not prevent the sale of these materials because such products offer individuals alternative visions of sexual identity; therefore, the materials themselves would not be considered illegal. Protecting the integrity of the imaginary body protects an individual's ability to choose what images will form and inform the repertoire of that body.

The second minimum condition of individuation is access to symbol systems, and the importance of this qualification is also twofold. It includes an individual's access to various means of acting in the world through symbol systems. Thus, any law needs to be assessed for its ability to promote or infringe on a citizen's potential for learning the intricacies of a symbol system, laying claim to the technologies necessary to enact that symbol system, and entering into public spaces where the products of that symbol system can be deployed. What is necessary, Cornell argues, is the "proliferation of imaginaries" through multiple symbol systems (*Imaginary* 104), which means that all people are owed by their society an education that ensures mastery of many different symbol systems. Like bodily integrity, access to symbol systems also includes an imaginary dimension. People need access to a repertoire of many symbol systems—many different ways of self-representation—so they can develop and explore a robust matrix of personae. The greater their mastery of different symbol systems, the more varied is their access to renarrating and resymbolizing the self. Reducing access to symbol systems impoverishes a person's possibilities for individuation. It truncates the project of developing a self and, through that self, happiness.[5]

Finally, protecting the imaginary domain is the most important of the three minimum conditions of individuation, for it links to both bodily integrity and symbol systems. In *At the Heart of Freedom*, Cornell asserts that an essential, and overlooked, element of the fight for women's legal and social equality is the "protection of each person's imaginary domain, that psychic and moral space in which we, as sexed creatures who care deeply about matters of the heart, are allowed to evaluate and represent who we are" (x). Borrowing from bell hooks, Cornell claims that the imaginary domain serves a "location of recovery," within which women can conceive of an identity and a reality that moves them out of matrices of abuse. "The imaginary domain is the space of the 'as if' in which we imagine who we might be if we made ourselves our own end and claimed ourselves as our own person" (8). She illustrates the work of the imaginary domain through an example from hooks, who describes the necessity of rescuing herself from a family matrix wherein she was "routinely tortured and emotionally persecuted" and finding that rescue in performance art, "in the ritual of inventing a character who could not only speak through me but also for me" (qtd. in Cornell 9). This "location of recovery" that hooks describes is what Cornell perceives as the imaginary domain, an essential element of selfhood and freedom. Within the imaginary domain, an individual can "re-present" the self in different guises and personas from an "other space," and thus embody a self "not ensnared in the matrix of abuse" (9).

Cornell is concerned with the ways in which these minimum conditions, particularly the protection of the imaginary domain, which relies on both bodily integrity and access to symbol systems, can be used to determine the responsibilities of the state for defending an individual's right to pursue personhood. But Cornell's precepts can serve as heuristics for creating, critiquing, and teaching composition with new media. Because this triad of factors emphasizes the material realities of human bodies, thus keeping at bay the simulacrum where the real is rendered inconsequential by a variety of social and legal factors, the three minimum qualifications provide a means to shape new media pedagogy that enriches identity formation and offers new modes of social engagement. One way to envision the possibilities of Cornell's triad for the identity building necessary for social

---

5. See Adam Banks, especially chapter 4, for an account of the cost of limited access for African American identity and social action.

action is to see them circulating through a protest event. Coco Fusco's performance art, especially her provocative *IDW*, provides a concrete enactment of Cornell's minimum qualifications in an artistic and activist context, offering a pragmatic illustration of the way new media can beneficially contribute to both identity formation and social action.

INDIVIDUATION, NEW MEDIA, AND SOCIAL ACTION

Cornell notes that artists serve an important function in terms of individuation. They "unleash the imaginary" by finding different ways to resymbolize and renarrate identity. By discovering new identities, these artists also discover new options for social action. Fusco does exactly that. Through her evocative feminist activist art, she demonstrates how people, especially women, might use new media to reshape subjectivities and realities that resist personal and social matrices of abuse, and, by so doing, enact social change. The roots of *The Incredible Disappearing Woman* are buried deep in Fusco's activism, particularly her desire to bring visibility to the women murdered and missing around the Cuidad Juarez area. In addition, Fusco uses new media to highlight the degree to which the entire realm of digital and virtual worlds can be a tool for social injustice as well as social justice. Encompassing live performance, film, still photography, and a simulated digital chatroom whose participants dictate the actions of the performers, the one-act play explores the entangled relationship between art and ethics, virtual bodies and real bodies, digital emancipation and economic deprivation. Cornell's minimum conditions of individuation circulate through *IDW*, suggesting the possibilities of a new media composition pedagogy that is imaginative, critical, and socially engaged.[6]

The drama consists of a complex amalgamation of stories within stories, media within media, and identities within identities. For instance, the set, which I described in my opening paragraph, features three different places that constantly shift identities, teetering always between the real and the imaginary. The major physical site consists of a diorama of an art museum exhibit: an examination table with a mannequin lying under a sheet (fig 1). The storyline connected to the diorama concerns a museum's efforts to resurrect a twenty-year-old transgressive performance art project involving an act of necrophilia with a rented corpse. In the back of the diorama is a screen where, during various moments in the play, the action and conversations of a museum opening are projected. Flickering characters involved in this storyline include the curator, docents, guests, and the controversial

---

6. My analysis of *The Incredible Disappearing Woman* is based on the script Fusco and two other actors performed at four international venues. Fusco generously provided the performed version of the script, which differs significantly from the 1999 version published in *The Bodies That Were Not Ours*.

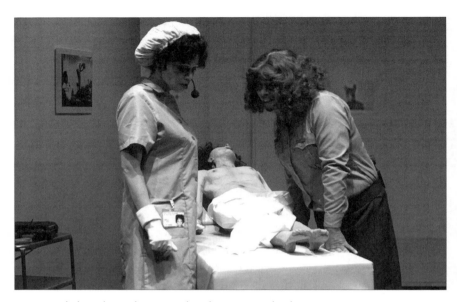

Figure 1: Chela and Magaly contemplate the corpse in the diorama

artist himself (fig 2). However, in the reality of the play, this diorama is not a museum opening at all; it is not the site of a re-incarnated performance art project. Instead, it is primarily a set created for the internet sex trade, which draws in the second storyline. The museum diorama is Room 13, designed for online clients with a taste for necrophilia. The third area of the stage, slightly separated from the diorama, is the actors' dressing area. Here, two of the three main characters, Rick (Magaly) and Julie (Chela), take their instructions from an off-stage manager who tells them that, for the evening's work, they are to assume the costumes of museum employees charged with preparing the museum for an opening. This small area integrates a third storyline that goes underground in the play: the account of people disappearing into identities over which they have no control in response to economic needs and at the behest of others who purchase them (fig 3).

Three troubling and implicitly linked phenomena, each trembling on the edge of what Fusco calls the abject interface of bodies and machines, inspire the sets and storylines of *IDW*, and each phenomenon highlights the importance Cornell's three conditions of individuation: bodily integrity, access to symbol systems, and deliberate, conscious maintenance of the imaginary domain. First, *IDW* directly and explicitly grapples with both the real and imaginary dimensions of bodily integrity. An initial inspiration for the play and the source of the diorama and film action is a literal necrophiliac moment from the 80s reincarnated at the turn of the millennium, and this storyline highlights the crucial issue of bodily integrity.

Figure 2: Flickering images frame Chela's words and actions.

Figure 3: Chela and Magaly perform for the clients.

The historical instance of necrophilia was part of a performance art project created by a Los Angeles-based male artist in the 80s, who videotaped his own vasectomy and included, as part of that project, an audiotape recording his final ejaculation of live semen into the body of a female corpse. The artist, unable to acquire a deceased body in the States, traveled to Mexico, where he was able to "rent" the body of a deceased woman, which he then used as a dead receptacle for his last live seed (195). To perform his art, the artist required "another place and another person [to] serve him in silence and then, disappear," Fusco says (196). While the performance drew condemnation in the 80s, Fusco recounts that the artist's work was unearthed for a major museum exhibit in Los Angeles twenty years later.

Both dimensions of bodily integrity—the enfleshed body and the imaginary body—concern Fusco in this troubling moment of art history. Beyond the violation to and of the body, ethically fraught as it is, Fusco protests the disappearance of that enfleshed body in the debates evoked by the project. This troubling moment is featured in the play through the action in the museum projected on the screen at stage back and through the characters' reenactment of that moment. At various points in the play, the curator, docents, and artist disinter the ethical debate, demonstrating through their conversation and actions the disappearance of the deceased body as a factor in the discussions of the art. *IDW* grapples with the absolute necessity of protecting the body, ensuring that bodily integrity—both the body's real and imaginary dimensions—is a focal point of ethical action and debates assessing any action's ethicality. But protecting the body extends beyond the debates about art. Not only does it encompass living bodies, but it also foregrounds the necessity for bodily integrity in identity formation: the repeated violation of the sex workers' real bodies and imaginary bodies.

Rick and Julie, as Magaly and Chela, cede control of their bodies, responding to the demands from their online clients to engage in various sexually charged actions: "stage a cat fight," "show some skin," and "dry hump." The clients dictate, and the sex workers respond. Layered on to this violation of bodily integrity in Room 13 is the violation of their bodies in the stories the characters recount. The third character, Dolores, half woman and half robot utility cart, tells of a tale of spousal abuse. During moments when a cataleptic ailment causes her to lose consciousness and mimic death, Dolores is beaten by her husband. Her priest counsels Dolores to pray while abused, using words that evoke violent religious images of penetration by an angelic flaming spear. Magaly was taken, tortured, and raped by the Chilean secret police; she lived only because she pretended to be a corpse during her rape. Chela loses her job, her livelihood, and access to her child when a sexual encounter with her factory supervisor, during which she is drugged insensible, goes awry. Repeatedly, the characters reveal in different ways the extent to which their physical and imaginary bodies are harmed.

Second, intertwined with the exploitation of bodily integrity is Cornell's concern with access to symbol systems. However, for Fusco, especially in *IDW*, the problem is the impoverishment or denial of that access. *IDW* grows out of Fusco's three-year investigation of the hundreds of murders and disappearances of mostly young female workers at the low-wage assembly-line factories that have sprung up in northern Mexico following NAFTA. Without a doubt, the literal loss of life highlights the need for bodily integrity. But equally important to these physical disappearances is the symbolic erasure of these women: their silence and their silencing within the symbolic order. The denial of access to symbolic power manifests itself in *IDW* through the reality of the sex workers' lives. For instance, Magaly and Chela perform according to the dictates of their internet clients, who speak to them but to whom they cannot speak back—except as anything other than what they are imagined to be by these clients. The buyers' words, always mediated by some digital technology, determine what the two do, but those words also determine the extent to which the characters can speak. Numerous times in the play, the physically absent but virtually present clients demand that the sex workers do more and say less. In addition, the clients control how the sex workers speak, not only insisting on a certain kind of conversational content but also imposing particular accents on those voices. For instance, one client, Sergei, continually orders Magaly and Chela to speak their improvised dialogue with an accent. Essentially, the workers are manipulated through a technological and symbolic interface, an interface that ensures their livelihood but over which they exercise no control.

Third, *IDW* attends to Cornell's commitment to the imaginary domain, which Fusco calls the "virtual imaginary." For Fusco, new media hold both promise and threat. She is tempted by the possibilities of the international reach of new media digitally disseminated, but this temptation is balanced by her fear of the disembodiment she associates with such dissemination. Because of the ease with which new media control, replicate, and distribute products, new media lure users into the erroneous belief that product is separate from producer and consumer. The misconception easily promulgated by new media is that the flesh of the audience/composer is unaffected by anything that might be done through new media itself. The malleable simulacrum is manipulated, not the real person. Thus, the only phenomenon affected is the immaterial product itself. It is exactly this false separation that Fusco aims to disrupt. Her strategy consists of what she calls a critical social-materialist orientation: performing new media in ways that constantly call attention to their existence as media. A social-materialist orientation protects Cornell's imaginary domain, as is evident in the revision the play underwent between the original published script (1999) and the final 2003 performance version.

Two major changes between the textual and performance versions highlight Fusco's efforts to protect the imaginary domain through a critical social-materialist orientation to new media: her choice to situate the action within the context of a virtual chatroom and the transformation of Dolores into a cyborg, a human utility cart serving as a mount for a laptop computer. The action of the 1999 version takes place in the museum, not in a simulated museum set staged for the sexual arousal of digitally mediated clients. The radical switch in scene and the deliberate sandwiching of virtual reality between bitter material realities opens the door to a critique of digital technologies. The continual and repeated violations of bodies—the sex workers perform nightly—is enabled by digital technologies that invite the clients to disregard the physical existence of those they view. The "jo-blo commandoes" perceive little actual difference between the projections of the screen and the antics of the sex workers. Both the flickering film images and the sex workers are designed for their enjoyment, to whom they are not answerable. With the distancing enabled by digital technologies, neither images nor workers deserve material or ethical consideration because both are categorized as not real, as unanchored from the real. By changing the venue from museum space to chatroom space, Fusco is able to critique the new media that enable the performance.

The second change concerns the character Dolores, who in the 2003 version becomes a half-human, half-machine utility cart. Dolores comes arrayed with a laptop computer—she is "topped" by that computer with all the sexual implications—and it is through the computer that the clients, two through typed commands and two through oral commands, dictate the characters' actions. The transformation of Dolores from poignant abuse victim taking confused comfort from violent religious imagery into a cyborg medium of the sex trade offers a searing assessment of attitudes fostered by unreflective use of technology, including new media. Crippled by technology and crippled as technology, Dolores symbolizes the degree to which new media embraced uncritically can hobble users.

IDW is a complex amalgamation of embodiment and disembodiment, imagination and material reality, virtuality and physicality. Through its performance and its critique of new media, it becomes a location of recovery, a product *of* the imaginary domain that simultaneously protects that imaginary domain even as it enlarges the scope of the imaginary domain. *IDW* highlights the ways in which Cornell's minimum conditions of individuation can take concrete form and serve an activist agenda. At the same time, *IDW* holds within it a lesson, a warning, about the nature of social action in an age permeated with the easily replicable products of new media. To protect bodily integrity, access to symbol systems, and especially the imaginary domain, author-artists who use new media for social action must be self-consciously critical of new media. As an exploration and comment on identity and social action through new media, Fusco, in combination with Cornell's theoretic construct, provides both an exemplar of the possibilities of new media for social action and a heuristic for generating new media writing pedagogy that keeps it real for both identity and social action.

AFFORDING NEW MEDIA IN THE CLASSROOM

While the eruption and wild proliferation of new media "posit new modes of consumption," Fusco says, they also "call for new concepts of citizenship and engagement with the public sphere" (192). Composition teachers who incorporate new media into their classrooms have a unique opportunity to foster these new concepts of citizen identity and public action. They can "afford" new media by returning continually to the three minimum qualifications of individuation that Cornell proposes and Fusco enacts; using these three qualifications as guidons, compositionists have a better chance fashioning a new media writing pedagogy that welds identity to social action and resists the temptation of digitally charged media to disembody users and disconnect consumers from the realities of abuse. Thus, inspired by Fusco, I take Cornell's minimum qualifications to conclude with descriptions of classroom activities that foster identity formation and social action through new media. I draw on the work of two undergraduate students responding to two different assignments to provide illustrations of outcomes: Jackie Desarro, who, while enrolled in an introduction to women's studies course taught by Carmen D. Siering at Ball State University, created a blog for what her instructor called an "activist project," designed "to extend what the students have learned in the classroom to the larger campus and/or local community in some way"; and Christina Hough, who, while enrolled in my upper-division composition theory and practice course, created a pop culture blog in response to an assignment requiring cultural critique disseminated through a digital medium. Initiated by different assignments, both students chose blogging as their vehicle and both students used their blogs as starting points for further activism.

1. Protecting Access to Symbol Systems

Without access to multiple symbol systems and technologies of production/dissemination, people are constrained in their options for individuation, Cornell asserts. Fusco dramatically illustrates the cost of symbolic impoverishment through the physical and cultural silencing of Magaly, Chela, and Dolores. The New London Group explicitly notes the importance of multiple symbol systems and technologies for social change. Designing "social futures" and fostering social change, they note, demands attention to modes of meaning making that extend beyond the textual, beyond print technologies, and beyond a single English (64). Thus, crafting activities that lend themselves to social action requires that teachers open up those assignments to new media options and encourage the use of multiple symbol systems. This does not mean that all assignments within a writing class must rely on digital media; however, it does mean that a significant portion of those assignments must include the use of digital media as an option.

Siering's activist project demonstrates one way of addressing the criterion of access. For example, her assignment does not stipulate that students use any particularly medium. In fact, they are instructed to choose their own topic, encouraged to work in groups, requested to photograph or videotape their projects, and urged to contact campus and local newspapers for additional exposure. Nowhere does Siering stipulate how her students are to accomplish their self-selected tasks. So some students created and physically distributed print brochures about feminist issues on a campus street corner; some created and posted flyers throughout the campus; some defied campus restrictions to draw chalk images on sidewalks. And some, like Jackie, chose to pursue a digital project. As Siering comments, "the internet provided a great opportunity for activism," and Jackie, a digital neophyte, discovered that potential. Inspired by her horrifying experiences with a dislodged Mirena intrauterine contraceptive device that required painful and expensive surgery to remove, Jackie designed a blog, *The Mirena Mishap*, to share her story with anyone who would listen.[7] The blog became her first salvo in an effort to "redirect the common experiences, anger, and sense of solidarity" of Mirena victims away from passive acceptance into active resistance. As she notes, her blog and the responses it evoked remind her "of how the women's movement first began—with just a couple of women talking to a few more and taking their personal experiences into the light of public activism."

An assignment that did not require new media but that provided space for digital options inspired Jackie to make her first foray into feminist activism. A different assignment, one stipulating that students engage in a digital cultural critique, led Christina to use multiple symbol systems to address the control exercised over women by various hegemonic institutions, from government to religion.[8] Taking advantage of the technological possibilities of the internet, Christina deliberately sought to design a blog where text, still photography/illustrations, and video talk back and forth. For instance, in her post "Christianity and Death," Christina opens with a painting of a woman who, with her feet tied and her arms supporting her, holds on her lap a tray of bloody instruments, evoking associations with female circumcision. This image is followed with a textual post surveying the role of Christianity in the subordination of women. The post concludes with a *YouTube* video, "Free Yourself from Religious Propaganda," that functions as Christina's call to action. Thus, through still images, words, and music, Christina lays out a problem—the historical subordination of women, especially through Christianity—and suggests a solution, all by means of different symbol systems. Through such a multifaceted array, Christina's blog communicates her feminist-activist agenda on overlapping and reinforcing levels.

---

7. Jackie's blog, *The Mirena Mishap*, is available at http://mirenamishap.blogspot.com

8. Christina's blog, *The Mind of Philonous*, is available at http://christinaphilonous.blogspot.com

While the use of new media technologies does not automatically ensure that the designer incorporates multiple symbol systems, it does encourage the incorporation of meaning-making modes that extend beyond language. In the process, assignments that allow for the use of new media increase students' access to symbol systems and thus increase their options for identity formation and social action.

2. Protecting Real and Imaginary Bodies

Intertwined with access to symbol systems is bodily integrity, which highlights the necessary consideration of physical and imaginary bodies. Even when created for an academic class, writing with new media is performance art, and performance art, Fusco explains, is almost inevitably centered on the artist's body. It is art designed to direct attention in specific ways to the body. But it is also *not* about the body. It both is and is not an amalgamation of the enfleshed and the imaginary body. Such a complicated interface between lived and imagined embodiment, with responsibility to both, lies at the heart of Fusco's *IDW* as Magaly, Chela, and Dolores struggle with the abuse of their real bodies and their ability to imagine themselves in different bodies. Practically speaking, for our classroom activities the criterion of bodily integrity translates into a deliberate focus on corporeal and imaginary bodies, something that we may accomplish by encouraging techniques such as witnessing and kinetic rhetoric.

Witnessing counters the dangers of digital passivity. New media, Fusco warns, foster a passive, not an active, access to symbol systems. The stance of the passive consumer is one small step from the stance of the detached creator, who produces an artifact through new media but remains separate from that artifact. Without an investment in the artifact, Fusco asserts, the producer too easily steps away from the implications of his or her product, just as the clients from the internet sex room in *IDW* eschew responsibility for their acts. Thus, media blogger Donna Bogatin scorns student activism in the digital age, claiming that it is "self-centered and effortless," a kind of point-and-click activism with low stakes in both digital and real worlds.[9] Fusco advocates countering such potential passivity through witnessing: "Following the methods that have been elaborated by other cyber-activist efforts, political engagement begins with assuming the role of witness, exercising pressure via oppositional surveillance tactics and refusing the role of passive consumer" (201). New media activities, then, in our composition classrooms might more effectively serve an activist agenda when a component of witnessing is deliberately integrated.

Jackie's blog demonstrates the potential of witnessing for shaping community and eliciting collective as well as individual action. To begin, her

---

9. See Lenhart, Kahne, Middaugh, Macgill, Evans, and Vitak for an alternative view.

initiating post recounts in simple language and heartbreaking detail her first-hand experience with a Mirena IUC. The difficulties began with "enormous amount of pain and pressure in my left abdomen," resulting from the migration of her IUC from her uterus to a position between her "left ovary and fallopian tube." In addition to the pain, Jackie describes her sense of betrayal: "I had previously researched this product and had never read any information about the device migrating. I felt let down by my doctor, and most of all the company, Mirena." Her health, as well as future pregnancies, threatened by the migration, Jackie underwent surgery, missing two weeks of her senior year in college and incurring immense medical debt. Through her straightforward and affecting account of her difficulties, Jackie stands as a witness to the very injustice she seeks to alter.

In addition, her moment of testimony invites similar instances of witnessing. Gloria Anzaldúa notes that "the ability to respond is what is meant by responsibility" (21), and through joint witnessing Jackie's blog invites a shared responsibility for the integrity of a woman's body. The sixteen respondents to Jackie's initial post disclosed similar experiences (and fears) concerning a Mirena IUC, revealed stories of difficulties connected with other birth control devices, or communicated offers to help. The power of a single witnessing elicited further witnessing, leading many respondents to encourage Jackie to take her efforts to publicize the dangers of IUCs one step further.

A second way that assignments can be created to protect bodily integrity through witnessing consists of practicing what Dene Grigar calls "kinetic rhetoric." Grigar analyzes the work of two feminist artists to suggest that effectively integrating new media into the composition classroom requires reconceptualizing composition as kinetic rhetoric and student writers as kinetic rhetors. She argues that the protest art of her subjects creates a rhetoric that repositions bodies, particularly women's bodies, as intrinsic to both the content and performance of new media artifacts. The protest art projects created by the artists she examines "break decorum [overt and covert rules of civilized behavior] and is accomplished through the use of the body," a process that includes both the artist's body and the audience member's body (112). The resulting kinetic rhetoric constitutes a means of persuasion that relies on physical activity and offers a "deliberate and sustained confrontation for the purpose of effecting change" (110). The two-prong emphasis the artists give to bodies as the subject of their art and bodies as integral to the experience of that art suggests that bodily integrity in the new media composition classroom can be fruitfully emphasized through sustained attention to writing as kinetic rhetoric, which requires students to see themselves not only as rhetors but also as artist-rhetors.

Christina's blog reveals an effort to construct a kinetic rhetoric by soliciting a kinetic response from her readers. Although lacking the digital expertise to fashion a game or a performance-art project similar to those created by the artist-activists Grigar studies, Christina does organize her blog so that entries speak to each other within and across the various posts. For instance, elements of her opening poem resonate to a music video accompanying a post on Christianity and death. Lines like "you are the nest in the tress" link to lyrics and images of "Free Yourself From Religious Propaganda" so that each component reinforces the other. In addition, the series of quotes in her third post, focusing particularly on feminist struggles, provides a context for a video from a Canadian news program about male equality that ends her last post. Thus, to experience Christina's blog fully, the reader must do more than sequentially scan the various entries, moving from top to bottom without retracing steps. Instead, the reader must physically engage with the site by scrolling back and forth across entries, constantly moving between opening poem and closing critique. The blog functions as a gestalt, requesting that viewers engage kinetically with the material, emphasizing the importance of their bodily engagement.

As both Jackie and Christina illustrate, the criterion of bodily integrity suggests new ways teachers might think about the media-body connection, inviting us to craft activities that approach new media as portals to both real and imaginary bodies. We can separate neither literacy nor rhetoric from embodiment. The need to emphasize bodily integrity and to protect bodily integrity, then, becomes integral to the teaching of composition with and through new media.

3. Protecting the Imaginary Domain through Materialist Critique

Cornell's third criterion, and, perhaps, the most important, consists of protecting the imaginary domain, the safe space of recovery within which we dream of different realities. One way composition teachers can design activities that protect the realm of the "as if" and "what if" is through the systematic inclusion of social-materialist critique. As Fusco demonstrates in *The Incredible Disappearing Woman*, a critical orientation is essential to a healthy and robust imaginary domain. It is not enough to employ new media to imagine identity and realities. New media composers must also self-critique. Otherwise, they risk technological seduction: the belief that technology is the only reality. Fusco asks: "How can technologies that are promoted as the means of dissecting the physical world, of extending our physical and mental capacities, and of creating an imaginative realm beyond the social be brought to bear imaginatively upon the social itself?" (199–200). Social-materialist critique is her answer. Thus, *IDW* is both a new media performance and a commentary on that performance. It attends to the ways in which new media constrain identity and the ways the material existence of new media impinge on (or grow out of) a particular set of social uses and discourses, a process that seeks to protect the potential of the imaginary domain.[10] What this criterion invites, then, are classroom activities that turn around on the performance of new media to extend or transform that performance through different kinds of commentary.

Jackie provides one example of protecting the imaginary domain through social-materialist critique. While her blog provides an enactment through new media of her tragedy—a narrative of her travails with the Mirena IUC—the aftermath functions as a critique of that narrative. She explains:

> From negative experiences with the hormones in birth control pills to doctors who treat women like uneducated lab rats, the stories the women shared on this blog showed me that more needs to be done about this dysfunctional birth control epidemic. The more I think about it, the more I'm sure this is a movement in the making. Women can only tolerate victim-blaming for so long before they recognize that their personal stories can, and should, have political impact.

Jackie's post-blogging activities thus serve as her social-materialist commentary, for she seeks to transform her trauma narrative into aggressive activism. The experience of witnessing via blogging brings to her a cadre of like-minded women, a discovery that changed her into a feminist activist, she says. As a result of this epiphany, Jackie not only plans to use her blog as a site of community activism for women with similar experiences—a place where they can share stories, sympathy, and support—but also a site where they can imagine ways of assailing this medical injustice together. As a community of activists, they can imagine a world where women are not medical victims and then systematically work to bring about change. To this end, Jackie announces that she has hired a lawyer to help her begin that process.

---

10. The importance of a social-materialist self-critique is highlighted not only by Fusco's performance in *IDW*, but also by the scholarship in computers and composition. Charles Moran, in his twenty-year retrospective of *Computers and Composition*, claims, in fact, that the decade of the 90s is characterized by such a critical orientation. Writing at the end of that decade, Cynthia L. Selfe argues for the importance of "paying attention" to technology, "thinking about what we are doing and understanding at least some of the important implications of our actions," a critical orientation to the complex intersections between digital technologies and literacy ("Technology and Literacy" 414). Finally, speaking specifically of new media, Anne Frances Wysocki contends that any medium becomes a new medium when users approach a communication technology with a self-reflexive critique of product and production (15). She argues that writing teachers are particularly well suited to practice critique because they "can bring to new media texts a humane and thoughtful attention to materiality, productions, and consumption, which," she points out, "is currently missing" (7). Particularly important to Fusco's agenda is her contention that social-materialist critique serves to protect what she calls the "virtual imaginary" and what Cornell calls the "imaginary domain."

A second example of a social-materialist critique that, like Jackie's, aims to protect the imaginary domain, is provided by Christina, particularly through the work she pursued outside my class. A student who dreams of pursuing an advanced degree in human rights, upon graduation, Christina came to me toward the end of our semester together to invite me to serve as the faculty advisor to a new venture she was undertaking with the help of two friends: the creation of an online magazine-forum where people could participate in a civic sphere that valued their poetic, rhetorical, and activist work. Conceived weeks after her blogging experience, *Everyday Adrenaline* serves a vision of the world wherein gender, racial, and environmental abuses are rectified.[11] At the heart of *Everyday Adrenaline* is an imagined world in which violence and injustice are the exceptions, not the rule. Thus, the online magazine-forum opens up a public space where participants can imagine a better world and work toward its realization. To this end, the cocreators have established a range of discussion topics, ranging from a general discussion forum with conversations focused on individual and community activism, to "topics of interest," like philosophy, humor, society, and science. In addition, the cocreators have created sites where members can post their creative material, seeing poetry, visual art, and rhetoric as essential to imagining different goals for world building. While her blog initiated her activism, Christina recognized the limits of that forum for initiating the kind of activism she desired. She critiqued and, through that critique, determined the necessity of devising a vehicle that provides a larger sphere of influence. In a post to *Everyday Adrenaline*, Christina articulates her vision:

> Do I only write to occupy myself; will anyone want to hear what I have to say? What if I can't say it strong enough or with words that work and are uncliched? Like, animals are our equals, god doesn't exist, and the only thing that can really matter is yourself and trying to make the world better. Everyone has different abilities, whether they are innate or socially constructed doesn't matter, and they all can implement for the greater good. While Brittney Spears is on the news with her ex-husband and children, there are starving people everywhere, rape, abuse, genocide, human trafficking; yes there are people trying to help, but imagine what could be done if we realized our true potential. We are the people, we are the problem, we have the power. There is no greater call to action. Words, language, supposed reality, alleged matter: these means give us the opportunity to stop all the major pain and suffering in the world.

Through *Everyday Adrenaline*, Christina systematically sets out to create a site that invites multiple participants and multiple kinds of participation in

---

11. *Everyday Adrenaline* is available at http://everydayadrenaline.com

the service of her larger goal of imagining a more humane world and working to protect that vision and bring that vision into being.

Regardless of the technology we privilege in our writing classrooms, regardless of our commitments to academic writing rather than performance art, affording new media requires attention to the minimum conditions of individuation. Teaching writing as a tool of social change requires a commitment to providing students with access to multiple symbol systems that offer a wide range of expression. In addition, such a pedagogical orientation demands as well a continual insistence on the importance of physical and imaginary bodies. Finally, writing for social action asks that we protect the imaginary domain so we can envision a different world, a world without abuse. We can afford new media for and in the socially active writing classroom if we remain sensitive to Cornell's minimum qualifications and enact them with the critical passion of Fusco's artist-activism.

PART 2
ACTIVITIES

MEDIATING BODIES ∧ MEDIATED BODIES

Following are activities that ask students to consider how they are embodied through—shaped by and shaping—relations that media encourage. Through articulating subject positions encouraged by different media and the activist possibilities of and for media, these activities ask students to take a mindful position in the media landscape.

ACTIVITY 1: TROPES OF EMBODIMENT

Growing out of issues of ethnicity, gender, and sexuality raised in "It's My Revolution" and "Drawn Together," this assignment asks students to consider how they identify themselves and then to examine online representations for these subject positions.

Objectives

- Explore popular representations of various subject positions.

- Interrogate the usefulness of particular categories for self-definition.

- Challenge tropes of embodiment.

Considerations

- This activity works from the self in order to open up discussions of race, class, gender, sexuality, and disability. If your class is homogenous, you may want to model a different identity to develop the discussion.

- This activity works best if the class members discuss their results together. This can be done via blog comments, a large in-class discussion, or in small groups.

- This activity can follow the social-tagging activity, using Delicious, described in the activities following part 1. This activity shows tagging related to photographs and identity as opposed to alphabetic texts, and so—with follow-up questions asking students to compare what is at stake when tagging writing and what is at stake when tagging or describing a photograph—can help students consider the complexities of tagging relative to media and identification.

Assignment

Overview

What identifiers do you use to refer to yourself? Are you a straight, Hawaiian, working-class woman? Are you a gay, disabled, white male? This assignment asks you to consider the accuracy of online representations for these categories.

Part 1

List the categories you think best describe you when it comes to race, ethnicity, class, gender, sexuality, and disability (as well as any other identifier important to you).

Part 2

Use your list to carry out *an image search* on Google for each identifier you wrote down. You will need to use different search terms (for example *white* will return very different images than *white people* or *white woman*). Take notes on the images that appear.

Part 3

Write a short response in which you address the following questions:
- Do the image search results match your understanding of this identifier? Why or why not?

- Were you surprised with the image results? Why or why not?

- What types of images would you like to see returned from your search?

- Do you believe the search results represent what most people picture when they think of this particular category of identification? In your opinion, is this an accurate representation?

- If someone developed a sense of this identification category based on the image search results, what would they think about people who identify with the category? What other sorts of representations would you wish to see show up in a search?

- What general conclusions does this activity encourage you to make about how people tag pictures online in relation to identity?

ACTIVITY 2: SOCIAL INTERFACES

This activity draws on all the chapters of part 2, asking students to consider the affordances and limitations of social-networking interfaces—and asking students to imagine otherwise. Through examining such interfaces, students confront how various multimodal design choices shape our understandings of self and each other.

Objectives

- Analyze rhetorically the design of online spaces.
- Complicate the concept of a universal user.
- Critique notions of effective design.

Considerations

- This assignment includes both in- and out-of-class work, but it is easily modified to for in-class use only.
- While the in-class work is designed for a computer lab, you can also provide printouts of social-networking sites for students to use.
- The final assignment asks students to create a social-networking site to represent themselves without consideration of others, but you could also ask students to design for others (for example, grandparents or local elementary school students).

In-Class Work

Pair up students and ask each pair to examine one social-networking site (SNS). So that the class looks across a wide range of such sites, assign sites in advance (such as Facebook, MySpace, Twitter, LinkedIn, Friendster, Bebo, Nexopia, Tagged, SkyRock, Orkut, and Babboo). To do detailed analyses, students will need either to have or to create a profile on the site they choose. If they don't feel comfortable doing so, just ask them to create a temporary dummy account.

Provide students with the following questions:

- If you are unfamiliar with the SNS, spend some time familiarizing yourself with the space. Do you find the SNS easy to use? Why or why not?
- Pay attention to the layout of the users' profiles. What element seems to be emphasized? (Notice the size and placement of the user's name, profile picture, information, friends, etc.)

- Do all user profiles look the same? If not, describe the key differences you see.

Regroup as a class, and have students briefly report on their findings. After these reports, engage the class in discussion around these questions:

- How do different SNSs emphasize different aspects of personality and/or identity? Consider age, ethnicity, class, religion, able-bodiness, occupation, location, values—any qualities that shape people.

- Does it seem that the layout of the SNS asks users to experience their relationships with their friends in particular ways? For example, how does Facebook's layout allow you to view/engage with your friends as compared to Twitter?

- Does the SNS ask you actively to think about the relationships you are establishing with others through the interface? Is there anything in the interface that asks you to stop and reflect on what you are writing or linking and how what you write or link might affect others and your relationship with them? Why might the SNS be designed to encourage—or not—such reflection?

- Is the SNS you examined one you already use? If not, is it one you might use if you had friends there? Why or why not?

- What type of people do you think are best suited to use the SNS you examined? Why?

Assignments

Overview

In class, you examined one SNS. This assignment asks you to spend time looking at two more, so that eventually you will have analyzed three SNSs. You will first write a short paper describing what you see as the audience and purpose for each SNS and how each design seems to compose its ideal user. Next, using any media available to you, you will create the interface for an SNS profile you feel would best suit the needs of you and your friends. Finally, you will present your SNS to the class.

Part 1: Report on Findings

After applying the questions from class to two more SNSs, write a short paper (two to four pages) that reports on your findings. Specifically, make a claim as to how each site composes its ideal user: Who does the interface of each site suggest would be its ideal user? Consider what this ideal user would want from their profile and their relationship (or lack thereof) with friends on the SNS. Make sure to describe specifically how the design and functionality work to suggest a certain type of user. If you're feeling stuck, consider what type of people would not necessarily find this SNS appealing.

Part 2: An SNS for your world

Now that you've examined the design and functionality of various SNSs, design your own. You can use software such as Photoshop or Paint, or you can draw or collage it on paper; use any medium available to you and with which you feel comfortable. Either way, you will design an SNS profile interface that you feel would work best for you and your friends. What do you want from an SNS site? What kind of relationships do you want to have with your friends? What type of interface do you want to look at when you're interacting with the site?

Part 3: The Presentation

Prepare and present a short (three to five minute) in-class presentation that will describe the choices you made in the design of your SNS.

In your presentation, describe the audience (what are you and your friends like?) and the site's purpose (what do you and your friends want out of SNS?).

Also describe how your design choices help to best serve this purpose for this audience by making connections between your purpose, audience, and design strategies.

ACTIVITY 3: VISUAL ACTIVISM

Growing out of "Visible Guerrillas" and "Affording New Media," this activity asks students to further consider the place of art and social action by exploring the affordances of public art.

Objectives

- Consider the role of visuals in creating rhetorical appeals.

- Examine the affordances of visuals for social action.

- Engage the role of context in rhetorical situations.

Considerations

- This activity is designed for one week of a class that meets two times per week. You can easily separate it out into three days by extending the discussion from day 1 into day 2.

Homework, Part 1

Ask students to familiarize themselves with Banksy (the political activist, graffiti artist, and painter) through looking at his website, www.banksy.co.uk, as well as by following the links from the *Wikipedia* entry on Banksy.

Ask students to write an informal response paper addressing the following:

- Do you consider Banksy to be an activist? Why or why not? (You will need to define *activist* in your writing.)

- What pieces did you find the most compelling? Why?

- Look through Banksy's street art (see the "Outdoors" link on his website or consider visiting http://www.boredpanda.com/80-beautiful-street-crimes-done-by-banksy). What piece do you think is the most persuasive for the audience that likely saw it? Why? What does it mean to be persuasive in this context?

Finally, ask students to email you the Banksy piece (or link to the piece) they *personally* found the most compelling; also ask them to email you the piece (or link to the piece) they thought was the most persuasive *for its particular audience in the piece's particular context* (remind them that context is about both place and time).

You will use some of these pieces in the next class.

In-Class, Part 1

Prepare a series of slides from the students' favorite Banksy pieces. Group them into "most persuasive for students" and "most persuasive given the audience/context."

Lead a discussion in which you first show the "most persuasive for them personally" slides. Ask students why they found this image compelling. Push them to go beyond the surface level answer (which often is "because it's funny, or sad, or touching"): ask them to consider what they needed to know, believe, feel, or have experienced in order for this art to move them in the way it did.

Now, look at the images they found the most persuasive given audience and context. Again, ask students why, and again, ask them to consider what the audience would need to know, believe, feel, or have experienced in order for the art to be persuasive in some way.

In order to get at the importance of context, you might ask students to imagine that this art was located somewhere entirely different. For example, what if the images he put on the Israeli West Bank barrier were instead on the side of building on your campus?

Goals for class discussion:

- Understand importance of context in rhetorical persuasiveness.

- Consider how audiences must come from a particular perspective and set of beliefs in order to find particular texts persuasive.

- If there is time, consider a discussion of whether or not they consider Banksy to be a social activist. Is graffiti a social act? Is street art different than graffiti? Why or why not?

Homework, Part 2

Ask students to choose one Banksy image and translate it from visuals to words. The context would still be street art in the same location, but this time instead of images they must convey a similar message in words. Ask them to prepare to share the image and their words in the following class period. They will need to bring the original image along with their translation.

In-Class, Part 2

Students will come to class with images and their translations. Put students into small groups and ask them to share their Banksy pictures and their translations of it into words. The goal of group work is to see what others have done, and to assess how successful they believe the translations are.

Regroup and ask students if anyone had a translation they felt would be as successful, if not more successful, than the original. Have the student share, and discuss as a group why this might be the case. If there is more than one example, share as many as there is time for. Now, ask students for an example of a translation that would be nowhere near as successful. Again, have the student share and discuss as a class why this might be the case.

In these discussions, ask students to pay particular attention to whether or not what the audience must know, feel, believe, or have experienced changes when the mode is switched from visual to linguistic.

Goals for class discussion:

- Understand the affordances of communicative modes.

- Consider how persuasiveness may change for different audiences when a meaning is conveyed through visuals versus words.

ACTIVITY 4: MOVING THROUGH AND SENSING A KNOWN ENVIRONMENT DIFFERENTLY

This activity asks students to experience campus in different ways than they usually do by asking them to produce a text that helps others experience campus differently.

Objectives

- Understand connections between mediating and being mediated.
- Explore writing that engages readers in nonvisual observation.

Considerations

- To carry out this activity, students need time to move about and explore their campus. This can be done as homework or as a class activity.
- Although two or three students working together often notice more than individual students about the sensuous possibilities of an environment, this activity does work when carried out by individuals.
- Depending on your students' abilities or interests, you could change the result of this activity to be a podcast or a brochure instead of a piece of writing.

Assignments

Overview

Working with two others, you are going to produce writing that helps others experience your campus as a nonvisual environment: you are going to produce a written campus tour that helps its audience experience notable smells, sounds, tastes, or touchable surfaces on your campus.

Part 1: What do you want others to experience on your campus?

With your two partners, explore your campus to determine which three to five smells, sounds, or touchable surfaces on your campus will help others learn something memorable or important about your campus. Perhaps your campus has unique tastes: a dairy that produces superb ice cream, a cafeteria known for its doughnuts, and a coffee shop with excellent mochas. Perhaps your campus is known for objects interesting to touch: lush lawns, old brick walls, and a hard metal monument. Perhaps your campus is a place of sounds: the busy street running through the middle, the drum circle that meets weekly in front of the library, and the wind funneled between the tall engineering and computer sciences buildings.

Explore the campus together to determine the sense through which you would like others to learn something interesting or unique about your campus.

Part 2: Develop a tour

With your two partners, write a campus tour that takes others to where they can experience the three to five smells, sounds, tastes, or touchable surfaces you want them to. Give your audience background for understanding why you chose what you did—but also write your tour so that others focus on the sense you have chosen and feel, with focus, what you want them to feel. What sort of descriptive language or instructions will most help them focus on, experience, and reflect on the sensuous experience of your campus you are offering them?

Part 3: Test your tour

Give your tour to someone else—a friend, family member, or classmate—and observe the person taking your tour. You do not want to talk to the person taking your tour, but—afterwards—ask what worked in your tour to help the person experience the sense you chose. Ask how the person experienced campus differently than when the person usually walks through campus.

Reflection

Write a short, informal reflection about what you learned from this activity and what you hope to use from it in the future. The following questions can help you shape your reflection.

In preparing your walking tour and as you explored campus yourself, what did you notice that you had not noticed before because you were now paying attention to different sensuous aspects of the campus environment? How might your composing of this text change how you experience your campus—or other places—in the future? Why do you think you hadn't noticed the aspects of campus you noticed through this activity? How do you think your senses have been shaped through previous experience and through the media you usually read or view such that you don't usually notice what you noticed with this activity?

How effective do you think your text was for others in shifting how they sense campus? What in your your text encouraged others to think differently about how they use their senses? If you were to revise this text—or could use any media available to you—how would you change it to be more effective in making others more alert to senses other than sight, and why?

WORKS CITED

Adam. "MySpace Profile." MySpace. Web. 25 October 2007.

Adorno, Theodor and Max Horkheimer. "The Culture Industry: Enlightenment as Mass Deception." Marxists Internet Archive. 2005. Web. 7 Feb. 2011.

Ahmed, Sara. *Queer Phenomenology: Orientations, Objects, Others.* Durham: Duke UP, 2006. Print.

Ahmed, Sara. *The Cultural Politics of Emotion.* New York: Routledge, 2004. Print.

Alexander, Jonathan. *Digital Youth: Emerging Literacies on the World Wide Web.* Cresskill, NJ: Hampton, 2006. Print.

Althusser, Louis. *Lenin and Philosophy and Other Essays.* Trans. Ben Brewster. New York: Monthly Review Press, 1971. Print

Anzaldúa, Gloria. *Borderlands/La Frontera: The New Mestiza.* San Francisco: Aunt Lute, 1987. Print.

Atwill, Janet M. *Rhetoric Reclaimed: Aristotle and the Liberal Arts Tradition.* Ithaca, NY: Cornell UP, 1998. Print.

Axelrod, Rise B., and Charles R. Cooper. *The St. Martin's Guide to Writing.* 7th ed. Boston: Bedford/St. Martin's, 2004. Print.

Banks, Adam J. *Race, Rhetoric, and Technology: Searching for Higher Ground.* Mahwah, NJ., Erlbaum, 2006. Print.

Barker, Dan. "Gender Differences between Graphical User Interfaces and Command Line Interfaces in Computer Instruction." Oct. 1991. Web. 26 Sept. 2001.

Barry, Lynda. *One Hundred Demons.* Seattle: Sasquatch, 2002. Print.

Bartholomae, David. "Writing with Teachers: A Conversation with Peter Elbow." *CCC* 46 (1995) 62–71. Print.

Baudrillard, Jean. "Requiem for the Media." *The New Media Reader.* Ed. Noah Wardrip-Fruin and Nick Montfort. Cambridge: MIT Press, 2003. 278–88. Print.

Baumgärtel, Tilman. "Immaterial Material: Physicality, Corporeality, and Dematerialization in Telecommunication Artworks." *At a Distance: Precursors to Art and Activism on the internet.* Ed. Annmarie Chandler and Norie Neumark. Cambridge, MA: MIT P, 2005. 60–70. Print.

Baym, Nancy K. "The Past, Present and Future of Human Communication and Technology Research." *Online Fandom.* 10 Oct. 2007. Web. 22 Oct. 2007.

Bechdel, Alison. *Fun Home: A Family Tragicomic.* Boston: Houghton-Mifflin, 2006. Print.

La Belle et la Bête. Dir. Jean Cocteau. Original distributors, 1946. Film.

Bellafante, Gina. "Twenty Years Later, the Walls Still Talk." 3 Aug. 2006. Web. 19 Mar. 2011.

Benjamin, Walter. "The Work of Art in the Age of Mechanical Reproduction." Marxists Internet Archive. 2005. Web. 7 Feb. 2011.

Benkler, Yochai. *The Wealth of Networks: How Social Production Transforms Markets and Freedom.* New Haven, CT: Yale UP, 2006. Print.

Bennett, Tony, and Diane Watson, eds. *Understanding Everyday Life.* Oxford: Blackwell, 2002. Print.

Berger, Asa Berger. *The Comic-Stripped American: What Dick Tracy, Blondie, Daddy Warbucks, and Charlie Brown Tell Us about Ourselves.* Baltimore: Penguin, 1973. Print.

Berger, John. *Ways of Seeing.* London: British Broadcasting Corporation, 1972. Print.

Berlin, James. "Rhetoric and Ideology in the Writing Class." *Cross-Talk in Comp Theory: A Reader.* Ed. Victor Villanueva. Urbana, IL: NCTE, 2003. 717–37. Print.

Bijker, Wiebe E. *Of Bicycles, Bakelites, and Bulbs: Toward a Theory of Sociotechnical Change.* Cambridge, MA: MIT P, 1995. Print.

Bishop, Wendy. *Ethnographic Writing Research: Writing It Down, Writing It Up, and Reading It.* Portsmouth, NH: Boynton/Cook, 1999. Print.

Blair, Kristine, and Christine Tulley. "Whose Research Is It Anyway? The Challenge of Deploying Feminist Methodology in Technological Spaces." *Digital Writing Research.* Ed. Danielle Nicole DeVoss and Heidi McKee, Cresskill, NJ: Hampton, 2007. 303–317. Print.

Block, Bruce. *The Visual Story: Creating the Visual Structure of Film, TV and Digital Media.* 2nd Ed. Walthem: Focal Press, 2007. Print.

Boal, Augusto. *Games for Actors and Non-actors.* Trans. Adrian Jackson. New York: Routledge, 2002. Print.

Bogatin, Donna. "Facebook 'Activism': How about a Greater Good." *ZDNet.* 9 Sept. 2006. Web. 14 Dec. 2008.

Bolter, Jay David, and Diane Gromala. *Windows & Mirrors: Interaction Design, Digital Art, and the Myth of Transparency.* Cambridge, MA: MIT P, 2003. Print.

Bolter, Jay David, and Richard Grusin. *Remediation: Understanding New Media.* Boston: MIT P, 1999. Print.

Bourdieu, Pierre. *Outline of a Theory of Practice.* Cambridge, UK: Cambridge UP, 1977. Print.

Brandt, Deborah. *Literacy in American Lives.* Cambridge, UK: Cambridge UP, 2001. Print.

Brodkey, Linda. "Writing on the Bias." *College English* 56.5 (1994): 527–47. Print.

Butler, Judith. "Against Proper Objects." *differences: A Journal of Feminist Cultural Studies* 6 (1994): 1–27. Print.

Campbell, Rebecca, and Sharon M. Wasco. "Feminist Approaches to Social Science: Epistemological and Methodological Tenets." *American Journal of Community Psychology* 28 (2000): 773–791. Print.

Card, Stuart K., Jock D. Mackinlay, and Ben Shneiderman. *Readings in Information Visualization: Using Vision to Think.* San Francisco: Morgan Kaufmann, 1999. Print.

Carrier, David. *The Aesthetics of Comics.* University Park, PA: Pennsylvania State UP, 2000. Print.

Castells, Manuel. *The Rise of Networked Society.* Oxford: Blackwell, 2000. Print.

Chute, Hillary. "An Interview with Alison Bechdel." *MFS Modern Fiction Studies* 52. 4 (2006). 1004–1013. Print.

Chytry, Josef. "Marx: Communism and the Laws of Beauty." *The Aesthetic State: A Quest in Modern German Thought.* Berkeley, CA: U of California P, 1989. 231–73. Print.

Cioffi, Frank L. "Disturbing Comics: The Disjunction of Word and Image in the Comics of Anrzej Mleczko, Ben Katchor, R. Crumb, and Art Spiegelman." *The Language of Comics.* Ed. Robin Varnum and Christina T. Gibbons. Jackson, MS: Mississippi UP, 2001. 97–122. Print.

Clark, Lynn Schofield. "The Constant Contact Generation: Exploring Teen Friendship Networks Online." *Girl Wide Web: Girls, the Internet, and the Negotiation of Identity.* Ed. Sharon R. Mazzarella. New York: Peter Lang, 2005. 203–220. Print.

Clark, T. J. *The Painting of Modern Life: Paris in the Art of Manet and His Followers.* Princeton, NJ: Princeton UP, 1984. Print.

Clifton, James A. *The Invented Indian: Cultural Fictions and Government Policies.* New Brunwich: Transaction, 1990. Print.

Cocteau, Jean. *The Art of Cinema.* Ed. André Bernard and Claude Gauteur. Trans. Robin Buss. London: Marion Boyars, 1988. Print.

Cocteau, Jean. *The Difficulty of Being.* Trans. Elizabeth Sprigge. New York: Coward-McCann, 1967. Print.

Cocteau, Jean. *The White Paper.* New York: Macaulay, 1958. Print.

"College Essay Contest." *New York Times Magazine,* 27 Sept. 2007. Web. 29 Sept. 2007.

Cooper, Marilyn. "Being Linked to the Matrix: Biology, Technology, and Writing." Forthcoming. Print.

Cornell, Drucilla. *At the Heart of Freedom: Feminism, Sex, & Equality.* Princeton, NJ: Princeton UP, 1998.

Cornell, Drucilla. *The Imaginary Domain: Abortion, Pornography, and Sexual Harassment.* New York: Routledge, 1995. Print.

Couture, Barbara. *Toward a Phenomenological Rhetoric.* Carbondale: Southern Illinois UP, 1998. Print.

Crain, Caleb. "Surveillance Society: The Mass-Observation Movement and the Meaning of Everyday Life." *The New Yorker,* 11 Sept. 2006: 54. Print.

Crowley, Sharon, and Debra Hawhee. *Ancient Rhetorics For Contemporary Students*. New York: Longman, 1998. Print.

Cruse, Howard. *Stuck Rubber Baby*. New York: DC Comics, 2000. Print.

Daniels, Les. *Comix: A History of Comic Books in America*. New York: Bonanza Books, 1971. Print.

Davis, D. Diane. *Breaking Up (at) Totality: A Rhetoric of Laughter*. Carbondale: Southern Illinois UP, 2000. Print.

Davis, Lennard J. "Bodies of Difference: Politics, Disability, and Representation." *Disability Studies: Enabling the Humanities*. Ed. Brenda Jo Brueggemann, Sharon L. Snyder, and Rosemarie Garland-Thomson. New York: MLA, 2002. Print.

Davis, Lennard J. *Enforcing Normalcy: Disability, Deafness, and the Body*. New York: Verso, 1995. Print.

Debord, Guy. "Society of the Spectacle." Marxists Internet Archive. n.d. Web. 7 Feb. 2011

de Certeau, Michel. *The Practice of Everyday Life*. Berkeley: U California P, 1984. Print.

Deloria, Philip J. *Playing Indian*. New Haven: Yale UP, 1998. Print.

Deloria, Vine, Jr. *Custer Died for Our Sins: An Indian Manifesto*. Norman: U of Oklahoma P, 1998. Print.

Derrida, Jacques. *Paper Machine*. Stanford: Stanford UP, 2005. Print.

Deutsch, Nancy. "Positionality and the Pen: Reflections on the Process of Becoming a Feminist Researcher and Writer." *Qualitative Inquiry* 10 (2004): 885–902. Print.

DeVoss, Danielle Nicole, et al. "Infrastructure and Composing: The When of new media Writing." *College Composition and Communication* 57.1 (2005): 14–44. Print.

Dickinson, Emily. "I'm Nobody, Who Are You?" *The Poems of Emily Dickinson*. Ed. Ralph W. Franklin. Cambridge, MA: Belknap, 1998. Print.

Dodge, Martin, and Rob Kitchin. *Atlas of Cyberspace*. London: Pearson Education, 2001. Print.

Drew, Julie. "Cultural Composition: Stuart Hall on Ethnicity and the Discursive Turn." *JAC* 18.2 (1998): 172–196. Print.

Dunn, Patricia Ann. *Learning Re-Abled: The Learning Disability Controversy and Composition Studies*. Portsmouth: Boynton /Cook, 1995. Print.

Ede, Lisa, and Andrea Lunsford. "Audience Addressed/Audience Invoked: The Role of Audience in Composition Theory Pedagogy." *Cross-Talk in Comp Theory*. Ed. Victor Villanueva. Urbana, IL: NCTE, 1997: 77–95. Print.

Edney, Matthew H. *Mapping an Empire: The Geographical Construction of British India, 1765–1843*. Chicago: U of Chicago P, 1990. Print.

Eisner, Will. *Comics and Sequential Art*. Tamarac, FL: Poorhouse, 1985. Print.

Elbow, Peter. "Being a Writer vs. Being an Academic: A Conflict in Goals." *CCC* 46 (1995): 72–83. Print.

Elbow, Peter. "The Shifting Relationship Between Speech and Writing." *CCC* 36.3 (1985): 283–303. Print.

Emig, Janet. *The Composing Processes of Twelfth Graders*. New York: NCTE Press, 1971. Print.

Enzensberger, Hans Magnus. "Constituents of a Theory of the Media." *The New Media Reader*. Ed. Noah Wardrip-Fruin and Nick Montfort. Cambridge: MIT Press, 2003. 259–75. Print.

Faigley, Lester. *Fragments of Rationality: Postmodernity and the Subject of Composition*. Pittsburgh: Pittsburgh UP, 1992. Print.

Felski, Rita. "The Invention of Everyday Life." *New Formations* 39 (1999–2000): 15–31. Print.

Finders, Margaret J. *Just Girls: Hidden Literacies and Life in Junior High*. New York: Teachers College P, 1997. Print.

Firth, Raymond. "An Anthropologist's View of Mass-Observation." *Sociological Review* 31 (1939): 166–193. Print.

Fleckenstein, Kristie. *Embodied Literacies: Imageword and a Poetics of Teaching*. Southern Illinois UP, 2003. Print.

Fleckenstein, Kristie. "Writing Bodies." *College English* 61.3 (1999): 281–306. Print.

Flower, Linda, and John R. Hayes. "A Cognitive Process Theory of Writing." *CCC* 32.4 (1981): 365–87. Print.

Ford, Andrew. "The Price of Art in Isocrates: Formalism and the Escape from Politics." *Rethinking the History of Rhetoric: Multidisciplinary Essays on the Rhetorical Tradition.* Ed. Takis Poulakos. Boulder, CO: Westview Press, 1993. 31–52. Print.

Foss, Karen A., Sonja K. Foss, and Cindy L. Griffin. "Introducing Feminist Rhetorical Scholarship." *Readings in Feminist Rhetorical Theory.* Ed. Karen A. Foss, Sonja K. Foss, and Cindy L. Griffin. London: Sage, 2004. 1–6. Print.

Foucault, Michel. *Discipline and Punish: the Birth of the Prison.* Trans. Alan Sheridan. New York: Random House, 1995.

Foucault, Michel. *The History of Sexuality, Vol. 1: The Will to Knowledge.* London: Penguin, 1998. Print.

Foucault, Michel. *The Uses of Pleasure.* Trans. R. Hurley. New York: Random, 1985. Print.

Fraser, Nancy. "Rethinking the Public Sphere: A Contribution to the Critique of Actually Existing Democracy." *Justice Interruptus: Critical Reflections on the "Postsocialist" Condition.* Ed. Nancy Fraser. New York: Routledge, 1997. Print.

Fulkerson, Richard. "Composition at the Turn of the Twenty-First Century." *CCC* 56.4 (2005): 654–687. Print.

Fusco, Coco. *The Bodies That Were Not Ours.* London: Routledge, 2001. Print.

Fusco, Coco. *The Incredible Disappearing Woman.* 2003. MS.

Gabriel, Teshome H., and Fabian Wagmister. "Notes on Weavin' Digital: T(h)inkers at the Loom." *Social Identities: Journal for the Study of Race, Nation and Culture* 3.3 (1997) EBSCO. Web. 9 Apr. 2008.

Gannett, Cinthia. *Gender and the Journal: Diaries and Academic Discourse.* Albany: State of New York P, 1992. Print.

Gardiner, Michael. *Critiques of Everyday Life.* London: Routledge, 2000. Print.

Garfield, Simon. *Extracts from Our Hidden Lives.* London: Ebury, 2005. Web. 2 Mar. 2009.

Garland-Thomson, Rosemarie. "Introduction: From Wonder to Error—A Genealogy of Freak Discourse in Modernity." *Freakery: Cultural Spectacles of the Extraordinary Body.* New York: NYU P, 1996. Print.

Garroutte, Eva Marie. *Real Indians: Identity and the Survival of Native America.* Berkeley, CA: California UP, 2003. Print.

Garza, Susan Loudermilk, and Tommy Hern. "Using Wikis as Collaborative Writing Tools: Something Wiki This Way Comes—Or Not!" *Kairos* (2005). Web.

Gee, James Paul. "Grading with Games: Interview with James Paul Gee." *Edutopia.* 27 August 2008. Web. 20 Dec. 2008.

Gee, James Paul. *What Video Games Have to Teach Us About Learning and Literacy.* New York: Palgrave Macmillan, 2003. Print.

George, Diana. "From Analysis to Design: Visual Communication in the Teaching of Writing." *CCC* 54.1 (2002) 11–39. Print.

George, Diana, and John Trimbur. *Reading Culture: Contexts for Critical Reading and Writing.* 5th ed. New York: Pearson Longman, 2004. Print.

Gibson-Graham, J.K. *The End of Capitalism (As We Knew It): A Feminist Critique of Political Economy.* 1996. Minneapolis, MN: Minnesota UP, 2006. Print.

Gibson-Graham, J.K. *A Postcapitalist Politics.* Minneapolis, MN: Minnesota UP, 2006. Print.

Glenn, Cheryl. *Rhetoric Retold.* Carbondale: Southern Illinois UP, 1997. Print.

Gloeckner, Phoebe. *A Child's Life and Other Stories.* Rev ed. Berkeley: Frog, 2000. Print.

Goffman, Erving. *Asylums.* New York: Anchor Doubleday, 1990. Print.

Goffman, Erving. *Behavior in Public Places: Notes on the Social Organization of Gatherings.* New York: Free Press, 1963. Print.

Goffman, Erving. *Stigma: Notes on the Management of Spoiled Identity.* New York: Simon and Schuster, 1986. Print.

Grigar, Dene. "Kineticism, Rhetoric, and New Media Artists." *Computers and Composition* 22 (2005): 105–12. Print.

Guerrilla Girls. "GuerrillaGIRLS: Fighting Discrimination with Facts, Humor and Fake Fur." 21 Nov. 2008. Web. 28 Mar. 2011.

Haas, Christina. *Writing Technology: Studies on the Materiality of Literacy.* Mahwah, NJ: Lawrence Erlbaum, 1996. Print.

Habermas, Jürgen. *Communication and the Evolution of Society*. Boston: Beacon, 1979.

Halio, M.P. "Student Writing: Can the Machine Maim the Message?" *Academic Computing* 4 (1990): 16–19. Print.

Hansen, Mark B. N. *Bodies in Code: Interfaces with Digital Media*. New York: Routledge, 2006. Print.

Hansen, Mark B. N. Embodying Technesis: Technology Beyond Writing. Ann Arbor: U of Michigan P, 2000. Print.

Haraway, Donna. "A Cyborg Manifesto: Science, Technology, and Socialist-Feminism in the Late Twentieth Century." *Simians, Cyborgs and Women: The Reinvention of Nature*. New York: Routledge, 1991. 149–181. Print.

Haraway, Donna. *Modest_Witness@Second_Millennium.FemaleMan© Meets_OncoMouse™: Feminism and Technoscience*. New York: Routledge, 1997. Print.

Harding, Sandra. *The Science Question in Feminism*. Ithaca: Cornell UP, 1986. Print.

Harley, J.B. "Maps, Knowledge, and Power." *The Iconography of Landscape: Essays on the Symbolic Representation, Design and Use of Past Environments*. Ed. D. Cosgrove and S. Daniels. Cambridge: Cambridge UP, 1988. 277–312. Print.

Harpold, Terry. "Dark Continents: A Critique of internet Metageographies." *Postmodern Culture* 9.2 (2009): n.pag. Web. 28 Mar. 2011.

Harris, Gardiner. *"As Physicians' Jobs Change, So Do Their Politics." New York Times*. New York Times, 30 May 2011. Web. 30 May 2011.

Hatfield, Charles. *Alternative Comics: An Emerging Literature*. Jackson, MS: Mississippi UP, 2005. Print.

Hawhee, Debra. *Bodily Arts*. Austin: Texas UP, 2005. Print.

Hawisher, Gail E., and Patricia A. Sullivan. "Fleeting Images: Women Visually Writing the Web." Ed. Gail E. Hawisher, and Cynthia L. Selfe. *Passions, Pedagogies, and 21st Century Technologies*. Logan: Utah State UP, 1999. 268–291. Print.

Hawisher, Gail E., and Cynthia L. Selfe. "The Rhetoric of Technology and the Electronic Writing Class." *CCC* 42 (1991): 55–65. Print.

Hayles, N. Katherine. *How We Became Posthuman*. Chicago, University of Chicago Press, 1999. Print.

Heidegger, Martin. *Being and Time*. trans. J. Macquarrie and E. Robinson. New York: Harper & Row, 1962. Print.

Henwood, Flis, Helen Kennedy, and Nod Miller, eds. *Cyborg Lives: Women's Technobiographies*. York, UK: Raw Nerve, 2001. Print.

Hess, Douglas. "Who Owns Writing?" *CCC* 57.2 (2005): 335–357. Print.

Hillocks, George. *Teaching Writing as Reflective Practice*. New York: Teacher's College P, 1995. Print.

Hockenberry, John. "This Is the Story of the Most Fearless Entrepreneur Ever: The Human Brain." *WIRED* Aug. 2001: 94–105. Print.

Hocks, Mary E. "Understanding Visual Rhetoric in Digital Writing Environments." *CCC* 54.4 (2003): 629–656. Print.

Holzschlag, Molly E. "Who Do You Blog For?" *Molly.com*. 14 Apr. 2006. Web. 29 Sept. 2007.

Hough, Christina. "General Discussion. Call for Action." *Everyday Adrenaline*. 5 Nov. 2007. Web. 4 Feb. 2009.

Hubble, Nick. *Mass-Observation and Everyday Life: Culture, History, Theory*. New York: Palgrave Macmillan, 2006. Print.

Ito, Mizuko. "Japanese Media Mixes and Amateur Cultural Exchange." *Digital Generations: Children, Young People, and New Media*. Ed. David Buckingham and Rebekah Willet. Mahwah, NJ: Lawrence Erlbaum, 2006. 49–66. Print.

Jahshan, Paul. *Cybermapping and the Writing of Myth*. New York: Peter Lang, 2007. Print.

Jamie. "MySpace Profile." MySpace. Web. 25 Oct. 2007.

Jay, Martin. *Downcast Eyes: The Denigration of Vision in Twentieth-Century French Thought*. Berkeley: California UP, 1993. Print.

Jenkins, Henry. *Convergence Culture: Where Old and New Media Collide*. New York: NYU P, 2006. Print.

Johns, Adrian. *The Nature of the Book: Print and Knowledge in the Making*. Chicago: Chicago UP, 1998. Print.

Johnson, Steven. *Interface Culture*. New York: Scribner, 1998. Print.

Johnson-Eilola, Johndan. "Little Machines: Understanding Users, Understanding Interfaces." *ACM Journal of Computer Documentation* 25.4 (2001): 119–127. Print.

Karl, Irmi. "On-/Offline: Gender, Sexuality, and the Techno-Politics of Everyday Life." *Queer Online: Media, Technology, and Sexuality*. Ed. Kate O'Riordan and David J. Phillips. New York: Peter Lang, 2007: 45–66. Print.

Kennedy, Helen. "Beyond Anonymity, or Future Directions for internet Identity Research." *New Media & Society* 8.6 (2006): 859–876. Print.

Kenney, Robert. "Coda." *The New Yorker* 15 Oct. 2007: 48. Print.

Kent, Steven L. *The Ultimate History of Video Games: From Pong to Pokémon and Beyond—The Story Behind the Craze that Touched Our Lives and Changed the World*. New York: Three Rivers, 2001. Print.

Kirtley, Susan. "Students' Views on Technology and Writing: The Power of Personal History." *Computers and Composition* 22 (2005): 209–30. Print.

Kitalong, Karla, Tracy Bridgeford, Michael Moore, and Dickie Selfe. "Variations on a Theme: The Technology Autobiography as a Versatile Writing Assignment." *Teaching Writing with Computers: An Introduction*. Ed. Pamela Takayoshi and Brian Huot. Boston: Houghton Mifflin, 2003. 219–233. Print.

Knowles, Brent, Preston Watamaniuk, Luke Kristjanson, Keith Soleski, Trent Oster, Bob McCabe, and Jim Bishop. *Neverwinter Nights: Instruction Manual*. New York: Infogrames Entertainment, 2002. Print.

Koepnick, Lutz and Erin McGlothlin. "Introduction."*After the Digital Divide: German Aesthetic Theory in the Age of New Media*. Ed. Lutz Koepnick and Erin McGlothlin. New York: Camden House, 2009. 1–22. Print.

Kramarae, Cheris, ed. *Technology and Women's Voices: Keeping in Touch*. New York: Routledge & Kegan Paul, 1998. Print.

Kress, Gunther. "English at the Crossroads: Rethinking Curricula of Communication in the Context of the Turn to the Visual." *Passions, Pedagogies and 21st Century Technologies*. Ed. Gail E. Hawisher and Cynthia L. Selfe. Logan, UT: Utah State UP, 1999. Print.

Kress, Gunther. *Learning to Write*. 2nd ed. London: Routledge, 1994. Print.

Kress, Gunther, and Theo Van Leeuwen. *Multimodal Discourse: The Modes and Media of Contemporary Communication*. London: Arnold, 2001. Print.

Kurzweil, Ray. "As Machines Become More like People, Will People Become More like God?" *Talk* Apr. 2001: 153–155. Print.

Kushner, David. *Masters of Doom: How Two Guys Created an Empire and Transformed Pop Culture*. New York: Random House, 2003. Print.

Lauer, Janice. "Rhetoric and Composition Studies: A Multimodal Discipline." *Defining the New Rhetorics*. Ed. Theresa Enos and Stuart Brown. Newbury Park, CA: Sage, 1993. 44–54. Print.

Lavin, Michael R. "The Comics Code Authority." *Comic Books for Young Adults*. 21 Dec. 2000. Web. 8 Aug 2007.

Lavin, Michael R. "Women in Comic Books." *Serials Review* 24.2 (1998): n.pag. Web. 8 Aug. 2007.

Lawthom, Rebecca. "What Can I Do? A Feminist Researcher in Non-Feminist Research." *Feminism & Psychology* 7 (1997): 533–538. Print.

Lee, Li-Young. *Behind My Eyes: Poems*. New York: Norton, 2008. Print.

Lefebvre, Henri. *Everyday Life in the Modern World*. New York: Transaction, 1984. Print.

Lefebvre, Henri. *The Production of Space*. Trans. Donald Nicholson-Smith. Oxford: Blackwell, 1991. Print.

Lenhart, Amanda, Joseph Kahne, Ellen Middaugh, Alexandra Macgill, Chris Evans, and Jessica Vitak. "Teens, Video Games and Civics." *Pew internet and American Life Project*. 15 Sept. 2008. Web. 2 Jan. 2009.

Lent, John A."The Comic Debates Internationally: Their Genesis, Issues, and Commonalities." *Pulp Demons: International Dimensions of the Postwar Anti-Comics Campaign*. Cranbury, NJ: Associated UP, 1999. Print.

Levy, Steven. "Ray Ozzie Has a Plan." *WIRED* Dec. 2008: 170–179, 214. Print.

Lincoln, Yvonna S., and Egon Guba. *Naturalistic Inquiry.* Beverly Hills, CA: Sage, 1985. Print.

Linder, Fletcher. "Speaking of Bodies, Pleasures, and Paradise Lost: Erotic Agency and Situationist Ethnography." *Cultural Studies* 15.2 (2001): 352–374. Print.

Link, Aaron Raz and Hilda Raz. *What Becomes You.* Lincoln: Nebraska UP, 2007. Print.

Lloyd, Genevieve. *The Man of Reason: "Male" and "Female" in Western Philoslophy.* 2nd ed. Minneapolis: U of Minnesota P, 1993. Print.

Lord, Erica. 12 Oct. 2007.

Lord, Erica. "MySpace Profile." MySpace. Web. 25 Oct. 2007.

Lu, Min-Zhan. "Composition's Word Work: Deliberating How to Do Language." *Composition Studies in the New Millennium: Rereading the Past, Rewriting the Future.* Ed. Lynn Z. Bloom, Donald A. Daiker, and Edward M. White. Carbondale: Southern Illinois UP, 2003. Print.

Lu, Min-Zhan. "An Essay on the Work of Composition: Composing English Against the Order of Fast Capitalism." *CCC* 56.1 (2004): 16–50. Print.

Lunsford, Andrea A., John J. Ruszkiewicz, and Keith Walters. *Everything's an Argument with Readings.* 4th ed. Boston: Bedford/St. Martin's, 2007. Print.

Madge, Charles, and Tom Harrisson. "Letter to the Editor." *The New Statesman* 2 Jan. 1937.

Madge, Charles, and Tom Harrisson. "They Speak For Themselves." BBC Radio script broadcast, 1 Jun. 1939, *BBC Home Services* (available through the Mass-Observation Archive, File Report A26).

Madge, Charles, and Tom Harrisson. *First Year's Work by Mass-Observation.* London: Lindsay Drummond, 1938. Print.

Malinkowski, Bronislaw. "A Nation-Wide Intelligence Service." *First Year's Work* 1937–1938. Ed. Charles Madge and Tom Harrisson. London: Lindsay Drummond, 1938: 81–121. Print.

Manet, Édouard. *Olympia.* 1863. Musèe d'Orsay, Paris.

Manovich, Lev. *The Language of New Media.* Cambridge, MA: MIT P, 2001. Print.

"The Mass-Observation Diaries: an Introduction." *Brighton: The Mass-Observation Archive and the Centre for Continuing Education,* University of Sussex, 1991. Print.

Marx, Karl, and Friedrich Engels. *The German Ideology.* Marx and Engels Internet Archive. Web. 20 May 2011.

McCloud, Scott. *Making Comics: Storytelling Secrets of Comics, Manga, and Graphic Novels.* New York: Harper Collins, 2006. Print.

McCloud, Scott. *Understanding Comics: The Invisible Art.* New York: Harper Collins, 1993. Print.

McGonigal, Jane. "Why I Love Bees: A Case Study in Collective Intelligence Gaming." *The Ecology of Games: Connecting Youth, Games, and Learning.* Ed. Katie Salen. Cambridge, MA: The MIT Press, 2008. 199–228. Web. The John D. and Catherine T. MacArthur Foundation Series on Digital Media and Learning.

McLuhan, Marshall. *The Gutenberg Galaxy.* Toronto: U of Toronto P, 1962. Print.

McLuhan, Marshall. *The Mechanical Bride: Folklore of Industrial Man.* Boston: Beacon Press, 1951. Print.

McLuhan, Marshall. *Understanding Media: The Extensions of Man.* New York: McGraw-Hill, 1964. Print.

McRuer, Robert. "Composing Bodies; or, De-Composition: Queer Theory, Disability Studies, and Alternative Corporealities." *JAC* 24.1 (2004): 47–78. Print.

Menand, Louis. "Woke Up This Morning." *The New Yorker* 10 Dec. 2007: 107. Print.

Merleau-Ponty, Maurice. *The Phenomenology of Perception.* Trans. Colin Smith. New York: Humanities, 1962. Print.

Mihesuah, Devon A. *American Indians: Stereotypes & Realities.* Atlanta: Clarity Press, 1996. Print.

Mill, John Stuart. *On Liberty.* London: Longman, Roberts, & Green, 1869. Print.

Miller, Susan. "Technologies of Self?-Formation." *JAC* 17.3 (1997): 497–500. Print.

Minahan, Stella, and Julie Wolfram Cox. "Stitch'nBitch: Cyberfeminism, a Third Place, and the New Materiality." *Journal of Material Culture* 12.1 (2007): 5–21. Print.

Minh-ha, Trinh T. Woman, *Native, Other: Writing Postcoloniality and Feminism.* Bloomington: Indiana UP, 1989. Print.

Mitchell, W.J.T. *Iconology: Images, Texts, Ideology.* Chicago: U of Chicago P, 1986. Print.

Mitchell, W.J.T. *Picture Theory.* Chicago: U of Chicago P, 1994. Print.

Mitchell, W.J.T and Mark Hansen. *Critical Terms for Media Studies.* Chicago: U of Chicago P, 2010. Print.

Monmonier, Mark. *How to Lie with Maps.* Chicago: U of Chicago P, 1996. Print.

Moore, Alan, and Dave Gibbons. *Watchmen.* New York: DC Comics, 1995. Print.

Moran, Charles. "Computers and Composition 1983–2002: What We Have Hoped For." *Computers and Composition* 20 (2003): 343–58. Print.

Mulvey, Laura. "Visual Pleasure and Narrative Cinema." *Feminism and Film.* Ed. E. Ann Kaplan. New York: Oxford UP, 2000. 34–47. Print.

Murray, Donald. "Teach Writing as a Process Not Product." *Rhetoric and Composition; A Sourcebook for Teachers and Writers.* Ed. R. Graves. Upper Montclair, NJ: Boynton/Cook, 1972. 89–92. Print.

Muzyka, Ray, Lukas Kristjanson, and James Ohlen. *Baldur's Gate Game Manual, Including Volo's Guide to Baldur's Gate.* Irvine CA: Black Isle Studios, 1998. Print.

Nakamura, Lisa. *Digitizing Race: Visual Cultures of the internet.* Minneapolis: U of Minnesota P, 2007. Print.

Naples, Nancy. *Feminism and Method: Ethnography, Discourse Analysis, and Activist Research.* New York: Routledge, 2003. Print.

New London Group. "A Pedagogy of Multiliteracies: Designing Social Futures." *Multiliteracies: Literacy Learning and the Design of Social Futures.* Ed. Bill Cope and Mary Kalantzis. London: Routledge, 2000. 9–37. Print.

Nielsen, Jesper, and Søren Wichman. "America's First Comics: Techiques, Contents, and Functions of Sequential Text-Image Pairing in the Classic Maya Period." *Comics and Culture: Analytic and Theoretical Approaches to Comics.* Ed. Anne Magnussen and Hans-Christiian Chrisitansien. Copenhagen: Museum Tusculanum, 2000. 59–77. Print.

Norman, Donald. *The Invisible Computer.* Cambridge, MA: MIT P, 1998. Print.

Norton, Rictor. "Cocteau's White Paper on Homophobia." *Gay History and Literature.* 9 Jan. 2000. Web.

Nyberg, Amy Kiste. "Comic Book Censorship in the United States." *Pulp Demons: International Dimensions of the Postwar Anti-Comics Campaign.* Ed. John A. Lent. Cranbury, NJ: Associated UP, 1999. 42–68. Print.

O'Riordan, Kate, and David J. Phillips, eds. *Queer Online: Media, Technology, and Sexuality.* New York: Peter Lang, 2007. Print.

Ong, Walter J. *Orality and Literacy: The Technologizing of the Word.* London: Routledge, 1982. Print.

Ong, Walter J. "The Writer's Audience is Always a Fiction." *Cross-Talk in Comp Theory.* Ed. Victor Villanueva. Urbana, IL: NCTE, 1997: 55–76. Print.

Onishi, Normitsu. "Thumbs Race as Japan's Best Sellers Go Cellular." *New York Times.* New York Times, 20 Jan. 2008. Web.

Packard, Becky Wai-Ling, and Paul F. Conway. "Methodological Choice and Its Consequences for Possible Selves." *Identity: An International Journal of Theory and Research* (2006): 251–271. Print.

Philips, Christa, Arthur Hagman, Aaron Sprinkle, and Queenie Ngai. *Arcanum: Of Steamworks & Magick Obscura.* El Dorado Hills, CA: Sierra On-Line, 2001. Print.

Powell, Malea. "Blood and Scholarship: One Mixed-Blood's Story." *Race, Rhetoric, and Composition.* Ed. Keith Gilyard. Portsmouth, NH: Boynton/Cook, 1999. Print.

Powell, Malea. "Down by the River, or How Susan La Flesche Picotte Can Teach us about Alliance as a Practice of Survivance." *College English* 67.1 (2004): 38–60. Print.

Powell, Malea. "Rhetorics of Survivance: How American Indians Use Writing." *CCC* 53.3 (2002): 396–434. Print.

Prensky, Marc. "Digital Natives, Digital Immigrants." *On the Horizon* 9.5 (2001): 1–6. Print.

Raley, Rita. *Tactical Media.* Minneapolis: U of Minnesota P, 2009. Print.

"The Regalia." *Wacipi PowWow.* Television, Twin Cities Public Television. TPT. 7 Aug. 2007.

Reinharz, Shulamit, and Lynn Davidman. *Feminist Methods in Social Research.* New York: Oxford UP, 1992. Print.

Reitberger, Reinhold, and Wolfgang Fuchs. *Comics: Anatomy of a Mass Medium.* Boston: Little, Brown and Company, 1971. Print

Reynolds, Nedra. "Interrupting Our Way to Agency: Feminist Cultural Studies and Composition." *Feminism and Composition Studies: In Other Words.* Ed. Susan C. Jarratt and Lynn Worsham. New York: MLA, 1998. 58–73. Print.

Rice, Jeff. "Networks and New Media." *College English* 69.2 (2006): 127. Print.

Rice, Jeff. *The Rhetoric of Cool: Composition Studies and New Media.* Carbondale, IL: Southern Illinois UP, 2007. Print.

Rifas, Leonard. "Racial Imagery, Racism, Individualism, and Underground Comix." *ImageTexT: Interdisciplinary Comics Studies* 1.1 (2004). n.pag. Web. Mar. 28 2011.

Ritchie, Joy, and Kate Roland. *Available Means.* Pittsburgh: U of Pittsburgh P, 2001. Print.

Robinson, Jerry. *The Comics: An Illustrated History of Comic Strip Art.* New York: G.P. Putnam's Sons, 1974. Print.

Robinson, John Manley. *An Introduction to Early Greek Philosophy.* Boston: Houghton-Mifflin, 1968. Print.

Romanyshn, Robert. "The Despotic Eye and Its Shadow: Media Image in the Age of Literacy." *Modernity and the Hegemony of Vision.* Ed. David Levin. Berkeley: California UP, 1993: 339–360. Print.

Rosenwasser, David, and Jill Stephen. *Writing Analytically.* 3rd ed. Boston: Thomson-Heinle, 2003. Print.

Ryan, Jennifer D. "Black Female Authorship and the African American Graphic Novel: Historical Responsibility in Icon: A Hero's Welcome." *MFS Modern Fiction Studies* 52.4 (2006). 918–946. Print.

Sabin, Roger. *Adult Comics: An Introduction.* London: Routledge, 1993. Print.

Sabin, Roger. *Comics, Comix, and Graphic Novels: A History of Comic Art.* London: Phaidon, 1996. Print.

Scheer, Robert. "Can Bill Gates Get His Nerd Back?" *Talk* Apr. 2001: 116–120, 182. Print.

Sedgwick, Eve Kosofsky. *Epistemology of the Closet.* Berkeley, CA: U of California P, 1990. Print.

Selfe, Cynthia, and Richard Selfe. "The Politics of the Interface: Power and its Exercise in Electronic Contact Zones." *CCC* 45:4 (1994): 480–504. Print.

Selfe, Cynthia L. "Lest We Think the Revolution is a Revolution: Images of Technology and the Nature of Change." *Passions, Pedagogies and 21st Century Technologies.* Ed. Gail E. Hawisher and Cynthia L. Selfe. Logan: Utah State UP, 1999: 292–322. Print.

Selfe, Cynthia L. *Multimodal Composition: Resources for Teachers.* Cresskill, NH: Hampton, 2007. Print.

Selfe, Cynthia L. "Technology and Literacy: A Story about the Perils of Not Paying Attention." *CCC* 50 (1999): 411–36. Print.

Sennett, Richard. *The Craftsman.* New Haven: Yale UP, 2008. Print.

Sheridan, David M., Jim Ridolfo, and Anthony J. Michel. "The Available Means of Persuasion: Mapping a Theory and Pedagogy of Multimodal Public Rhetoric." *JAC* 25 (2005): 801–44. Print.

Sheridan, Dorothy, et al. *Writing Ourselves: Mass-Observation and Literacy Practices.* Cresskill, NJ: Hampton, 2000. Print.

Shipka, Jody. "A Multimodal Task-Based Framework for Composing." *CCC* 57.2 (2005): 277–306. Print.

Shusterman, Richard. *Performing Live: Aesthetic Alternatives for the Ends of Art.* Ithaca, NY: Cornell UP, 2000. Print.

Siering, Carmen D. "Teaching Everyday Feminist Activism: How Taking It To the Streets Helps Students Become Everyday Feminist Activists." *Beyond "Burning Bras": Feminist Activism for Everyone.* Westport, CT: Praeger, 2009. Print.

Silverman, Kaja. "Fassbinder and Lacan: A Reconsideration of Gaze, Look, and Image." *Visual Culture: Images and Interpretations.* Ed. Norman Bryson, Michael Ann Holly, and Keith Moxey. Hanover, NH: Wesleyan UP, 1994. 272–301. Print.

Sirc, Geoffrey. "Box-Logic." *Writing New Media.* Ed. Anne Frances Wysocki, et al. Logan: Utah State UP, 2004. Print.

Smith, Dorothy E. *The Everyday World as Problematic: A Feminist Sociology.* Milton Keynes: Open Press, 1988. Print.

Sobchack, Vivian Carol. *Carnal Thoughts: Embodiment and Moving Image Culture.* Berkeley: California UP, 2004. Print.

Spatt, Brenda. *Writing from Sources.* 7th ed. Boston: Bedford/St. Martin's, 2007. Print.

Spender, Dale. *Nattering on the Net: Women, Power, and Cyberspace.* North Melbourne: Spinifex, 1995. Print.

Stiegler, Bernard. "Memory." *Critical Terms for Media Studies.* Ed. W.J.T Mitchell and Mark Hansen. Chicago: U of Chicago P, 2010. 64–87. Print.

"Stigma." *Merriam-Webster Online Dictionary.* Merriam-Webster. 2012. Web. 16 April 2012.

Stone, Allucquére Roseanne. "Split Subjects, Not Atoms; or, How I Fell in Love with My Prosthesis." *Configurations* 2.1 (1994): 173–190. Print.

Street, Brian, ed. *Cross-Cultural Approaches to Literacy.* Cambridge, UK: Cambridge UP, 1993. Print.

Sullivan, Laura L. "Cyberbabes: (Self-) Representations of Women and the Virtual male Gaze." *Computers and Composition* 14 (1997): 189–204. Print.

Sullivan, Laura L. "Wired Women Writing: Towards a Feminist Theorization of Hypertext." *Computers and Composition* 16 (1999): 25–54. Print.

Tensuan, Theresa M. "Comic Visions and Revisions in the Work of Lynda Barry and Marjane Satrapi." *MFS* 52.4 (2006): 947–64. Print.

Trimbur, John. *The Call to Write.* 4th ed. Boston: Houghton Mifflin, 2008. Print.

Trimbur, John. "Taking the Social Turn: Teaching Writing Post-Process." *CCC* 45 (1994): 108–11. Print.

Turkle, Sherry. *Life on the Screen: Identity in the Age of the internet.* New York: Simon and Schuster, 1995. Print.

Varnum, Robin, and Christina T. Gibbons. eds. *The Language of Comics: Word and Image.* Jasckson, MS: Mississippi UP, 2001. Print.

Vygotsky, Lev S. "The Genesis of Higher Mental Functions." *The Concept of Activity in Soviet Psychology.* Ed. J.V. Wersch. Armonk, NY: M.E. Sharpe, 1981, 144–188. Print.

Wahlstrom, Billie. "Communication and Technology: Defining a Feminist Presence in Research and Practice." *Literacy and Computers.* Ed. C. Selfe and S. Hilligoss. New York: MLA, 1994. 171–185. Print.

Webb, Patricia. "Reconceptualizing Classroom-based Research in Computers and Composition." *Computers and Composition* 23 (2006): 462–476. Print.

Wegenstein, Bernadette. *Getting Under the Skin: Body and Media Theory.* Cambridge: MIT Press, 2006. Print.

"Why Do We Blog?" *Sandhill Trek.* Nov. 2004. Web. 29 Sept. 2007.

"Wikipedia." *Wikipedia, The Free Encyclopedia.* 2 Mar 2009. Web. 2 Mar. 2009.

Willard, Tom. Rev. of *The Electronic Word: Democracy, Technology, and the Arts,* by Richard A. Lanham. *Rhetoric Review* 13.2 (1995): 440–443. Print.

Wills, David. *Prosthesis.* Stanford, CA: Stanford UP, 1995. Print.

Wilson, James C., and Cynthia Lewiecki-Wilson. "Disability, Rhetoric, and the Body." *Embodied Rhetorics: Disability in Language and Culture.* Ed. James C. Wilson and Cynthia Lewiecki-Wilson. Carbondale: Southern Illinois UP, 2001. Print.

Wood, Denis and John Fels. *The Power of Maps.* New York: Guilford, 1992. Print.

Wysocki, Anne Frances. "Opening New Media to Writing: Openings & Justifications." *Writing New Media: Theory and Applications for Expanding the Teaching of Composition.* Logan: Utah State UP, 2004. 1–42. Print.

Yancey, Kathleen Blake. "Made Not Only in Words: Composition in a New Key." *CCC* 56.2 (2004): 297–328. Print.

Young, Iris Marion. *Justice and the Politics of Difference.* Princeton: Princeton UP, 1990. Print.

Zorbaugh, Harvey. "The Comics—There They Stand!" *Journal of Educational Sociology* 18.4 (1944): 196–203. Print.

INDEX

ABOUT THE AUTHORS

KRISTIN AROLA is an Assistant Professor of English and Director of the Digital Technology and Culture program at Washington State University. Her essays on digital pedagogy and representation have appeared in *Computers and Composition, Harlot: A Revealing Look at the Arts of Persuasion,* and *The Journal of Literacy and Technology.* She is also co-author of the *IX: Visualizing Composition* series and has recently co-edited the third edition of *CrossTalk in Comp Theory.*

At the University of Wisconsin-Milwaukee, ANNE FRANCES WYSOCKI teaches written, visual, and digital rhetorics. Lead author of *Writing New Media: Theory and applications for expanding the teaching of composition* and *The DK Handbook,* she has also designed and produced software to teach 3D visualization and geology. Her new media pieces have won the Kairos Best Webtext award and the Institute for the Future of the Book's Born Digital Competition.

...

JONATHAN ALEXANDER is Professor of English and Chancellor's Fellow at the University of California, Irvine, where he also serves as Campus Writing Director. He is the author or editor of seven books, including *Literacy, Sexuality, Pedagogy: Theory and Practice for Composition Studies* and the co-authored *Finding Out: An Introduction to LGBT Studies.* In 2011, he was honored with the Charles Moran Award for Distinguished Contributions to the Field of Computers and Writing.

JEN ALMJELD is an Assistant Professor of English at New Mexico State University. Her research interests include new media theory, identity, gender, and composition pedagogies with recent publications in upcoming collections *Girls, Cultural Productions and Resistance* and *Preparing Writing Teachers for the Multimodal Age.* She is also currently co-authoring a multimodal textbook called *CrossCurrents: Cultures, Communities, Technologies.*

KRISTINE L. BLAIR is Professor and Chair of the English Department at Bowling Green State University, where she teaches in the doctoral program in Rhetoric and Writing. She serves as editor of both *Computers and Composition* and *Computers and Composition Online.* In 2007 she received the Technology Innovator Award from the Conference on College Composition and Communication's 7Cs Committee, and in 2010 she received the Computers and Composition Charles Moran Award for Distinguished Contributions to the Field.

JAY DOLMAGE is an Assistant Professor of English at the University of Waterloo in Ontario, Canada. He is the editor of *The Canadian Journal of Disability Studies.* His essays on rhetoric, writing, and disability studies have appeared in *Cultural Critique, Rhetoric Review,* and the collection *Rhetorica in Motion: Feminist Rhetorical Methods & Methodologies* (University of Pittsburgh Press, 2010). He also recently edited a special issue on disability studies for the journal *Open Words.*

JASON FARMAN is an Assistant Professor at University of Maryland, College Park in the Department of American Studies and a Distinguished Faculty Fellow in the Digital Cultures and Creativity Program. He is author of the book *Mobile Interface Theory: Embodied Space and Locative Media* (Routledge, 2011), which investigates the impact of mobile media on practices of everyday life and the production of lived, embodied spaces. He has also published recent articles on locative media, digital mapping, game studies, and surveillance technologies.

KRISTIE S. FLECKENSTEIN is Professor of English at Florida State University. She is the author of *Vision, Rhetoric, and Social Action in the Composition Classroom*, winner of the 2009 W. Ross Winterowd Award for Best Book in Composition Theory, and *Embodied Literacies: Imageword and a Poetics of Teaching*, winner of the 2005 Conference on College Composition and Communication's Best Book of the Year Award. In addition, she has co-edited two books and published more than 40 articles and books chapters that cluster around her research interests of visuality and rhetoric, feminist theory, and composition pedagogy.

DR. MATTHEW S. S. JOHNSON is a rhetoric-composition specialist at Southern Illinois University Edwardsville. His work on composition and game studies has appeared in *Dichtung Digital*, *College Composition and Communication* and *College English* as well as the collections *Writing and the Digital Generation*, *From Hip-Hop to Hyperlinks,* and *TechKnowledgies*. He was guest editor of the "Reading Games: Composition, Literacy, and Video Gaming" special-issue of *Computers & Composition* and serves as Reviews Editor for the *Journal of Gaming and Virtual Worlds*.

BEN MCCORKLE is an Associate Professor of English at Ohio State University at Marion, where he teaches courses on composition, the history and theory of rhetoric, and digital media production. He is the author of the book *Rhetorical Delivery as Technological Discourse: A Cross-Historical Study*, published by Southern Illinois University Press. He has also published essays in various journals and edited collections, including *Computers and Composition Online*, *Rhetoric Society Quarterly*, and *Composition Studies*.

DAVID PARRY is an Assistant Professor of Emerging Media at the University of Texas at Dallas. His work focuses on the cultural effects of the digital network. He has published and presented on topics including social media and protests, digital games, digital literacy, and the future of digital scholarship. He recently edited *Ubiquitous Surveillance*, part of the Living Books series. He can be found at http://www.outsidethetext.com.

KRISTIN PRINS writes about digital technologies, contemporary craft, and first-year writing as a graduate student at the University of Wisconsin-Milwaukee. She teaches writing and serves as an administrator in UWM's first-year writing program, a position that includes mentoring new instructors and advising students. Currently, she is working on a book-length manuscript exploring the connections between craft and digital technologies in writing courses. Alongside her academic work, she makes traditional and digital handicrafts.

AARON RAZ LINK is an historian and philosopher of science, an MFA in writing, and a graduate of the Dell'Arte International School of Physical Theatre. Currently, he teaches at the Pacific Northwest College of Art. His book *What Becomes You*, a memoir in two voices (with Hilda Raz), was a 2008 Lambda Literary Award finalist. Selections from his current book project on performance can be found in *Water-Stone Review*, *Prairie Schooner*, and *Fourth Genre*.

JACQUELINE RHODES is Professor of English at California State University, San Bernardino. Her work focusing on intersections of rhetoric, materiality, and technology has appeared in *College Composition and Communication*, *Enculturation*, *JAC: A Journal of Composition Theory*, *Computers and Composition*, and *Rhetoric Review*, among other venues. Her book *Radical Feminism, Writing, and Critical Agency: From Manifesto to Modem* was published by SUNY in 2005.

KAREN SPRINGSTEEN is an Assistant Professor of English and the Writing Center Director at SUNY Potsdam. Her most current essay, "Closer to Home: Veterans' Workshops and the Materiality of Writing," details her community literacy work with members of the national Warrior Writers project (www.warriorwriters.org). The essay argues that there can be less of a disconnection between war and home than many civilians think, *if* we look to veterans who are already speaking, writing, and publishing and to civilians who are already listening, reading, and standing with veterans of the global war on terror.

PAUL WALKER is an Assistant Professor at Murray State University in Murray, KY where he coordinates the first-year composition program and directs the Purchase Area Writing Project. His research in environmental rhetoric, writing theory, and assessment has appeared in *Composition Studies*, *Writing on the Edge*, *Rhetoric Review*, and *Composition Forum*. He is currently finalizing his forthcoming book, *Teaching in Context: Composition in First-Year Learning Communities* (Hampton Press).